THE SOCIAL
AND LEGAL STATUS OF
WOMEN

THE SOCIAL AND LEGAL STATUS OF WOMEN

A Global Perspective

Winnie Hazou

New York
Westport, Connecticut
London

Library of Congress Cataloging-in-Publication Data

Hazou, Winnie.
    The social and legal status of women : a global perspective /
Winnie Hazou.
        p.   cm.
    Includes bibliographical references.
    ISBN 0-275-93362-8 (alk. paper)
    1. Women—United States—Social conditions.   2. Women—Legal
status, laws, etc.—United States.   3. Women—Cross-cultural
studies.   I. Title.
HQ1421.H39   1990
305.42'0973—dc20   89-72096

Library of Congress Catalog Card Number: 89-72096
ISBN: 0-275-93362-8

First published in 1990

Praeger Publishers, One Madison Avenue, New York, NY 10010
An imprint of Greenwood Publishing Group, Inc.

Printed in the United States of America

∞

The paper used in this book complies with the
Permanent Paper Standard issued by the National
Information Standards Organization (Z39.48-1984).

10 9 8 7 6 5 4 3 2 1

Contents

Preface

This book is essentially about change. While change is an inescapable fact of modern life, social change has a particular significance. Steven Vago explains social change in terms of "a restructuring of the basic ways in which people in a society relate to each other with regard to government, economics, education, religion, family life, recreation, language, and other activities" (1981:239). The interconnection and interdependence of law with other social institutions cannot be ignored, and while the answer to the "chicken or the egg" question concerning the relationship between law and social change may not always be obvious, we must recognize the interplay. Past experience shows us that laws merely reflect prevailing social norms and institutionalized customs. This contributes to their effectiveness. At the same time, however, social engineering to remedy inequities is a basic trait of modern law. "The law—through legislative and administrative responses to new social conditions and ideas, as well as through judicial reinterpretations of constitutions, statutes, or precedents—increasingly not only articulates but sets the course for major social changes" (Friedmann 1972:513).

This is true not only in the United States but also in other countries. At times law successfully directs immediate fundamental change, as when the Soviets and the Chinese both used legislation to guide social change and restructure society following their revolutions. At other times, law enforcement is hampered by an encrusted culture that accepts gender inequality as normal.

Modern law in the United States is both the cause and the effect of social change in the lives of women, although the relationship is extremely complex and controversial. However, the relationship need not be thoroughly understood. In general, in Western societies the legal changes that affect women have resulted from altered social conditions, a gradual shift in attitudes and values, and a heightened consciousness in a highly urbanized and industrialized environment. New laws give official recognition to these de facto conditions, and they mandate uniform compliance. On the other hand, in traditional societies where there are high illiteracy and low female employment rates, social change in the status of women must usually be precipitated by law if it is to come about at all. Without laws mandating equal treatment in such areas as marriage, inheritance, employment, and education, the achievement of equal social status for the world's women would take even longer to become a reality.

This book is divided into two parts. The first part analyzes the social and legal changes that affect women in important areas of their lives. It analyzes the changes in American society by combining a sociology of women with a sociology of law to depict the interplay of the effects of changing customs and law on the life-styles and expectations of women. The persistence of outworn stereotypes, the discriminatory laws of the past, and the effects of modern law are discussed. In the second part of the book, the United Nations (UN) treaties that affect the status of women are examined in order to enlarge the perspective and show that gender equality is a desired goal for people everywhere. Representative countries in different geographical locations are then examined to ascertain the status of women and the current social and legal changes in each culture.

The author recognizes that the law is the most important tool available to people to shape social justice. The formulation of international law at the United Nations influences social change on a global scale. The international rules being formulated by that world body have as an ideology the conviction that the development of women, along with men, is necessary in order to have a better world in the future. Countries that ratify the treaties pertaining to the rights of women are mandated to incorporate formal norms of gender equality in their societies. Other countries, since they are members of the global community, are also beginning to feel pressure to conform to the international standards. In part because of the efforts of the United Nations, future generations of men and women will enjoy greater freedom and equality and will be better able to develop their full potential.

Part I

The Experience in the United States

1

Introduction

It is an inescapable fact of human existence that people are born into human groups and are expected to live out their lives according to informal and formal group norms. All social life is affected by the political mandates of a particular society. However, in complex societies such as the United States and other Western countries, few persons have much more than a vague impression of judicial prescriptions of their own legal rights. This is especially true for women, who often have only a smattering of knowledge concerning the specifics of the sundry laws that apply to important basic events in their lives such as marriage, divorce, inheritance, work, and crimes against women. While ignorance of the law is a widespread and deplorable phenomenon among the general public, and while it would benefit all citizens to remedy that situation, women should be especially eager to acquire a knowledge of the law since traditionally women as a group have had to endure a lower legal status than men. Recent accelerated social changes have modified that status of inequality, however, as new life-styles and values in various countries have begun to be reflected in their laws.

Just as social life is an ongoing process, the legal system of the United States is also dynamic, and constitutional amendments as well as statutes, ordinances, and court decisions largely reflect the mores of the social era during which they were enacted. Over time, societal values change and new legal rules come into being, although the two processes do not necessarily occur simultaneously. At times there are enormous lags between the intent of the laws and the concurrent social realities. Another complication besides culture lag has to do with regionalism. Not only do laws reflecting traditional norms and others reflecting emerging values coexist at a given time, the laws and court decisions may also vary among legal jurisdictions in different parts of the country. Such inconsistencies prevail unless federal legislation or Supreme Court decisions render them invalid. Thus, far from being static, a society's laws represent a process, a development, and even a transformation of an entire area of social activity. When the circumstances of people's lives are altered, changes can be expected on the macro level of society. Conversely, when innovative laws have been enacted, there is a tendency to adjust behavior in the face of authority. On both social levels, the attitudes toward women have been changing.

For purposes of clarity, the concept *status of women* simply means position of women in relation to the position of men in all the fields of society in which human beings act. Measuring indicators usually involve any of five major fields: (1) women's legal rights (analysis of discriminating laws and effect of new laws); (2) education (comparison of percentages of boys and girls in school); (3) societal integration (participation in labor force and government compared to men); (4) economic position (wage differentials); and (5) sociopsychological position (dominate or subordinate in interaction) (Hommes 1978). Although references to these indicators will be made, the focus of this book is legal rights, as they are often a prerequisite force that sets in motion a series of changes affecting other aspects of women's social status. The issues addressed will pertain specifically to women's lives and the changes that have occurred in the traditional status of women, including the present emerging consciousness and aspirations for free life-styles, work parity, and flexibility of gender roles, and the legal recognition of social equality with men. In Part 1, the more iconoclastic laws and court decisions that are pertinent to the so-called gender issue in the United States will be discussed. There are myriads of laws enacted by the federal government and the states that affect the lives of women. The best that can be aimed for in one volume is an introduction to some representative statutes. I will discuss the past social and legal status of women, and then depict some legal changes and also the direction of change in the general social understanding of the rights of women. The two areas of study, the sociology of women and the sociology of law, are combined because in combination they afford an understanding of past discrimination against women and the altered present social and legal status of women.

LAW AND WOMEN

The sociological approach to law concerns the examination of the legal system in relation to the other institutions. Law is one of the major underpinnings of social integration, contributing codes of conduct, form, and coherence to social interaction. Without the general acceptance of rules of order and the mechanisms for their enforcement, chaos would generally result. Simply stated, laws are the formalized and enforceable symbolic representations of the culture's ideological beliefs, preferences, and mores. The content of law can be examined by exploring the social sources of law along with changes in attitudes and values. For example, an altered technological system affects other major institutions in society since it influences social organization within the family, as well as the stratification, labor, educational, religious, and medical systems.

Changing social needs often require adjustments in the lives of individuals and a modification of the culture. Social scientists seek to understand the social forces influencing the informal and formal processes of the social order. Although, in a broad sense, law is a reflection of a society, in a social system undergoing rapid change the correlation of social norms and legal norms is far from perfect. For example, although in the United States more than half of the working-age women are in the labor force, which was previously the domain of men, the assumptions inherent in much of the law place women and men on an unequal footing.

Explanations of what is considered correct in a society are often based on long-standing tradition. People have certain behavior expectations because in society "It has always been done that way." The problem with such an approach is the tacit assertion that original decisions were made on the basis of inherent truths rather than learned preferences and rational expediencies. Such an erroneous perception is not conducive to questioning, reassessment, or doubt concerning the application of customary mores to present circumstances, nor does it lead to an analysis of the traditional power bases of the past.

In the United States there has also been change concerning the impetus of law and an enlargement of its impact on society. Early law was a restatement of customs and an expression of values and norms prevalent in the culture. Modern law, however, has often been a catalyst for social change. An example of this is the 1964 Civil Rights Act which mandated an end to discriminatory practices that were part of the culture. In spite of legal changes, however, there is still a reluctance on the part of some persons to alter ingrained habits of thought and behavior and accept the changing gender roles in principle, even though antidiscrimination laws have mandated changes. This results in the previously mentioned lag. Such a phenomenon is of concern to social science researchers, whether they seek knowledge by surveying the effects of the social institutions on women (a top-down perspective) or by studying the impact that women and their changed circumstances have on family, education, government, and the economy (a bottom-up approach).

WOMEN IN SOCIETY

It is fitting to examine the social structure as it influences and is influenced by a single segment of the population because women as a group have historically been viewed as psychologically and socially different from men. Therefore, they were not to be included in public life, as the following quote by Thomas Jefferson illustrates: "Were our state a pure democracy there would still be excluded from our deliberations women, who, to prevent depravation of morals and ambiguity of issues, should not mix promiscuously in gatherings of men."

Although women's experiences vary according to class, ethnicity, race, marital status, geographic location, religion, and age, they receive categorical treatment from society and the laws reflecting that society. Although women have been treated as members of a socially limited category, they have not in the past formed the type of group consciousness and distinct values, life-styles, and self-perceptions that are characteristic of subcultures. Indeed, women have seldom had a strong perception of sharing a common fate as a group in the past; hence they have not had access to the support and sustenance commonly found in having a separate community of one's own kind. Such enlightenment might have led to a kind of group dynamics for social change. Women are and always have been a major segment of the population. Whether they are traditionalists or feminists by conviction, or any gradation in between, much can be gained in self-understanding by acknowledging the social forces that influence attitudes and behavior.

One result of unexamined and biased thinking is the different treatment often accorded by the courts and legislatures to men and women solely because of their sex when theoretically all persons are equal under the law. This can be seen in differential treatment on the basis of sex in such areas of the law as contracts, social security, selective service, work hazard protection, and spousal benefits. Thus, the study of both the experience of women and the sociology of law as it pertains to women helps readers to understand the interconnection between the two topics. This can aid in adapting to the status quo by clarifying the confusion that results when society is undergoing rapid social change. The basic structures in Western societies took a long time evolving, and were accepted as natural by both men and women. Year after year, very little changed. The social innovations that resulted from technological breakthroughs that have been accumulating since the beginning of the (broadly called) Industrial Revolution have disrupted many of the encrusted patterns of social interaction that reflected gender superordinate-subordinate relationships. Some of the changes are informal (such as the so-called sexual revolution), but many are being formalized into law (as with the Equal Pay Act). The manifest function of these new rulings is the protection of civil rights through the prevention of sex discrimination. Change is not always smooth, and sometimes an uneven and disruptive influence is reflected in the relationships of men and women involved in the everyday process of adjusting to society's altering view of reality.

It is incumbent on everyone to seek understanding of these influences on patterns of interaction in a given society. As societies develop and their members interact over a period of time, their interpersonal exchanges in certain fairly broad and fundamental areas of life follow increasingly predictable patterns. People come to learn what is expected of them and what they can expect of others. These interrelated understandings are functional and involve the important social prerequisites that must be fulfilled for the survival of the group. This process of developing orderly, stable, and increasingly predictable forms of social interaction is called institutionalization. An institution is an enduring cluster of values, norms, statuses, roles, and expectations that develops around the basic needs of a society. If viable organized life is to continue, basic requirements of the society must be met such as the replacement and socialization of members, the production and distribution of goods and services, and the espousal of a shared ideology and system of social control to ensure approved behavior. Once patterns of behavior become institutionalized, they are expected to be binding on all group members. These patterns are not final and definitive, however, and change does occur with repercussions throughout the system. A good part of this book is concerned with recent changes and adjustments in social institutions.

What is termed *conventional wisdom* is all-pervasive in a society, and it is seldom questioned either by those in the system that it benefits the most or those it helps the least. The chapters that follow will highlight the institution of the family and the place of women in the economy, and then will analyze the institutionalized allotment of power available to women in order to probe the implicit understanding of women's special sphere in the society. It is hoped that this will give perspective and coherence to innovations in social roles which at times appear to result in misunderstandings and chaos. I will review the assumptions concerning sex that were prevalent in past circumstances, and also the emerging altered social conditions, which require a rethinking of traditional mores and a reformulation of legal pronouncements. Landmark legislation that can be designated as a catalyst in the formalization of the changes will also be included. Theoretical approaches to the sources of law will be applied as an aid to understanding how inequality becomes reflected in the legal system of a particular era. Although I must omit many interesting and important cases which reflect the new emerging status of women, the trend toward greater legal equality of the sexes will be apparent.

If there is an ideological underpinning for the study of women's status and the law, it is the fact that inequality cannot be justified in a society that espouses egalitarian principles. Egalitarianism is the concept that all persons have worth, dignity, and human rights regardless of social rank, race, ethnicity, or gender. In an egalitarian society individuals are judged by achieved criteria and not ascribed ones. That is, achievement is of more consequence than birthright. Of course, this is idealistic, and sex, a major ascribed characteristic, has been and to some extent still is a basis for unequal treatment under the law. However, women have benefitted from recent social, cultural, and legal changes as social dynamics have altered encrusted habits of thinking and behaving, leading to greater recognition of full citizenship and autonomy for women. While of necessity only some of the new legislation can be identified in this book, the direction of the change is of most consequence.

THE UNITED NATIONS AND THE GLOBAL PERSPECTIVE

It must not be overlooked that the concept of egalitarianism is not unique to the United States. The changes in attitudes and conditions that have been leading to greater equality between men and women have been occurring in many industrialized Western societies. Some European nations have been more vigorous than the United States in the legalization of changes that aim toward equality between the sexes. This will be of concern in Part II of this book.

Influences between countries cannot be avoided in a world of mass communications and transportation. It therefore becomes meaningful to look at the influence of the discussions and formulations of the United Nations, the world political and social body, with regard to the changing status of women because the conventions and other legal instruments of the United Nations concerning human rights carry great weight. The United Nations was formed in 1945, and almost since its inception one of the concerns of this august body has been the political, economic, and sociocultural rights of women. In 1946 the Economic and Social Council of the United Nations created the Commission on the Status of Women.

To date there have been more than twenty different international legal instruments dealing specifically with women that emanated from bodies of the United Nations. These instruments represent long and serious deliberations by the member nations. Their authoritative communications denounce sex discrimination on a worldwide scale. These international documents concerning the status of women are extremely influential as each one represents an international consensus on the particular problems of treatment of women in such areas as education, marriage, and employment. Most of the documents are formal conventions. A convention has the effect of a treaty and is legally binding on the member nations that ratify or accede to it. As of this writing, the latest convention on this topic is the Convention on the Elimination of All Forms of Discrimination Against Women, which came into force on September 3, 1981. Not only does it include nondiscrimination norms, it also imposes obligations on the countries to foster joint-parental familial responsibilities and to employ efforts to eliminate sex-role stereotyping. Such UN treaties have great worldwide influence in building the consensus necessary for passing nondiscriminatory legislation in the various countries. They thus influence the lives of many individuals. Although we cannot determine which influences are most important in the passage of any legislation, we do know that in the United States legal reforms have evolved only slowly.

Some UN documents regarding the elimination of the unequal status of women predated the U.S. Equal Pay Act of 1963 and Civil Rights Act of 1964, which are directed at discrimination and mandate change in the United States. In the global arena, sex stereotypes have often been based not only on historical practice but also on religious teachings. Major religious tenets of the Christian, Jewish, and Islamic faiths place women in subordinate social roles. These religions influence the lives of many of earth's inhabitants who literally accept the admonishings of their holy books. Economic conditions also have relevance. However, regardless of religion or type of economy, strides toward more respect for human worth regardless of gender have been made in many countries. Some countries have made attempts to abide by the prescriptions of the international agreements concerning the status of women that were signed at the United Nations. In order to illustrate this trend toward greater parity of the sexes in various countries, this book presents case studies from different geographical areas, which should be enlightening concerning the quality of change, if any, in the lives of women in different parts of the world. The case studies represent Argentina, Sweden, Egypt, India, and China. These countries have different types of government, different levels of economic development, and different religious and cultural underpinnings. They are also typical of other nations within their geographic locations.

The final chapter of this work gives a global perspective on the emerging process of change in the status of women and discusses the spreading universality of the concept of sexual equality. Since we all inhabit the same world, it is only a question of time concerning the adoption of various aspects of equality between women and men in the many countries that make up the world community.

2

The Socialization of Women in the United States

It is obvious even to the most casual observer of the human scene that men and women often act differently. They seem generally to be concerned with dissimilar aspects of the social condition, and their behaviors do not appear to result from coercion. Further observation shows that their activities fall into certain recurring patterns that are compatible with each other. This is not surprising, as sociological analysis shows that human needs and interests are best assured when society is organized in predictable ways. The various statuses (positions within a hierarchically ordered society) and roles (behavior patterns associated with certain statuses) are functional and an integral part of the social structure. Within the social system individuals can and do occupy many statuses, such as housewife, mother, teacher, neighbor, student, accountant, secretary, and executive. The research question concerns just how it happens that people undertake the different roles. In particular, how does it happen that a woman's activities are quite similar to those of other women and a man's behaviors bear a greater similarity to those of other men?

One explanation of this social phenomenon requires the belief in biological determinism. Biological determinism is the conviction that there are qualities inherent in the physical being that cause certain behaviors. In this view, women's anatomical makeup leads to particular attitudes, values, and subsequent behavior patterns that are different from men's. Thus, an ascribed status (a status that is assigned by birth such as race, age, and sex, and over which a person has no control) is the master status in a person's life.

Another explanation concerns social determinism, the belief that human behavior is the result of conditions in the social world. In this view, the newborn's personality is a tabula rasa, a clean slate. Whatever becomes marked on the slate is due to the person's interaction with the social environment, which consists first of kin in the family milieu and then of friendships and work associates. Overlaying these groups is the culture, which influences the personal response to life's contingencies as well as the way other people respond to the individual. In modern industrial societies people are judged mostly on the basis of achieved status, a status attained largely by the individual's personal efforts.

This dichotomy concerning inherited versus social attributes is often referred to as the nature versus nurture debate by social scientists who seek to understand the bases of human behavior. Regardless of which polarity one tends to favor, it is through the process of socialization within a culture that people learn and internalize the attitudes, values, and appropriate behaviors that allow them to become responsive, participating members of the society. Individual self-identity is gradually acquired, along with motivations and the requisite knowledge to perform adequately in the social roles enacted during the course of a lifetime in keeping with that identity. These assumed values, beliefs, and desired behavior patterns must be transmitted to the young in order for a culture to be perpetuated, and so from the day of birth the child is socialized to fit into society. Although socialization is a unique experience for all persons and, due to personal idiosyncracies, is never the same even for similarly situated members of society, there is nonetheless, a general consensus and an acceptance of overall cultural patterns.

CULTURE, GENDER ROLES, AND SOCIAL STATUS

Cultures are unique to a given society; they evolve as generalized collective solutions to the problems inherent in the human condition in particular localities. Cultures are material and also ideational, and represent a way of doing things as well as an accepted point of view. Artifacts and behaviors are symbolic representations of the culture. Most cultures have rigid ideas about what constitutes masculine and feminine traits; these beliefs may vary across cultures.

One study suggests that if certain sex-appropriate behaviors were inherited by men and women they would be universal throughout the human species. Anthropologist Margaret Mead's research showed that personality traits such as passivity or aggression are learned rather than innate in the individual (Mead: 1968). Mead studied three preliterate societies and found that the culturally assigned gender roles were different in each one, and different from roles in the United States. In one culture the women were active, dominant, impersonal, and managers of the economy, while the men were emotionally dependent and adorned themselves to gain the attention and affection of a woman. Women obviously had a high status in this culture. Mead's finding, which suggested that our assumptions about what are normal male or female personality traits can vary by society, is important in refuting the rampant belief that anatomy is destiny. To a large extent, socialization is destiny.

Social status is related to other positions in a society. Status implies a hierarchical arrangement of positions to which have been socially ascribed not only varying degrees of power and prestige but also a set of rights and obligations that are expected to be fulfilled. The acquisition of a particular social status is related to the perceived traits of men and women. In many patriarchal societies, ascribed status (status over which one has no control) has been the major determining factor for women. In virtually all societies, men have more power, prestige, and privileges by virtue of their sex. It is generally accepted that low status involves a lack of control over the material or social resources in the society, and a general lack of choice in unfolding of one's destiny. This social imbalance has evolved in spite of the fact that both sexes are equally necessary for human survival.

Nearly all human behaviors are prescribed by the culture of which the people are a part. Individual survival depends on group survival. Although the circumstances have varied, human beings have had the same physical needs universally. Therefore, there have evolved many similarities concerning women and men in the social arrangements of all groups. It is often a matter of speculation as to how the differential social statuses evolved from preliterate societies to the present day, but by using the perspective of anthropologists, much information can be gleaned.

In their studies of preliterate peoples and social bonding, anthropologists have constantly stressed the importance of group or societal behavior. Tribal custom is interpreted in terms of its contribution to social cohesion and integration. The individual is not studied per se; rather, anthropologists study role behavior and group interaction. The function of customs and socially prescribed behavior is to contribute to group solidarity and survival. Therefore, all systems exist primarily to maintain the social structure and enhance social integration. A woman occupies a definite position in society and is one of the supports of the network of social relations; her role has a raison d'être in its particular manifestation in a given society. In early societies women were valued, as was all human life, and they were influential in decisions of the small society.

As cultures became more complex and the economy became based on monetary exchange, women were more and more relegated to nurturing others in the home while men worked outside the home for wages. Men took the role of head of the family, and, in spite of the importance of domestic work for the orderly continuation of the society, women's status was lowered. Today the inherited doctrines that are part of the culture have perpetuated distinctions in gender roles since they articulate what it means to be a male or female. In many societies women are exploited as domestics within the home (see Chapter 8). The caste-like status differentiation has become normal and accepted by all, even the less privileged sex. Women have been socialized into believing in their inferiority of endowment; they accept a special woman's sphere which is ascribed at birth, and they do not generally question their unequal status.

Socialization into Separate Spheres

Socialization is a major factor in the perpetuation of a culture and the acquisition of gender-role identification, as has been suggested. Socialization for gender roles starts from birth as the parents enact their understandings of proper behavior by using a pink blanket for a baby girl and a blue one for a baby boy. Thus, by symbolism, parents initiate a whole syndrome of gender-role differentiation that relegates a child to one of two possible scenarios of child rearing.

The sex typing of children does not consist only of purposive behavior such as blanket choice. Parents are not always aware of the differential treatment they give to their male and female offspring. Studies have shown that male babies are handled less often, played with more roughly, and thought of as stronger than females; while female babies are cuddled, handled gently, and talked to more often than males (Kagan and Lewis 1965, Komarovsky 1953). The treatment of baby girls by mothers may initiate the female bonding process in the infants, according to one study (Goldberg and Lewis 1969). As children get older, girls are protected more and encouraged to be dependent and weak while boys are permitted more leeway in their play activities (Kagan 1964).

It would be very difficult to circumvent the set of social expectations concerning gender even if parents made an effort to do so, because these beliefs permeate other aspects of life as the child matures. As long as society places such importance on an anatomical difference and shunts the sexes into different tracks in life, boys and girls will grow up to be different from each other in the socially expected ways. This is a type of self-fulfilling prophecy; the differences are accepted as correct by the individuals themselves, who quickly learn the rules and do not question them. Once the definitions of the self as male or female are acquired they influence all the other roles the individual enacts throughout his or her lifetime. The potent impact of gender socialization helps shape the individual's destiny as a member of society. As a result, not only is personal choice largely eliminated, there is also a problem in the fact that the gender-role tracks are not equal. Boys learn that they are members of the superior sex while girls learn that they are relegated to subsidiary, nurturant, and dependent roles. The justification has always revolved around the naturalness of the aggressive/passive dichotomy for boys and girls.

Many studies of sexual characteristics have been undertaken in an effort to understand trait variances in individuals, but they have not demonstrated unequivocal, innate differences in behavior between males and females. Apparent personality differences, such as those categorized as assertive or conforming behaviors, are largely the result of the internalization of sex-appropriate behaviors associated with the gender roles people are expected to perform. Differences between men and women in style, dress, and behavior, (whether verbal or nonverbal) help define gender roles in the same way that actors on a stage use costumes, gestures, and props to give validation to roles they are playing. A major difference is that the sex role becomes so thoroughly a part of the person's psyche as well as his or her physical and social self that it is perceived as innate. Men and women have internalized the belief that their physical differences justify relegation by society to different courses in life, which may ultimately accord them unequal chances for the acquisition of their society's resources.

Theories of Gender-Role Socialization

It must be noted that the words *sex* and *gender* cannot be used interchangeably. The word sex pertains to a person's anatomical structure, and sex role concerns behaviors determined by that anatomy. For females this includes pregnancy and lactation. The term gender role concerns the socially created expectations for female attitudes and behaviors. A gender role is an all-encompassing social construction, involving the self-concept of the woman (her gender identity), and including psychological and personality traits as well as the social roles assigned to her sex. Traditional gender roles revolve around the notion that women are naturally people-oriented, and the general expectations are that women are nurturant, emotional, passive, and dependent on men. According to society, the degree of a woman's "femininity" depends on how well she enacts her gender role. Therefore, a gender role is a social invention that is more complex than a sex role. It involves a blend of social and psychological behaviors, as well as the values, attitudes, and norms that the society designates as appropriate for the female.

The socialization process starts in early childhood. Just how it evolves and succeeds is of concern to those who eschew genetic explanations for the differential behavior patterns of males and females. There are two main theoretical approaches through which sociologists attempt to analyze and explain the processes underlying the learning of accepted gender-role behaviors of human beings—the social learning model and the cognitive development model. Both these explanatory models reject the notion that gender is biologically determined, and instead attempt to explain how it is acquired in the context of society.

Social Learning Theory

This model of gender-role development bases the explanation of the emerging identity on role playing in early childhood. It involves the concepts of reward and punishment, conditions arising in the external environment. A child's behavior that is rewarded by others is more likely to be repeated than behavior that has elicited punishment. Inappropriate performances are likely to be discontinued. The experiences of acceptance or rejection contribute gradually to the child's self-identification as male or female. This theory emphasizes the assumption that children have a need for rewards and that personality traits are mainly learned (Bandura and Walters 1963). A variation of this theory is the modeling perspective, which includes observational learning. It incorporates the recognition that individuals are capable of generalizing from live and symbolic models such as movies and television to similar situations without having to experience them personally. Thus, through observation, children learn probable outcomes for behaviors before they actually perform them. There are countless numbers of models in society to emulate, whether actual or fictional, and social learning is facile and subtle (Mischel 1966).

In summary, children learn gender-typed behavior in the same manner that other behavior is learned—through observation, rewards and punishments, and imitation of adult models. The process begins at a very early age as the child learns to conform to parental and cultural expectations of sex-appropriate behaviors. Specific and constant reinforcements given early in life often have far-reaching effects on later behavior; once the gender identity is acquired, it is difficult to alter. For women, the traits that are encouraged and rewarded are not functional for acquiring the power and material resources that are available in the society.

Cognitive Development Theory

Another explanation of gender-role learning comes from cognitive development theory. From this perspective a child's gender identity is not learned from others, but instead the child's self-labeling as male or female results from the active structuring of his or her own experience. The stress is on the child as a thinking person who organizes what he or she learns concerning gender roles and connects it with his or her body and world. By the age of three, children have categorized themselves as male or female and then seek to act like one or the other. On that basis, self-socialization follows, along with the categorization by the child of other people. Thus, gender identity is a cause of gender-role learning rather than a result of it (Kohlberg 1966).

Once the sex-specific gender-role identity is acquired, it remains an integral part of the individual. Consequently, a girl acts a certain way because she knows she is a girl and not because she is rewarded for doing so, and she expects similar behavior from other girls.

Artifacts facilitate the learning process during infancy and young childhood, as they supply subtle messages to children concerning expected behavior. The selection of toys by parents reflects their perceptions concerning sex appropriateness. For example, trucks, machines, and erector sets for boys, and dolls, sewing kits, and tea sets for girls reflect parental agreements concerning the expected future activities of their children. Additional passive messages are incorporated into children's books, wherein most pictures and texts show men as active manipulators of their worlds, and women in domestic roles that are auxiliary to men. The belief that boys and girls are inherently different and so require differential treatment tends to be a self-fulfilling prophecy as boys and girls internalize ideas concerning gender-appropriate behaviors (Deckard 1983, National Organization for Women 1972, U'Ren 1971). Recent content analyses of children's school books have highlighted the inequalities in story line and pictures. The analyses have brought about some change, and some publishers are now printing children's texts that better reflect the real world. However, there does not seem to be much change in the toys adults buy for boys and girls.

Furthermore, it should be noted that the socialization process for any individual can be influenced by extraneous factors such as the family's class, ethnicity, and race, and also by the peer group, the geographical area, and the present ideological stances of the society. These are strong forces that serve as invisible lenses through which the child views the world. Whatever the circumstances of the individual, there is a close connection between the socialization process, the mores of the group, and the stereotypes accepted by the society.

The Devaluation Process: Social Stereotypes

Attitudes toward women become normative and are sustained through the use of stereotypes. A cultural stereotype can be understood as an over-simplified generalization by which we attribute certain traits to any person in a group without regard to individual differences. Stereotypes save time and afford an ease of personal cognition in the myriad contingencies that arise in everyday life. In the society, stereotypes are functional in that they become common knowledge. They are so pervasive that they serve as important reference points in the observation of a group, suggesting the formation of attitudes toward it and the subsequent treatment of that segment of society. While time and effort are saved and ease of interaction is gained, the process is blatantly unfair to members of the stereotyped group.

Women are particularly affected, and their options are limited by stereotypes. A crucial determinant of one's self-concept concerns how one is defined and categorized by others in the social environment. Stereotypes concerning women usually are based on an implicit understanding that certain traits or characteristics are hereditary and therefore natural, and as such are not considered within the realm of purposeful social change. The beliefs that women are naturally passive, domestic, overly emotional, often erratic ("It's a woman's prerogative to change her mind!"), and totally incapable of leadership are among the more traditional stereotypes. Even those people who are victimized by the stereotypes tend to believe they are true, and their behaviors are governed accordingly. Most women behave in the way others expect them to; many accept the negative label as correct, play the part, and do not question their place in the society.

History has shown that once stereotypes are established they are not easily eradicated. They continue among succeeding generations and under changed structural conditions. Difficulties can arise when socialization processes become at odds with new realities in the lives of women, as when adults who influence children were raised under different social conditions themselves and have outdated understandings and values. Cultural lag results. This concept refers to the disparity between reality and the expectations created by a socialization process that is no longer entirely relevant in a rapidly changing society. This lag can make it difficult for women to work out new norms and roles, since there can be a lack of supporting cultural values, role models, and reinforcing social networks for a new life-style.

Complicating the issue are beliefs concerning the alleged naturalness of gender differences held by social scientists who employ certain assumptions about basic differences when they devise scales for the measurement of masculinity and femininity traits of human personalities. In their models they assume that there are basic and extremely important differences in the lives of men and women. These assumptions concern bipolarity, unidimensionality, continuity, normal distribution, consistency of content, and the importance of the differences (Tresemer 1977).

Assumption of Bipolarity

It is generally assumed that relations between men and women are based on a dichotomy, and that any alleged "feminine" characteristic at one end of the continuum is the opposite of a given "masculine" characteristic at the other end. This assumption is epitomized in the use of the expression "the opposite sex." It ignores the fact that there is a great overlap of traits between the sexes. It is an oversimplification that leads to the so-called common knowledge that men have innate qualifications for carrying out instrumental (doing, leading, or building) tasks, while women excel at expressive (nurturant, emotional, and passive) behaviors.

Emile Durkheim, one of the early classical sociologists, in 1893 used the terminology "intellectual versus affective functions" to describe sexual differences that he felt resulted from physical evolution. He wrote that

woman leads a completely different existence from that of man. One might say that the two great functions of psychic life are thus dissociated, that one of the sexes takes care of the affective functions and the other of intellectual functions. (Durkheim 1964:60)

Different points of view result from the use of selective perception and the desire to justify existing arrangements. However, it is a scientific fact that traits such as sensitivity, leadership, decision making, artistic ability, and empathy are not the monopoly of either sex.

Assumption of Unidimensionality

It is generally assumed that there exists only one dimension of masculinity and femininity. This is an oversimplistic explanation of gender; scales that are used to measure other traits for degrees of difference among people are usually multidimensional. For instance, in the measurement of racial and age differences, more complex scales are recognized as necessary since over-simplification could lead to erroneous conclusions or only half-truths. Differences between men and women are equally complex.

Assumption of Continuity

This evokes images of a graded interval with zero at the center representing apparently androgynous traits (neutral qualities) and with masculine and feminine at the two extremes. It is assumed that building things (a "mas-culine" task) is the opposite of nurturing a baby (a "feminine" task). The difficulty with this model lies with the impossibility of clarifying just how one activity is the direct opposite of the other. Toys are some of the artifacts used for encouraging certain behavior expectations in children, and we clas-sify some playthings as masculine or feminine. However, it is difficult to prove that a truck is the opposite of an apron or that building blocks are the opposite of tea sets. Nonetheless, such artifacts are given to either girls or boys depending on how society has classified the toy.

Assumption of a Normal Distribution

It is assumed that for each sex there is a similar distribution of gender traits. However, studies of gender-role typologies show that isolating traits for one gender is unrealistic, as there may be contradictions and overlap-pings. This is apparent in many professions. For instance, the occupation of minister, which has traditionally been a male profession, requires nurturant personality traits, and the Mother Superior in a monastery requires lead-ership skills. Sociologists suggest that if both sexes are socialized similarly there will be random distribution of personality traits.

Assumption of Consistency of Content

The assumptions of the universality of certain gender traits span the ages, cover vast periods of time, include all classes and races, and cover large geographical locations. This all-inclusiveness has been disputed by many anthropological studies (especially those of Margaret Mead), and yet the ideas concerning the universality of dichotomous gender roles do not fade away. Furthermore, the consistency is expected to pertain in all contingen-cies, and the feminine woman is asked to be nonaggressive and nurturant even when her current situation requires decision making and leadership. A related and important issue concerns the individual physical or class-related circumstances that can modify self-identity and influence gender-role behavior in spite of societal expectations. For example, in the United States the black woman is a dominant type as she is often the head of her family and also the breadwinner. In this way people experience their biological equipment and social circumstances differently.

Assumption of Importance

Given that the average man's body is larger than that of the average woman, and that men and women have different functions in the biological process of procreation, one can ask whether these factors are of such a degree of difference as to justify the socialization of individuals to inhabit what amounts to two different social worlds. Today many people feel that the importance of the physical differences between men and women have been exaggerated, and that in most spheres of life where men and women are encouraged to develop their full potentials spiritually and intellectually, there is little difference in personality trait development.

The assumptions contained in the above scales generally ignore the fact that the similarities of personality traits between the sexes are far more numerous than the differences. The use of dichotomous scales thus becomes a Procrustean manner of fitting men and women into slots and thereby allowing social life to continue in its traditional way. For those individuals relegated to the superior status, this is a great convenience.

The Persistence of Stereotypes

The topic that requires analysis is the longevity of these stereotypes in spite of undeniable social changes that have negated the alleged frailty of the female. Culpability lies in the persistent generalized attitudes that are inherent in the main institutions of our society such as the family, the economy, the religion, the educational system, and the polity. A medium for the transmission of information (including the expected attitudes, values, and desired behavior) is the communication system. Informal communication between individuals, whether verbal or tacit (by speech, posture, dress, and routine mannerisms), is important in the persistence of stereotypes since meanings are commonly shared and reinforced. The presentation of the sexes in the mass media also subtly reinforces the old power structure. Let us consider various means of communication and their subtle relationship to the perpetuation of stereotypes.

Sexism and Language

Human culture as we know it would be impossible without language. Languages provide the vocabulary and concepts that are needed by a people; they are important instruments in the socialization process within a society. Language reflects the basic conditions of a people and its ideology, as it serves as a repository of modes of thought. By studying a language's vocabulary and semantic structure, the basic orientation of a people can be known. For example, the language of the Hopi Indians has no future tense. Because of that it is understood that life for the Hopi is a continual process of becoming, of day-to-day importance.

Language is also reflective of the most powerful group in a society and can become a tool for their interests, since ideas are conveyed through the vocabulary. One linguist wrote of the English language: "Emotive words acquire the connotations by reflecting the sentiments of the dominant group in a society—in our case white Anglo-Saxon males" (Strainchamps 1971:252). The major premise of some word usages is that males are superior to females. Let us examine how language reinforces gender-role identity. In a patriarchy (a society where males as a group have authority over females as a group) the masculine assumption of superiority is rampant. In everyday usage the male pronoun is employed to represent persons who may be either male or female when the sex is unknown by the speaker. This convention insults women by ignoring them. Employment of the male pronoun is so ingrained in our culture that its habitual use is unthinking. Jane Williamson, Diane Winston, and Wanda Wooten quote two instances of actual pronoun usage which, although ridiculous upon reflection, are correct according to our language. One example is a remark from a group insurance brochure: "If the employee becomes pregnant while covered under this policy, he will be entitled to . . . " Another example is a remark made by a New York state assemblymember: "Everyone should be able to decide for himself whether or not to have an abortion" (1979:162). There have been a few attempts by publishers to avoid the use of the male generic, and the double pronoun "he/she" is used occasionally today, but general conversation has not been altered to reflect that reality while still remaining grammatically correct.

Even more telling of the male power base in society is pronoun usage in religion. Religion is a basic underpinning of spiritual values for many, and it is meaningful that the supreme Being is presumed to be male. This sex designation is so ingrained in the culture that when feminists urge a troubled person to "Pray to God; she'll understand!" it is considered a good joke.

Male nouns have been used also to designate the sex deemed appropriate to fill certain positions. For example, the terms *chairman* and *alderman* have carried with them the elimination of any possibility that females could be authority figures. The suggestion that females are physically frail is connoted in the words *policeman* and *fireman*. The use of the common words *man-power* and *man-made* ignores the input of the female's efforts in the production of goods and services.

There are many linguistic practices that make it plain that male and female equivalents of the same words do not necessarily have the same connotations, and show that our culture has different attitudes and feelings toward men and women. This has been referred to as the semantic derogation of women. One study of the historical patterns of word usage concludes that many words concerning women that were once neutral have acquired derogatory connotations over the years (Schulz 1975). For example, the words *Sir* and *Mister* are titles of courtesy, while their female equivalents, *Madam* and *Mistress* have become words often used to designate a brothel-keeper and an unmarried sexual partner. Pet names for women have also followed a downward path. Words commonly used by men are *doll* (a child's toy), *kitten* (a baby cat), *baby* (a newborn human), *girl* (a very young female), *pixey* (a fairy or imaginary being), and *bird, bunny, chick*, and *minx* (members of the animal kingdom). These words rob adult women of their maturity and dignity. The process of deprecation vulgarizes a word, and when such a word is used in connection with women it can acquire an obscene or debased connotation, often implying sexual wantonness. For example, the word *hussy* originally meant *housewife* but in common parlance it now connotes "a brazen, lewd woman or prostitute" (Schulz 1975:66). Even a seemingly innocuous term such as *person* has been used sarcastically or humorously by some men to ridicule modern women's desire for semantic inclusion in occupation titles.

Other writers corroborate these findings, and also see the differential attitudes and feelings about men and women as being rooted in the linguistic structure. Words that formerly had no negative connotations (*dame, broad, nymph, bitch*) are now used in derogation of women. However, the male equivalents have not been downgraded, and when one wants to insult a male, the use of female referents are often used. For instance, a man is called a *sissy* (diminutive form of sister) or referred to as a *bastard* or *son of a bitch*, both terms derogating the honor of the man's mother. Laurel Richardson (1988) pointed out that one can conclude from the language that females do not have a fully autonomous and independent existence. As evidence, she mentioned that the words *he* and *man* can be used grammatically to refer to both men and women. Also, pronoun usage perpetuates alleged personality attributes and career aspirations, since nurses and secretaries are referred to as *she* and doctors and engineers as *he*. In addition, women are defined in terms of their sexual desirability to men, since there are different connotations for unmarried older persons: the male is an *eligible* bachelor while the female is an *old spinster*. Language not only reflects but also shapes visual images and suggests appropriate feelings and attitudes. Thus, language influences values and is an important socializing agent. It is not a neutral force in any society, and sexist language is damaging to women.

Sexual differences concerning language usage have been recognized by law. Swearing has been seen as a masculine and virile form of expression. It has the power to intimidate the "weaker sex" and in order to protect them, a law was passed in California that prohibited the use of obscenities in front of women and children. This was an instance of discrimination against one sex, in this case men, but in a subtle way it also perpetuated the alleged weaker status and need for protection of women. It had other consequences also, as females could be denied access to certain clubs and jobs on the grounds that their presence would legally limit the freedom of expression of males. Drinking in public bars has been considered a masculine activity, the use of alcoholic beverages a male prerogative, and the tavern a place where so-called masculine language can be used with impugnity. Because of that fact, women were prohibited by law from becoming bartenders in many states. This changed when the United States Supreme Court struck down the California law in the case of *Sail'er Inn, Inc. v. Kerby* (1971), and decided that this statute interfered with freedom of expression. This decision invalidated other similar state laws. The Court decided that excluding women from the occupation of bartending violated not only California's own constitution, but also the equal protection clause of the Fourteenth Amendment to the U.S. Constitution and Title VII of the Civil Rights Act of 1964.

It is obvious that times are changing. Since vocabulary embodies conceptual and cognitive notions, and since social environments do not remain static, if a language is to remain adaptive it too must change. Outmoded linguistic practices can impede people in their attempts to meet new contingencies. There are new cultural realities concerning gender. Lacking adjustments in vocabulary usage, there will be a discrepancy between linguistic habits and social reality. Although it may be gradual and subtle, such a process of language adaptation to the new realities of women's lives may be occurring at present. Words like *chairperson, firefighter, police officer,* and *mail carrier* are replacing the designations that connoted males.

Nonverbal Communication

In the socialization process, nonverbal communication is also of great importance for the transmission of attitudes and values. It gives subtle cues concerning the conduct of interpersonal relationships. The available studies show that different self-images and statuses are tacitly communicated by the use of gestures, postures (ways of standing, walking, and sitting), facial expressions, demeanors (ideas conveyed through one's dress, bearing, and deportment), and etiquette. These nonverbal cues observed in normal interaction communicate and constantly reinforce the theme of male dominance, activity, and independence, and the counter-theme of female submissiveness, passivity, and dependence (Goffman 1967). Many examples can be cited concerning the efficacy of nonverbal communication in the maintenance of cultural stereotypes. Two cases, demeanor and etiquette, will be discussed.

Demeanor

It is only women in our society who are assigned a decorative function. Their success in life often depends to a large extent on how attractive, young, and sexually desirable to men they can appear to be. Much time, effort, and expense are spent to achieve success in the physical aspects of their lives, since acceptance and happiness depend to a large extent on close approximation to the cultural stereotype. For a woman, this affects how others regard her and even her own self-esteem. She must remain slim and use cosmetics effectively to look as pretty as possible and so be pleasing to men. Although looking attractive is an asset for men also, it is a cultural expectation mostly for women.

The clothing designed for women also contributes to an air of allurement and gives others the message of femininity. Short skirts which show the contours of the legs, tight sweaters and jeans which accentuate the female form, long hair and the cultivation of long fingernails which require time and attention, and high-heeled shoes which restrict freedom of movement all reinforce the female stereotype of feminine appeal based on physical attraction rather than mental perspicuity. These props also give the message that the female incorporates and adheres to the unequal norms concerning the male activist, who has choices, and the female passivist, who waits to be selected on the basis of her appearance.

Etiquette

The rules of conduct involved in everyday interaction go unquestioned. Laurel Walum (1974) analyzed one rule of gender etiquette that appears on the surface to be the mere exercise of good manners but is actually fraught with meaning as it conveys the message that men and women are not perceived as equals. This is the common "door ceremony." When a man and woman are walking together down a hall and they come to a closed door, the woman waits while the man goes ahead and opens the door for her to pass through. Then the man follows. So thorough is the socialization process that this habitual routine is almost automatic and has remained unquestioned. Walum argues that such a seemingly trivial common ceremony is in fact quite nontrivial, and has an impact on the maintenance of cultural values. In a simple way it affirms not only the nature of the social order, but also its morality. The door ceremony functions to bind society together, as all rituals do, in that generalized social norms are being adhered to. Both parties in the ritual understand the notions incorporated in the concepts of masculinity and femininity, and both are playing their roles. This involves the social stance that the male is the doer; he is self-confident, strong, and worldly, the authority in control. Man alone is capable of facing the unknown behind the closed door. The female unthinkingly acknowledges all this as she waits. She communicates that she accepts the passive role, and signals her frailty, weakness, and dependence on a male to help her through her daily activities. Through a simple common courtesy, men and women tacitly confirm gender stereotypes and communicate the acceptance of the patriarchal social order (Walum 1974).

The interaction patterns that are part of the daily personal habits of men and women contribute to the stability and predictability of society. As such they are functional, although they do not necessarily benefit particular individuals. While modern laws do not mandate behavior that is deferential to women, the interaction routines such as the one described are manifestations of ideas ingrained in the culture. These revolve around the patriarchal notion of male superiority, and the need for a female to marry and live her life under the aegis of a man. Males are seen as the protectors of women, who are weak and incapable of managing on their own. These concepts have formed the basis of domestic law (see Chapter 4). They are also the foundation of work laws, as "for women's own good" women have legally been barred from freedom of the choice of occupations and certain employment opportunities (see Chapter 5).

On the informal level, perceptions vary as to how these gender assignments are to be interpreted. Man as authority, doer, decider, protector, and virile he-man can take the pleasant form of door opener or it can be manifested in selfishness and even violence against women (see the discussion of wife-battering and rape in Chapter 6). Men and women do not always realize that both behavior patterns emanate from the same ideology, that of sexual inequality. Having a door held open for one can be too big a price to pay for inferior social status, lack of power, and lack of opportunity in the labor market.

Television and Communication

Another major way that gender stereotypes are reinforced is through the mass media. The print and audiovisual media comprise an enormous part of what we call "big business." Billions of dollars are involved, and millions of people are reached. Television is the entertainment medium that reaches the most homes. Its portrayals of people are passively accepted as normal, even though gender stereotypes form the basis of most character delineations. The passive indoctrination continues for an average of five to seven viewing hours each day, research has shown.

Many surveys have been conducted to analyze television presentations of female roles. After one survey, conducted by the United States Civil Rights Commission in 1977, a report that was highly critical of the television industry was released. It attacked the television industry for the constant portrayal of a social structure where males are in control of their lives and are seen as "more serious, more independent, and more likely to hold prestigious jobs." On the other hand, women "were younger, often unemployed, more 'family-bound,' and often found in comic roles. Those women who were employed were in stereotyped and sometimes subservient occupations" (Parrillo 1980:25).

Stereotyping of women in television advertising is also rampant; women are still portrayed as individuals who are unable to

make a decent cup of coffee or buy the right dog food, who require laundry instructions from a man who probably does not wash his own clothes, and who spend the major part of the day cleaning the toilet bowl and admiring their reflections in the dinner dishes. (Friedman 1977:xiii)

Such programming unobtrusively reinforces the old gender stereotypes and also socializes the young into the accepted patterns. While television has tremendous potential for changing these images, instead it seems to be in the business of upholding the old, hackneyed role definitions of women. (See Davidson and Gordon 1979, Gerbner and Gross 1976, Richardson 1988, Tuchman 1978.)

Devaluation and Social Status

One strategy used for the maintenance of dominance is the inferiorizing and devaluation of women by viewing them as being all alike, a categorical perception based on physical attributes. One social scientist, Edwin Schur (1984), listed four types of evidence for this allegation. First, there exists in our social and economic system pronounced sexual inequality. This is reflected in our stratification scheme. Women are in the lower echelons of the socioeconomic and occupational prestige ladders, and thus receive a low evaluation within the society. Second, women are objectified and are perceived categorically. Modes of perception that negate women are sometimes implicit, and sometimes explicit or even blatant. The everyday treatment of women suggests that they are not being valued as individuals but rather are perceived as being all alike, as evidenced in daily interaction. For example, women are perceived to need the door opened, their bag carried, and so forth. Third, devaluation is evidenced in cultural symbolism. Schur agreed that common language usage often slights, derogates, trivializes, or unnecessarily sexualizes women. The symbolism is also a part of the message of the mass media. Pornography, whether soft-core or hard-core, adds much imagery that is blatant and sexually objectifying to the cultural symbols. Public manifestations include the use of words like *bunny, doll,* and *minx* in reference to women, the pictorial depiction of their sexual characteristics and of exaggerated bodily dimensions in many magazines, and advertisements that allege their extreme preoccupation with soiled clothes and shiny dishes. The fourth evidence that Schur suggests concerns the victimization of women. Devaluation is confirmed in the context of women's relation to the definitions of deviance. This concerns not only the many "deviances" imputed to women under our male normative system, but also the fact that male offenses against women have not been strongly condemned. For instance, wife battering has been viewed as family squabbling, men have not been apprehended in the crime of prostitution, and in rape the onus has been on the female victim to supply corroborative evidence that she was indeed raped and is not lying.

These four major grounds for acceptance of the notion that women have a devalued status are convincing. Under such conditions, aspirations are discouraged and opportunities restricted. Such systematic devaluation becomes a self-fulfilling prophecy for a woman, and the realization of her full potential may be thwarted. Stereotypes concerning her lack of ability to cope with the outside world will thus be reinforced. In effect, the woman does become inferior socially and economically since avenues of endeavor leading to the acquisition of resources are denied to her. Her lower position relative to men is blamed on her alleged physical and mental handicaps and not on the restrictive social forces that have condemned her to that state. When her lack of ability is not blamed, her subordinate status is attributed to God's will; the following lines from an 1873 Supreme Court decision are typical of the social attitudes that prevailed:

The civil law, as well as nature herself, has always recognized a wide difference in the respective spheres and destinies of man and woman. Man is, or should be woman's protector and defender. The natural and proper timidity and delicacy which belongs to the female sex evidently unfits it for many of the occupations of civil life. (*Bradwell v. Illinois* 1873)

Indeed, the Court was reflecting the common knowledge of its day.

Socialization and Law

It is more efficient to impose values and norms on the individual and affect social control through the socialization process rather than through formal legal pronouncements. Once the culture's mores become internalized, the individual regulates his or her own behavior to conform to the culture. Thus self-policing, rather than formal external coercion, is usually based on the person's belief in the correctness of the norms of the culture, and thus the system is perpetuated. Acceptance and compliance with general cultural norms are widespread and includes people who benefit the most from the system as well as those who benefit the least. However, informal rules are not always enough.

In large, complex, heterogeneous societies the socialization process is insufficient to ensure unanimity of understandings and the smooth human interaction that an orderly society requires. Different groups perceive society from different vantage points, and become convinced of the correctness of their perspectives and norms. The modern pluralistic society with its accelerated pace of social change requires written laws, prescribed punishments, and enforcement agencies to ensure that general overall rules will be adhered to. Laws serve as guidelines for behavior when there is doubt concerning the norms.

The task of obtaining a gender-neutral society is not a facile matter. While innovations and adaptations in gender roles are occurring in the informal norms, change has proven to be a slower process on the formal level. The disparate social conditioning of males and females has been effective in the past in laying a foundation for sex discrimination in the society and the law. Unequal treatment has generally not been questioned until comparatively recently. Modern household amenities have facilitated the acceptance of both a private and a public life for women. Economic and family changes are now making it very difficult for lawmakers to sustain the myth of female inferiority. Increasingly more women have found it necessary to simultaneously raise children alone and enter the marketplace, and many have proven themselves capable in leadership roles, thus refuting the stereotypical images of women.

A catalyst that is starting to change attitudes is modern law which mandates equal treatment in the labor market and in education and family systems. This compels social changes. Many of the existing discriminatory older laws are being reinterpreted today in the courts to reflect the reality of women's lives. When archaic laws that treat women differently from men remain on the books, they often are ignored or unenforced. Thus, there is a close relationship between law and social change. Later chapters detail the past circumstances, present realities, and new legal pronouncements in major areas of everyday life. First the sociology of law itself will be discussed.

3

The Nature of Law

The sociology of law seeks to formulate, categorize, and verify the general interrelations between the law and other social factors. To this end, the task of the social scientist is to identify the various sources of law, show how they affect the functioning of modern law, and highlight the interaction of the legal system with the activities and relationships that comprise the social system.

Law is a major institution of social integration, as it helps regulate human interaction by supplying coherence, stability, and limitations for personal behavior patterns. Human freedom is defined as freedom within the formal and informal boundaries set by the society. Formal decrees are necessary when the informal sanctions that function to ensure acceptance of the mores are inadequate. An understanding of why laws are needed, however, does not sufficiently explain the process by which a society comes to have certain laws and why some of them are differentially enforced. For this it is necessary to understand the social sources of law.

It is a matter of record that in the United States there have been disparate assumptions concerning the rights of men and those of women. This is true in spite of the assertion in the Delcaration of Independence that "all men are created equal." In addition, the U.S. Constitution guarantees "equal protection of the laws," although there have been, and still are, differential applications of the law on the basis of sex.

THE BASES OF LAW

There are several generally accepted theories concerning the origin of law. A theory is a comprehensive explanation concerning some aspect of how society works. It directs one's thinking on the subject by offering explanation and allowing predictions to be made concerning future contingencies. In short, a theoretical viewpoint governs the way that a social phe-nomenon is seen and understood. Where law came from and why it devel-oped as it did are questions that can be approached by using theoretical perspectives that concentrate on (1) law as a natural phenomenon, (2) law as custom, (3) law as emanating from the structure/function of a society, and (4) law from the conflict perspective that deals with the maintenance of power. A brief introduction to these perspectives will enlighten the later discussions of the legal inequality of the sexes in certain areas of human endeavor.

Law as a Natural Phenomenon

The notion that there are inherent in human existence certain fundamental legal principles for the guidance of human conduct that are open to human cognition is an old one. It was generally accepted that these legal principles emanated from some supernatural force or abstract universal truth. This belief views law as coming from a higher source and existing regardless of human enactments. The force is everywhere and is everlasting. All philo-sophies of natural law share a basic common belief that certain principles are deeply grounded in the general plan of life and are an integral part of all social groups.

The theory of natural law is grounded in the assertion that the basic qualities of man's nature are knowable, and they should be the basis for the social and legal ordering of human beings. It requires the acceptance of the concept of a moral universe "whose laws have as much claim on men as those of the physical universe itself." The theory holds that "laws come either directly from God or are inevitable rules made in harmony with the nature of things" (Kidder 1983:58).

In the United States, ideals of natural law can be deduced from the references in the Declaration of Independence to "the Laws of Nature's God" and to the "self-evident" truths "that all men are created equal and endowed by their Creator with certain inalienable rights." Natural law is also acknowledged in the Bill of Rights, the first ten amendments to the U.S. Constitution, which insure the maintenance of the individual's God-given rights. Religiosity sustains the legal system and religious precepts help establish the legitimacy of authority. For example, ideas of justice and the relationship of women to men were decreed and fulfilled by a type of logic determined by the cosmological order. The subordination of women to men was thought to be enforced by nature, by reason, and by revelation. Therefore, it has had legal sanction, as the two previously cited court de-cisions show. Legal inequality was based on the alleged natural delicacy of women (see Chapter 4), an attribute that was largely a myth.

The distinction between facts and values can become obscured in the theory of natural law, which has much in common with theological beliefs.

If people perceive law to be based on a natural ordering that morally compels obedience, the resulting behavior is not too different from behavior that is based on ethical and spiritual principles felt to be required by a deity. The major difference is that theological principles are accepted on faith while natural law is felt to be knowable through right reasoning. Both ideologies, natural law and theology, result in a general acceptance of principles, since people are loath to violate rules based either on compelling forces over which they have no control or on the imperatives of a supernatural being.

In the seventeenth and eighteenth centuries the natural law philosophers looked to *right reasoning* as a guide for discerning the most perfect form of law based on eternal postulates of reason and justice (Vago 1981). Right reasoning, it should be pointed out, is a criterion that cannot be verified through empirical scrutiny, and so it lends itself to interpretation by the more powerful individuals in society.

An analysis of the word *natural* alone does not afford total enlightenment as to its social and legal usage. At best, the concept *natural* is enigmatic and does not allow clarity of definition. It is a vague term that can incorporate social recommendations that solidify the social order, or involve deterministic forces toward phenomena over which people have no control. While there is doubt as to its precise meaning, the standardized usage of the term natural as applied to women's social roles is unequivocal. Natural law rationale has been used to keep women working as unpaid domestics in the home and has prohibited them from competing for the power and resources that society has to offer. They have been barred from education and occupations of power and prestige. Women did not even have control over their own bodies, as society (as reflected in the law until recently) deemed it unnatural to use contraceptives to prevent unwanted pregnancy since the so-called natural order of things would be disrupted.

It has been viewed as natural that women should live out their lives inhabiting a separate sphere from men by remaining in the home to serve as nurturant and homemaker, and the laws have effectively prevented them from doing otherwise. As Christine Pierce (1971) pointed out, the concept *natural* in common language usage has a social interpretation that involves recommendations of what is desirable and acceptable, since what is truly preordained or determined is inevitable and legislation concerning these things would be unnecessary. It can be concluded that the ultimate evaluation of what is considered natural in a society is made by those in power.

Law as Institutionalized Customs

Law has also been perceived as a formal restatement of the customs prevalent in a society. The customs themselves have arisen as an expression of the values and norms that developed in the society as it sought solutions to the problems of group life. What a society accepts as truth and as common knowledge are often reflected in its formal rules. Customs evolve over time, and through informal enforcement processes they become so much a part of everyday life that conformance is largely habitual and unthinking. However, there has not always been a perfect correlation between customs and laws.

The classic example of such incompatibility was the 1919 Volstead Act, which became the Eighteenth Amendment to the U.S. Constitution. It banned the sale of alcoholic beverages. Since it was customary for people to drink alcohol, and since serving cocktails and wines at dinners and social gatherings had long been a folkway, citizens who were otherwise law-abiding found creative ways to circumvent the law. It proved almost impossible to enforce, and fourteen years later the Twenty-First Amendment to the Constitution was passed to end the era of prohibition. This points out the difficulty of changing customs by legal means if the population is generally opposed to the change. William Sumner, an early writer on folkways, asserted that there must be a basic compatibility between a society's customs and its laws if the laws are to be enforceable (1906).

When legally mandated social change runs counter to internalized expectations, some people seek creative ways to circumvent the law. There are many examples of this in relation to women's quest for legal recognition in the labor market. It was long the ideology that women were inferior to men, and under common law it was the custom that women were generally confined to domestic work in the home. Unfortunately, cultural norms tend to remain rather stable over time, even when social and economic circumstances have undergone metamorphoses. Today, despite passage of the Equal Pay Act in 1963 and Title VII of the Civil Rights Act in 1964, women still are concentrated in the largely segregated traditionally female occupations, which usually involve domestic skills. Notwithstanding the legislation concerning equal rights, men in personnel and decision-making positions have found ways to circumvent the law. For example, for years height and weight requirements were commonly used to flout antidiscrimination laws concerning gender, until this was declared unconstitutional by the Supreme Court in 1973 (see Chapter 5).

The theory that law is based on custom makes the assumption that the original choices were based on correct preferences that were learned, and disregards the notion that for individuals thinking is often subconsciously acquired and irrational. However, customs are functional for the society and they contribute to orderly social interaction. It is not always known how customs came into existence. Anthropologists feel that early customs enabled a group to survive by giving an overall coherence to the culture. When the external environment changes, however, new and appropriate responses are called for. The extent to which a society is successful at this adaptation is a guage of internal consistency. There are irrational contradictions in a society that on the one hand alleged that women are a weak sex, overemotional, feather-brained, and in need of protection from men, and on the other hand required them to do heavy work in the fields or work long daily hours operating heavy machinery in the burgeoning factory system during the era of massive immigration to the United States. The reality seems to be that when monetary profits are involved, ideology can be bent, and when workers are socially devalued they can be paid less for their labor.

The theory that law originates in custom also helps us to understand why some laws are irrational, since the customs on which they were based may have also been irrational. For instance, the Supreme Court's *Dred Scott* decision of 1857, (*Scott v. Sanford*:1857) which proclaimed that a black slave had no civil rights, was based on custom that alleged that black adults remained at the inferior level of children. Concerning sex, when it is taken for granted in the culture that there are inherent qualitative differences between the sexes, the perception will become formalized as the rationale for legal discrimination between men and women. For instance, the refusal of Congress to pass legislation to give women the franchise since, according to custom, they were incapable of intelligent public decisions, was responsible for preventing women from having this political power until 1920. Clearly, there are times in the relationship between custom and law when law must take a dominant role in modifying customary ideas and bringing about uniform social change.

There are other problems besides the irrationality of many customs. One problem has to do with population pressure. With the increasing diversity and size of the U.S. population, law based on the harmony of generally accepted mores and customs can no longer be taken for granted. Public opinion no longer serves to ensure conformity in a heterogeneous society, for the ideology of pluralism includes a recognition of diverse and even competing customs regulating the behavior of various ethnic and economic groups. A force that supercedes customs is thus required to reconcile diverse customs and interests if cooperation and coordination are to be achieved. For a large and varied population, a formal legal system, which is based on the awareness of both national and individual needs, and which can be effective in its application to altered circumstances in times of accelerated social change, is mandated.

Structure/Function Theory of Law

Another perspective of the origin of law concerns the social structure itself and the need for the maintenance of organized social activity. Within the society, statuses and roles represent a structure of relationships between people of different ranks with varying power and wealth. All societies are hierarchically structured systems with each of their parts contributing to their survival. Functional analysis deals with the consequences of any social phenomenon on the entire social structure. A law is a manifestation of the normative system, and it contributes to social control. The source of control over the individual is embedded in the social structure and the institutions, which are viewed as coercive in nature. Change in one part of the system influences changes in other parts in order to adjust the whole. For instance, if there is an increase of crime in a city, there may also be an increase in the criminal justice system to compensate for it. Society has a tendency to seek this balance. Thus, stability is maintained, the status quo is justified, and social change is neutralized and de-emphasized. Society has laws because legal configurations serve an important function, that of ensuring that equilibrium will be maintained at all times. Thus, law is an element in the social structure that contributes to the survival of the society.

An early structuralist, Emile Durkheim, who wrote during the turn of the century, analyzed society's need to preserve solidarity by creating and preserving certain mechanisms to keep people cooperating (Durkheim 1964). His analysis is that as societies grew larger and more heterogeneous due to specialization and diverse values, social consensus could no longer be taken for granted. As individualism developed, norms became de-sanctified, and organic solidarity based on the differences resulting from the division of labor emerged. The function of law changed from being a reflection of generally accepted customs to being a means of preserving harmonious relationships and reconciling diverse customs and interests. Law was thus a response to the ambivalence created by the society's increasing complexity. Generally, law provides uniformity, and as such it fills the voids caused by the imbalances of social change which otherwise threaten the fabric of social life.

A distinction can be made between manifest and latent functions of activities within the social system. When applied to law, manifest functions concern the intended and overt functions of a particular piece of legislation. Latent functions are the unintended and covert consequences that are not officially recognized but that can have important consequences (Merton 1967). For instance, the so-called protective laws were passed so that the exploitation of women employed in factories would be curtailed (see Chapter 5). These laws had the latent effect of justifying discrimination and limiting the amount of wages a woman could earn, since they prevented her from earning overtime pay, and made her ineligible for many of the more remunerative jobs in factories. Lack of adequate wages often made women dependent on men for sustenance, and reinforced the officially held notion that a woman's primary status was that of housewife. Thus, the protective laws were functional for maintaining the status quo.

An attribute of stratified society is the organized pattern of unequal privilege, power, and wealth. A limitation of structure/function theory concerning the basis of law has been a general lack of interest in the personal motives of those who control and use legal power. Those in power in society are able to produce laws that are in their own interests and thus to perpetuate the pattern of inequality. Laws that make divorce difficult, contraceptives hard to obtain, and abortions illegal, and that prescribe restrictive rules in employment, are subtle reminders that a woman's role is that of domestic and child producer within the confines of marriage. In the past, women were socialized to accept the social role of nurturant, and a type of self-fulfilling prophecy operated as women specialized in domestic activity in a male-dominated home—woman's place, by social definition. These unequal relationships have a tendency to persist long after social circumstances have changed.

The structure/function perspective seeks to justify the inequalities within a society by explaining them in terms of their function in permitting organized groups to cope with their environments in a structured way. Law is but one element of the many interlocking systems that contribute toward this end. Others, such as the conflict theorists, however, question the assertion that past laws that mandated social inequality for blacks and women came into being because the society needed them for its survival.

Conflict Perspective

A growing orientation in the sociology of law is that of the conflict theorists. They view social life in terms of the tension and conflict between individuals and groups. The social world is characterized by a continual struggle and clash of interests. Law is viewed as a manipulative device of the powerful elites to establish and maintain their dominance over other classes in a society. The emphasis is on power relationships, which are made legitimate by law.

Conflict theorists reject the assumption of consensus, an assumption inherent in natural law, custom, and structure/function theories. Instead, society is composed of many classes of antagonists who use law as one tool in the promotion of their own interests and superiority. This manipulation of power for self-interests is facilitated because law has an ideological as well as a coercive role. As societies become complex, law has to accommodate competing power centers, so it has to appear not to favor any one of them. It therefore adopts the appearance or ideology of promoting equality. To this end, the law "developed generality (its commands applied to everyone regardless of class) and autonomy (the legal establishment became a separate competing power unbeholden to any single elite)" (Kidder 1983:196). Since law carries with it the notions of universal justice and the common good, the concept is seldom questioned by those who benefit the least from the system. "The promotion of the rule of law dampens the resistance of poorer classes by obscuring the real, imbalanced consequences of the system" (Kidder 1983:89). Thus, the system supports domination and exploitation more effectively than if brute force were used.

Conflict theorists speak of social change as a salient fact of life. Law in the simpler societies of the past relied on the existence of common understandings and integrated community networks, which resulted in general social consensus and a stable and orderly society. Modern society, however, is often polarized into different interest groups. Specialization, or the division of labor in society, perforce produces a hierarchical social order since all specialties do not command the same amount of social appreciation and material wealth. Inevitably, some groups dominate others. The basic problem for those in power is the maintenance of their position. The elites thus have a need to legitimize their situations and make specific and orderly the rules of accepted interaction among the groups in society.

Present post-industrial society has encouraged increasing individualism, and hence an increasing tension between group consensus and private interest. One result is that different groups vie for domination in a milieu where change is ubiquitous. A different kind of social solidarity emerges, as do different kinds of law. In-group members must often make token concessions to out-group members in an attempt to appease them and maintain the status quo. Thus, conflict brings about change, such as the redistribution of power or material resources.

The crucial question concerns who in society has the power to effect action. Power becomes concentrated, and no matter which model of social power in the United States is accepted, an analysis makes it obvious that power is not a democratic concept. Power is not equally shared by all citizens. However, when the power division runs along sex lines, one is led to question the conditions that legitimated such inequality.

Often laws are the result of the interests of a few who have the power to impose their ideas on the masses. According to Austin Turk, there are five kinds of power that accrue to those who control the established legal system:

1. Physical force, which may be used to restrain dissidents;
2. Economic power, which supplies a system of rewards and punishments to the benefit of those who control the system;
3. Political power, whereby certain political structures and their norms are supported instead of others, thus constituting a method of control;
4. Power to influence the ideological environment, which helps promote unquestioned compliance and acceptance as inevitable and desirable; and
5. Diversionary power, which helps mask real sources of inequality and the key ingredients that centralize power by getting some people involved in minor law suits and political movements (1976:276).

Conflict theorists see law as a social phenomenon, not an inevitable natural product. Many statutes are interpreted as an outcome of conflict situations whereby the ruling elite have moved to consolidate their privilege, power, and economic strength over other groups in society. In this perspective it is assumed that the legal institution is not value-neutral but rather is oriented to special interests. Conflict theorists wish to debunk myths about society and expose the machinations of the interest groups that seek to acquire and retain power. Law is used as an instrument of power, and conflicting groups contend to satisfy their interests against those of others.

However, social change is an inescapable fact of social life. If the incumbent power structure changes, laws can be modified to reflect that situation. New social definitions can also emerge. Out-groups such as minorities and women can seek more legal representation and control over the formal rules that govern their lives. The most hopeful avenue leading to social equality for women has been modern law, which has increasingly recognized their needs for equal treatment.

ROOTS OF LAW IN THE UNITED STATES

Whatever the perspective concerning the basis of law in society, the reality is that we do live under a coercive legal system. People everywhere live by the rule of law. This includes the whole spectrum or organized life, whether the group is a preliterate community adapting to harsh environmental conditions or a complex and technologically advanced urban-industrial society with a heterogeneous population.

In the United States there are many legal rules emanating from many political jurisdictions. The enactment of laws is the province of the legislative, administrative, and judicial bodies of government, and their legal pronouncements are the result of special social circumstances and precipitating factors. A brief review of the English common law tradition and of constitutional law in the United States is useful for understanding women's legal status, since it can be said that the former tradition is the underpinning for sexual inequality and in the latter body lies the hope of changing it. Later chapters will be concerned with certain landmark laws and Supreme Court decisions concerning women's rights.

Old English Common Law

The basis of U.S. law in colonial times was the English system of common law. Starting in the twelfth and thirteenth century, common law was built up in England over the centuries on a case-by-case basis as a result of the kings' judges' decisions in the settlement of disputes. As a situation arose it was judged in the courts in terms of the prevailing understandings of reasonableness. These decisions were recorded and became the precedents on which later decisions in similar cases were based. The laws themselves were not written, and the principle of law had to be inferred from the previous case decisions.

When the first English settlers came to the North American continent they brought with them the concept of the supremacy of law and the common law tradition. Colonial governments, as extensions of the government of

England, continued to follow it. After independence, the basic English system of law was, in general, continued as a matter of expedience, unless it was in violation of the Constitution of the United States or in conflict with state laws. During the nineteenth century, this common law was transformed into U.S. statute law. State legislatures examined each area of the English common law, extracted the basic principles, and arranged them in a systematic collection of statutes. The object was to restate, modify, or clarify the concepts embodied in the precedents. The two main categories or collections of these statutes subsequently became known as the penal code and the civil code (Alexander 1975).

Today many of our laws retain the terminology and ideology of English common law. For instance, in many states the definition of rape still includes the archaic words, "carnal knowledge of a woman." U.S. laws vary somewhat from state to state in spite of a common base, however; this is because each state made its own judgment concerning which principles should be extrapolated. Today, when no specific statute has been enacted concerning a particular situation, the relevant common law principle still applies and is still enforceable. Thus, the early legal concepts and legal procedures still have vitality, and although there are other influences on law such as the need to adapt to the dominating themes and conditions of particular eras, the conceptual underpinning is still the common law tradition.

Constitutional Law

Constitutional law is the body of law that not only delineates the political organization and powers of government, but also sets limitations on the exercise of governing power. The U.S. Supreme Court is vested with the power of interpreting the fundamental principles of law based on the Constitution.

The rights and freedoms that U.S. citizens expect are guaranteed to them by the U.S. Constitution and its amendments. Its underlying ideology was first put forth in the Declaration of Independence, which states that "no citizen shall be denied the right to life, liberty, and the pursuit of happiness." The Constitution was formulated during a time when the country had a rural, agrarian economy and a population of fewer than four million people. With profound insight, the founding fathers made provisions for amendment and for interpretation by the Supreme Court of the United States, in order to render the Constitution elastic, dynamic, and vital, and to allow its essential principles to continue to be applied during changing times. Congressional laws, judicial decisions, and amendments have contributed to the growth, adaptability, and application of the Constitution. Through such means the founding documents have proven remarkably flexible through the years.

There are many different but simultaneous legal realities due to the fact that there are various legal jurisdictions enacting legislation. The U.S. Constitution allots to the states jurisdiction over certain aspects of social life. For instance, state laws have long been involved in the regulation of marriage, and have specified the minimum age for marriage, health requirements, and grounds for divorce. In an area such as domestic law, therefore, the statutes of the fifty states can vary considerably. This is attributed somewhat to differences in social circumstances in various regions of the country, but is mainly attributed to the extent of the lingering influences of the region's early colonizers at the time the state laws were formally encoded. While English common law was the major influence, French and Spanish jurisprudence lingered in a few southern states that had originally been settled by those countries.

U.S. constitutional law is a unique system within the country. The federal government and the states, counties, and towns all pass laws that pertain to their levels of jurisdiction. The laws are binding unless they are overridden by the Constitution, the U.S. Congress, or the federal court system. In addition to varying legislation, judges' decisions in similar cases also may differ by legal jurisdiction. This decentralization of lawmaking and legal interpretation leads to regional variations and contributes to the lack of a single consistent stance on ideology concerning the legal equality between the sexes. The U.S. Constitution guarantees "due process" and "equal protection of the laws" for all citizens. In recent times, in the absence of an amendment such as the proposed Equal Rights Amendment, which would automatically render discriminatory state laws unenforceable, these two clauses have proven useful to women in their legal challenges to what they perceive to be discriminatory laws.

The Declaration of Independence states that "All men are created equal"; at the time of its drafting, the word *men* was used in the literal and not in the generic sense. In practice, it meant white men only. Women were not guaranteed equality in all areas with men. After many years of political and social activism, women were able to have some impact in overturning encrusted habits of thought. Ultimately, legal means had to be sought for the redress of grievances. Bringing suits in the courts for the purpose of invalidating discriminatory state law became a means of forcing a more equitable interpretation of the founding documents of the country. Thus, judicial review has in recent years functioned as a powerful generator of individual rights, and has been a catalyst for social equality.

Judicial Review: The U.S. Supreme Court

The constitutionality of any law in the country, whether state or federal, may be challenged. The U.S. Supreme Court renders the final verdict on all matters involving the federal Constitution since it is empowered with interpreting its fundamental principles. In the landmark *Marbury v. Mad-*

ison case in 1803, Chief Justice John Marshall asserted the justification for the power of the Supreme Court to review the constitutional validity of actions taken by other branches of government. Marshall said that:

Certainly all those who have framed written constitutions contemplate them as forming the fundamental and paramount law of the nation, and consequently, the theory of every such government must be, that an act of the legislature, repugnant to the constitution, is void. It is emphatically the province and duty of the judicial department to say what the law is. Those who apply the rule to particular cases must of necessity expound and interpret that rule. If two laws conflict with each other, the courts must decide on the operation of each.

So, if a law be in opposition to the constitution; if both the law and the constitution apply to a particular case ... the court must determine which of these conflicting rules govern the case. (*Marbury v. Madison* 1803)

The rule that the Supreme Court has the final authority has now been law for more than 185 years, even though the Constitution does not specifically state that the last word in articulating and enforcing individual rights rests with the judiciary. The Supreme Court has almost complete control over its docket, and it can decide not to hear a case without giving a reason. If an appeal is accepted for review by the Court, a majority decision of the nine justices is necessary to invalidate the law that is being challenged. When a law is judged unconstitutional, the decision has a sweeping effect, and all prior similar laws are rendered unenforceable. The decision has the effect of overriding the law. Thus, the Supreme Court deals with matters of law as they pertain to individual rights and also affect the reality of people's lives.

For example, the 1973 Supreme Court decision legalizing abortion, *Roe v. Wade*, rendered unconstitutional many state laws prohibiting abortion on demand. Included in the rationale of the Court in that case was the statement, "the word person as used in the Fourteenth Amendment, does not include the unborn." However controversial the status of the fetus may be (see Chapter 4), this decision became the law of the land, and some statutes had to be revised or ignored since any state laws denying a woman an abortion before a certain period in her pregnancy would not be upheld in court.

Another example of judicial review concerns the alleged right to privacy. The Supreme Court has been charged with interpreting what is meant by privacy since the concept is not referred to specifically in the Constitution. In their decision in a case involving the sale of contraceptives, the justices alleged that the sale and use of contraceptives could not be prohibited by the state, since the right to personal privacy superseded even the Bill of Rights, and since the marital relationship was intimate to the degree of being sacred (see *Griswold v. Connecticut* 1965 in Chapter 4).

As will be seen from later discussions, other more recent Supreme Court decisions have been instrumental in changing encrusted attitudes and in overturning legal statutes that denied women full equality and protection of the laws. Although their decisions have not always been popular with the states, the Supreme Court justices represent the final authority.

In the struggle for equal rights, the most common formal guarantees to be invoked are often the fundamental rights in the Fourth, Fifth, Ninth, Fourteenth, and Nineteenth amendments. A brief explanation of some of the passages from these documents will be useful for the later discussion of the cases based on them.

Constitutional Bases of Court Decisions Affecting Women

When the Constitution of the United States was being written, the founding fathers were understandably concerned with the means by which the new government would function. After they had completed the main body of the Constitution, they felt concerned that they had taken for granted some basic values in which they believed and which had to be made more explicit before they felt that the document was fully acceptable. This was done through the adoption of the Bill of Rights, the first ten amendments to the Constitution. These rights were viewed as fundamental in a free society, and were not to be abridged by the federal government. Later, more amendments were adopted. To date, twenty-six amendments have been added to the U.S. Constitution.

The procedure for the adoption of an amendment is not a facile one. Once an amendment has been proposed in Congress, it must be ratified by three-fourths of the states. At times, many years elapse before an amendment is adopted. The proposed Equal Rights Amendment, which passed Congress in 1972, failed to be ratified by three-quarters of the states. The proposed amendment read simply: "Equality of rights under the law shall not be denied or abridged by the United States or by any State on account of sex." That is, in the determination of equal rights of U.S. citizens, sex should not be a factor. The passage of an amendment would have by itself rendered sex-discriminatory laws invalid. However, women have had some success in challenging discriminatory laws on the basis of other amendments.

Fourth Amendment

This amendment concerns the right of the people to be secure in their persons, houses, papers, and other effects, against unreasonable searches and seizures. It implies that an individual's personal privacy shall not be violated, and that the right to privacy is just as important as any other right that is carefully and specifically delineated.

Fifth Amendment

This amendment concerns legal rights. It contains the self-incrimination clause which states that no person shall be compelled to be a witness against him- or herself. Also, no person shall be deprived of life, liberty, or property without due process of law. This guarantees personal rights and enables citizens to create a zone of privacy that they cannot be forced to surrender.

Ninth Amendment

This amendment states that even if certain rights are not specifically enumerated in the Constitution, they shall not be construed as denied to the people. This aimed at preventing the denial of a fundamental right simply on the technicality that it was not specifically mentioned in the Constitution, since it was not possible to list all rights that are due the people.

Fourteenth Amendment

This amendment states that all persons born or naturalized in the United States are citizens of the United States and of the state wherein they reside. No state shall make or enforce any law that shall abridge the privileges or immunities of the citizens of the United States, nor deny to any person within its jurisdiction the equal protection of the laws. The Fourteenth is one of the most far-reaching amendments, since it provides that the basic rights of citizens that are protected by the federal government are not to be abridged by the states.

In spite of the fact that the U.S. Constitution has contained the "equal protection" clause since 1868, such citizens as blacks and women have not always enjoyed equality under the laws. This situation has been challenged with much success in the past two decades, as discussed in the following chapters. Today, many challenges to state laws discriminating against women invoke the "equal protection of the laws" clause of the Fourteenth Amendment.

Nineteenth Amendment

This amendment concerns women's suffrage. It states that the right of citizens of the United States to vote shall not be denied or abridged by the United States or any state on account of sex. Although some states had permitted women to vote, it was not recognized as a national right until 1920 when the Nineteenth Amendment was adopted.

Social Science in the Courtroom: The Brandeis Brief

In the United States the judicial system plays a part in the creation of law. This is a feature of the basic system of checks and balances between the legislative, executive, and judicial branches of government. Although law made by judges emanates from the decisions of specific cases, the impact goes beyond the particular case. Justices are required to give reasons for their decisions based on legal principles. These are written and become public. The decisions then become precedents that will guide the resolution of similar cases in the future. This contributes to continuity and consistency in legal decisions, allows predictions to be made, and assures fairness for persons affected by the decisions since the case is fitted into a larger pattern.

Although the decisions of previous cases become part of the foundation for later decisions, the *Muller v. Oregon* case in 1908 started a precedent that led to the possibility that social facts as well as legal precedents could be taken into consideration when deliberating a case. The *Muller* case concerned the legality of discrimination in the form of protective labor laws for women only. These were laws that prohibited women from working in certain occupations reserved for men. The laws also imposed weight-lifting and hours-of-work restrictions on women but not on men. The Court upheld such laws, arguing that women were different from men and so needed special protection. To substantiate their argument, the justices relied on the massive amount of data compiled by Louis D. Brandeis, which later became known as *The Brandeis Brief*. It was a 113-page compilation of statistics concerning the physical differences between men and women, the social effects of the introduction of machines in industry, the impact of overwork on "female functions" and childbearing capacity, the disastrous effects of long hours of work on the health of women and the welfare of future generations. It was documented by testimonials from doctors and others on the nature and functions of women, and contained much additional information (Babcock, Freedman, Norton, and Ross 1975). In short, Brandeis cited sociological, physiological, and medical data to substantiate the majority decision, an excerpt of which reads:

The limitations which this statute places upon her contractual powers, upon her rights to agree with her employer as to the time she shall labor, are not imposed solely for her benefit, but also largely for the benefit of all. Many words cannot make this plainer. The two sexes differ in structure of body, in the functions to be performed by each, in the amount of physical strength, in the capacity for long-continued labor particularly when done standing, in the influence of vigorous health upon the future well-being of the race, the self-reliance which enables one to assert full rights, and in the capacity to maintain the struggle for subsistence. This difference justifies a difference in legislation and upholds that which is designed to compensate for some of the burdens which rest upon her. (*Muller v. Oregon* 1908)

The Court was impressed by the brief and accepted the validity of taking into account sources other than the judicial in justifying decisions. Thus, the bases on which decisions rest have been widened. Brandeis later became an associate justice of the Supreme Court from 1916 to 1939.

In his analysis of the role of the social sciences in judicial lawmaking, Daniel Moynihan stated that "the range of what is material in lawsuits is now greatly expanded—or will be as the courts submit to the logic, or perhaps it may be better to speak of the spirit, of the social sciences"(1979:23). Although in the *Muller* case average physical size and medical data were used to show the weakness and vulnerability of women, and therefore to justify unequal protective laws, a trend was started for the introduction of social science data in future cases, many of which have been favorable to women. For example, statistics have been used effectively in some women's rights cases, as when litigators have introduced sociological data to show the actual situation of women and the effects of stereotypes on equality, thus influencing the Court to abandon inaccurate and paternalistic views.

CASE: *Taylor v. Louisiana* (1975). This more recent case is cited as an example of the change in the Court's philosophy. Louisiana law permitted the automatic exemption of women from jury duty based on the notion that they were the center of home and family life. The law was challenged on the ground that the Sixth Amendment to the U.S. Constitution guaranteed trial by a jury drawn from a fair cross-section of the community. The fact was that few women had ever served on a jury in Louisiana because they invoked the exemption, leaving the world of such activity to men. In this case a convicted criminal defendant used the situation to challenge his conviction on the grounds that no women had served on his jury.

The importance of this case revolved around the fact that data provided by the plaintiff concerning the reality of women's lives influenced previous positions that had been taken by the Court concerning the "natural sphere of women." Pertinent excerpts from this aspect of the Court's ruling include the following:

Statistics compiled by the Department of Labor indicate that in October, 1974, 54.2% of all women between 18 and 64 years of age were in the labor force. . . . Additionally, in March, 1974, 45.7% of women with children under the age of 18 were in the labor force; with respect to families containing children between the ages of six and seventeen, 67.3% of mothers who were widowed, divorced or separated were in the work force, while 51.2% of the mothers whose husbands were present in the household were in the work force. Even in family units in which the husband was present and which contained a child under three years old, 31% of the mothers were in the work force. . . . While these statistics perhaps speak more to the evolving nature of the role played by women who happen to be members of a family unit, they certainly put to rest the suggestion that all women should be exempt from jury service based solely on their sex and the presumed role in the home. (*Taylor v. Louisiana* 1975)

Sociological facts have become important adjuncts for inclusion in Court deliberations as they are vital when an understanding of the total situation is required. The major institutions such as the family, economy, education, and government are interrelated, and change in one sphere affects changes in another. Law does not exist in a vacuum, but rather is intertwined with the social, economic, and political structure of our culture. Thus, social science has a place in the courtroom.

Standards of Review Used by the Supreme Court

The equal protection clause of the Fourteenth Amendment represents a broad concept, and over the years the Supreme Court, through its interpretive decisions, has shaped it and given it scope and meaning. The Court applies particular standards of review to particular cases under deliberation. The justices must decide which of three distinct tests are applicable to ascertain whether the law in question violates the equal protection clause— the reasonableness test, the suspect classification test, or the intermediate test. A brief explanation will enlighten later case discussions showing how the tests have been applied to women's issues.

The Reasonableness Test

This criterion deals with the purpose of the state law and asks whether it is reasonable for state purposes to treat two classes of people differently. It is a test of rationality, and it has also been called the *rational relationship* test. If the Court decides that there was a reasonable purpose for the law and that the two classes of citizens merit different treatment, then the state law stands.

Most laws do discriminate and differentiate between classes of persons without being illegal. For example, the federal law that provides social security payments only to those over sixty-five years of age who have been members of the work force discriminates against those individuals who never worked, and the state laws which make school attendance compulsory for children under certain ages discriminate between children and adults. Such discrimination between classes of persons has a rational basis and does not violate the equal protection clause since there are valid reasons to differentiate between the groups. The test of reasonableness is a lenient one, and it places the burden of proof of the unreasonableness of a state law on the claimant.

In practice, the reasonableness test does not prohibit all official discrimination. If in the Court's view a compelling state interest is served, it permits state action that differentiates on the basis of race or nationality, and the Court has thus upheld laws concerning school district segregation (Freeman 1984). Under this standard, sex is a reasonable basis for classification and for official discrimination when it can be justified that a compelling state interest is involved. The previously mentioned *Muller v. Oregon* case involved such a test. The Court justified sex discrimination based on the belief that women needed special protection because they were an inferior class of persons, and it was rational and in the state's interest to protect them in the marketplace and preserve them for maternal functions. The *Muller* decision was cited in future cases, and the legal basis in various states for the different treatment of women was confirmed in such diverse areas of social endeavor as education, suffrage, and employment benefits.

In the history of the Supreme Court there are many examples of conflicting decisions. Recent Supreme Court decisions have recognized that no legitimate purpose would be served by state laws that discriminate between male and female workers, male or female students, or other groups of persons similarly situated. The simple test of rationality has been used to declare such discriminatory laws unconstitutional. The following two cases show how social attitudes have changed between 1948 and 1971.

CASE: *Goesaert v. Cleary* (1948). In 1948 the Supreme Court upheld a Michigan law that limited the types of jobs available to women. In this case, Valentine Goesaert, Margaret Goesaert, Gertrude Nadroski, and Caroline McMahon, the appellants, brought action against Owen J. Cleary, Felix H. Flynn, and G. Mennen Williams who were members of the Liquor Control Commission of the State of Michigan. In this case the proscription was against bartending. This proscription was claimed to be an infringement of women's economic and personal rights. The Court justified drawing a sharp line between the sexes, and upheld the state law on the grounds that the state's purpose was to prevent moral and social problems. Prohibiting women from bartending was seen as a reasonable way of preventing these problems.

CASE: *Reed v. Reed* (1971). This 1971 case concerned a challenge to an Idaho law that gave preference to men as administrators of the estates of decedents. Cecil R. and Sally M. Reed were separated, and when their son died intestate (that is, without leaving a will), both parents wanted to be appointed to administer his estate. Although both were equally entitled and qualified, Idaho courts automatically appointed the man. The court ruled that when both relatives apply to the Court, the word *female* should be omitted since it could not be of consequence in the matter, and that the state's excuse of "administrative convenience" for male preference had no rational basis. Automatic preference for the male in such cases were declared unconstitutional.

The Strict Scrutiny or Suspect Classification Test

A more stringent standard than the reasonableness test is the strict scrutiny or suspect classification test. It is used for laws affecting certain fundamental rights, and has generally been applied to racially discriminatory laws. When a law sets up a suspect classification, such as when blacks and whites are treated differently, the law is examined by the Court very closely, with what is called *strict scrutiny*. It looks critically at whether the purpose of the law is of overriding importance, and whether the classification that the law establishes is necessary for accomplishing that purpose. That is, using the strict scrutiny test, the degree of closeness of the correlation between the purpose of a law and the means to achieve it are examined. The burden of proof is on the state to demonstrate a "compelling State interest" for a given law which is being contested on the grounds of the equal protection clause of the Fourteenth Amendment. Many discriminatory state laws have been found unconstitutional by the Court when they failed this strict scrutiny.

The Court has not as yet included sex in its considerations of discrimination under this test. To date, the Court has not in general successfully grappled with the question of women's constitutional status; it has refused to officially extend to gender classifications the same strict scrutiny that it applies to race, alienage, and national origin. However, although sex was not officially included as an inherently suspect classification, the Court has rendered decisions favorable to women based on stricter criteria than those applied under the reasonableness test, as the following case shows (Cary and Peratis 1981, Kay 1988).

CASE: *Frontiero v. Richardson* (1973). The Frontiero case concerned the U.S. Government's denial to its female employees, on the basis of administrative convenience, of the substantive and procedural benefits granted to males. Air Force Lieutenant Sharron Frontiero challenged a law that provided automatic dependency allowances for males in the uniformed services while imposing a restriction on women's dependents. Women had to prove that they paid at least one-half of the spouse's living costs, while allowances were unquestioned for males' spouses even if they earned more than their husbands. The system had been based on old stereotypes. The Court, by a plurality decision, ruled in favor of Lieutenant Frontiero, and decreed that spousal benefits had to be paid regardless of sex.

This case achieved prominence because four of the nine justices were of the opinion that the gross and unjustified stereotypical distinctions between the sexes still pervaded society, and that romanticized paternalism served to keep women in a cage, not on a pedestal. They felt that sex was similar to race and national origin since it is an immutable characteristic determined solely by the accident of birth. That is, these four justices felt that classifications based on sex were inherently suspect, and should therefore be subject to strict judicial scrutiny. Although the *Frontiero* case did not legally change the standard of review used in sex discrimination cases, the plurality decision did have an influence on some later decisions, and some state courts did adopt the strict scrutiny standard (Cary and Peratis 1981, Kay 1988:28).

The Intermediate Test

Since 1976 another standard of review has been applied to some sex discrimination cases. It falls between the reasonableness and the strict scrutiny tests, and has come to be referred to as the intermediate test. When this criterion is used, the state has to prove that the law has an important purpose and that the classification is substantially necessary to achieve that purpose. It is harder for a state to meet this test than the reasonableness test, but less difficult than meeting the requirements of the strict scrutiny test.

The first time this new test was applied was in the case of *Craig v. Boran*

(1976). Men and women were treated differently under an Oklahoma law, as men could not buy 3.2 beer until age twenty-one but women could buy it at age eighteen. Oklahoma justified its law on the basis that sex differences showed up in statistics concerning traffic accidents, and it was a measure to improve traffic safety. Males between the ages of eighteen and twenty-one were arrested at a rate ten times higher than females that age. The Court's decision was that "classification by gender must serve important governmental objectives and must be substantially related to achievement of those objectives" (Freeman 1984:387). The Court ruled that discrimination such as that contained in the Oklahoma law was not reasonable, as regulating drinking and driving could not be done on the basis of sex, and traffic safety, a common good, could be accomplished in a different manner. The Oklahoma law was declared unconstitutional.

In actual practice, in recent cases that have been accepted by the Supreme Court for review, there has not been an automatic and unequivocal application of any particular one of the three tests by the justices. As it stands today, in the absence of an equal rights amendment, the Court has a great deal of flexibility concerning which standard of review to apply in a particular case. Each case has been judged according to particular circumstances. For instance, sometimes the more lenient reasonableness test has been invoked, as in the case of *Kahn v. Shevin* (1974), which allowed beneficial tax treatment for widows because of past economic discrimination against women. Sometimes the strict scrutiny test is used, as in the *DeFunis v. Odergaard* case of the same year, when the Court refused to uphold a law that gave special treatment to minorities who have been stigmatized in the past, on the basis that this would place a "stamp of inferiority" on them due to the law's tacit assumption that they could not succeed on their own merits.

In 1979, in the *Orr v. Orr* case, the Court used the intermediate test to invalidate an Alabama law that required only husbands and not wives to pay alimony to ex-spouses after divorce. The Alabama law was not sex-neutral, and as such it violated the equal protection clause of the Fourteenth Amendment. The Court ruled that whichever spouse had the greater income had to pay alimony if the other spouse was financially needy (Cary and Peratis 1981, Ross and Barcher 1983).

What is important is that family status is no longer a determinant of women's legal status. The Supreme Court continued to invalidate state laws that reinforced role stereotyping and economic dependence of women. When discriminatory statutes were upheld by the Court, compelling grounds had to be found other than the mere fact of being female.

MODERN LAW AND SOCIAL CHANGE

Social change in a complex society is a product of sundry factors and the relationships among them. These include technological innovations, discoveries, global conflicts, economic cycles, intergroup frictions, individualism and accelerated competition, emerging group consciousness, and rising expectations. It is virtually impossible to outline a definitive cause-and-effect relationship for most of the changes that have become part of our social system.

The legal system itself has not been immune to influences from the altered societal needs and expectations of the population in adjusting to new contingencies. Although it is a powerful integrative mechanism in society, it is not a static phenomenon. It is a living and dynamic instrument, and it reflects past consciousness and present new themes in a changing society.

There have been important social changes that the country has faced. These include (1) the decline of the kinship-based system with its fixed statuses, (2) an emergent mobile, socially fragmented, and pluralistic mass society characterized by large-scale organization with new legal problems, and (3) an increased attention to the furtherance of the general welfare (Selznick 1968). A response to some of these trends has been legislation that has aimed to maximize individual freedoms. For example, Congress passed the Equal Pay Act in 1963 and the Civil Rights Act in 1964 mandating an end to discrimination in employment. Women were included in these new guarantees of equal rights.

The courts have also had a significant impact, even though court decisions concern specific issues raised by particular parties to a dispute. Court interpretations have recognized a broader right to privacy in the last forty years. Close scrutiny is given in the review of cases where basic liberties are threatened. Deliberations and decisions have been more concerned with the preservation of the fundamental civil liberties guaranteed by the Bill of Rights, and there must be compelling reasons for the state ever to abridge them (Friendly and Elliott 1984).

Court decisions are pragmatic solutions to problems within the context of law. Laws can be adjusted for the purpose of achieving stated goals. Harold Berman explains:

While accepting the English doctrine of precedent, whereby a court is bound to follow previous decisions of analogous cases, American courts have generally been more creative in interpreting earlier cases in order to adapt the law to changing conditions. Also American courts have not accepted the English doctrine that the highest court can never overrule its own precedents; the United States Supreme Court, as well as the Supreme Courts of the various states, have on occasion declared simply that one of their previous decisions was wrong and would not be followed. (1961:14)

Women as a group have been gaining in the process. Much of modern law attempts to offer workable analyses of legal rights to prevent confusion and to offer practical solutions to problems that arise during the periods of rapid social change. Today, many rules and procedures are being modified to ensure the incorporation into U.S. society of groups that had been discriminated against with legal impugnity in the past. Many changes are coming about through judicial reinterpretation of existing legal documents.

Today an important characteristic of U.S. law is the recognition of only functional differences among people, not intrinsic differences. That is, a women might be refused a job in a traditionally male occupation such as professional football player for being too small or too slow (functional difference) but not for being a female per se (intrinsic difference) (Galanter 1966). When rights are abrogated and women appeal, they now often get favorable Court decisions based on the Fourteenth Amendment. If an equal rights amendment to the United States Constitution is ever passed, it will invalidate any existing discriminatory practices and reduce the public's dependence on judicial review in the acquisition of gender equality.

Changes in attitudes are occurring in many aspects of everyday life such as the family, the workplace, the educational system, the government, and politics. In the following chapters certain areas of the law in which sex-based discrimination has been present will be identified, and the underlying social conceptions and misconceptions on which legal discrimination is based will be examined.

4

The Family: A Major
Social Institution

The modern concept of the ideal marriage is that it is a socially recognized union in which both partners are legally equal. The underlying basis of the ideal marriage is romantic love, and within the marriage each individual is expected to continue to pursue personal growth and self-fulfillment.

There were vastly different expectations about marriage prevailing in the United States two centuries ago. In those days, upon marriage, the two persons became one legal entity, and that entity was male. This legal situation was summed up in *Commentaries on the Law of England* (1765) by Sir William Blackstone, the noted English legal scholar, whose writings became the authority long referred to by English and U.S. lawyers. Blackstone wrote, "By marriage, the husband and wife are one person in law: that is, the very being or legal existence of the woman is suspended during the marriage." In effect, the wife was not thought to have a separate existence, and she lost many civil rights, including rights over her children, rights to sue or be sued, rights to sign contracts, and even rights to property previously held in her own name (DePauw and Hunt 1976:11).

The theoretical underpinning for this was the feudal doctrine of coverture (the subsuming of a wife's identity under the husband's), which itself partly reflected long-standing biblical notions of the unity of the flesh of husband and wife. In early England, the doctrine of coverture effectively kept women in a state of civil invisibility. A good wife's duties consisted of working hard at her domestic chores, and being quiet, passive, and absolutely obedient to her husband.

Since love was not a great consideration, a woman's happiness rested on the hope that she would marry a good and benevolent man. This was especially true because it was lawful for the husband to discipline and "chastise" his wife, as was explained and justified by Blackstone:

The husband also . . . might give his wife moderate correction. For, as he is to answer for her misbehaviour, the law thought it reasonable to entrust him with this power of restraining her, by domestic chastisement. . . . [T]he courts of law will . . . permit a husband to restrain a wife of her liberty, in case of any gross misbehaviour.

These are the chief legal effects of marriage during the coverture; upon which we may observe, that even the disabilities which the wife lies under are for the most part intended for her protection and benefit; so great a favourite is the female sex of the laws of England. (Blackstone 1765:442–445)

The difference between chastisement and beating is one of degree, and it rests on personal perception. The denial of personal autonomy for the woman was rationalized as being for her own good in the manner that children are corrected by parents who understand life and who must therefore guide their offspring who do not know any better.

Social inferiority and legal subordination were the married woman's lot— a situation she could do nothing to change. If she was unhappy and suppressed, her discontent was privatized and she led a life of quiet desperation, or at best a life of pragmatic adaptation. If she remained single, she might not fare much better. Aside from the social ridicule and the stigma of being labeled an old maid, she would still be under the authority of a man, her father. Since marriage did bring social approval and some psychological and physical comforts, it was generally preferable to subordination to a father (Depauw and Hunt 1976).

Of course, it cannot be presumed that all wives were unhappy with their lots, nor that many women rejected the situation, so successful was the socialization process of the society and so engrained the historical concept of natural male dominance. The economic system was based on households, and although the husband was the absolute head and master of the household, there were some legal compensations for the woman. After marriage the husband became responsible for the woman's support and, upon the husband's death, under common law she was entitled to inherit one-third of his estate since she had acquired dower rights upon marriage. However, when a woman married she lost more than rights to property; she lost much autonomy over her own body. The husband had a right to her sexual services, and could coerce her into obedience if she became rebellious (Babcock, Freedman, Norton, and Ross 1975). In effect, the wife was the ward of her husband and was commanded to obey him. Under the patriarchal system, both husband and wife assumed statuses upon marriage that neither one could easily alter or terminate.

ORIGINS AND EVOLUTION OF FAMILY ROLE RELATIONSHIPS

Hunting and Gathering Societies

The earliest forms of human association and the origins of the differential status of men and women that are epitomized in the family cannot be definitively known. Some primates, humankind's nearest relatives, do live in monogamous family groups; some do not. Among those that do, male dominance does not naturally follow, and when it does come about it seems to be an adaptation to a particular environment.

There are analogies between humans and the higher primates. One is the need to suckle and nurture a relatively helpless newborn. The female body is specialized for this role, leaving the male free for the role of defense of the group. The anthropologist Kathleen Gough stated that among nonhuman primates

Where defense is important, males are much larger and stronger than females, exert dominance over females, and are strictly hierarchized and organized in relation to one another. Where defense is less important there is much less sexual dimorphism (difference in size between male and female), less or no male dominance, and a less pronounced male hierarchy. (Gough 1979:49)

Among humans, evidence shows that economic life was built mostly around the sexual division of labor. Educated guesses agree that male dominance became an early form of male-female interaction because it was functional for the circumstances that people faced. Out of the sexual division of labor there developed a family unit, as well as group cooperation for survival. It is presumed that in early hunting and gathering societies, social life was comparatively egalitarian since anyone could seek out the available food supplies. Besides nurturing, women's food-gathering activities were important for group survival.

As hunting for game also became a means of sustenance, the division of labor based on sex became pronounced. Hunting was confined mostly to males. It is hypothesized that the division of labor, based originally on the need to produce new members of the society and the sole ability of the females to bear and nourish the offspring, led to a more passive role for women. The male role became that of activist and provider, and he developed skills that gave him mastery over prey. Social status accrued to males who could hunt effectively, since meat had scarcity value for a group. The female's task, the gathering of wild foodstuffs, was simple and commonplace. Furthermore, women did not require the help of other women to pick food, whereas men needed to cooperate with each other to capture wild game. This strengthened the ties of male groups, and led to what Lionel Tiger (1969) called *male bonding*. When differences between tribes developed, warfare also strengthened the position of males. Warfare not only made possible a differential accumulation of wealth, but also permitted a gradual domination over the family unit and a devaluation of woman's status.

Gradually groups began herding animals rather than hunting them, and cultivating food in place of gathering wild growths. There was a decline in nomadism, and people began to live in rather permanent settlements. Anthropologists who have studied agricultural and herding societies are in agreement that a tightly organized paternal and hierarchical family structure was functional for that pattern of subsistence. It was necessary to adhere to certain basic rules and customs for raising food, since idiosyncratic individual behavior of a member could endanger survival needs. Leadership was required, and the society became more stratified. It is speculated that since men were already involved with animals because of hunting, animal husbandry and agricultural decisions fell to them. Men gained dominance over the material processes of production in agricultural societies for the same reasons—biological imperatives—that led to their absorption with and mastery in hunting and warfare. Control was extended and exercised over women also. Social inequality grew as a consequence. Since more groups were able to live together, kinship became the prime organizing principle, with males dominant in the extended family. Settled life made possible the production of goods on a greater scale than before. A surplus developed, and production for exchange became possible.

Later, the rise of the state and the growth of the stratification system had the effect of reinforcing the ensconced male dominance. By the time of the writing of the Old Testament, a woman's place in society was limited to the female circle. Her worth and status depended on pleasing her husband and bearing his children, she being the "vessel for his seed," as the Bible stated. She was largely excluded from community religious ritual and was generally held in a subordinate and dependent social position. In colonial American society, relations between husband and wife were influenced by the teachings of the Bible. In various biblical verses, wives are admonished to be quiet and obey their husbands. St. Paul stated: "Women must keep quiet at gatherings of the church. They are not allowed to speak; they must take a subordinate place, as the Law enjoins. If they want any information let them ask their husbands" (1 Cor. 14:34–35); and "Wives, be subject to your husbands; that is your proper duty in the Lord" (Col. 3:18–19). Such writings gave religious sanction to the curtailment of women's legal rights and to their subordinate position in marriage (Richmond-Abbott 1979).

The coming of the Industrial Revolution exacerbated the lower status of women. The movement of the married couple away from the seat of the extended family to the locations of the factories was a process required in the new economy. It can be said that the factory system, which helped strip a wife of the emotional support of her extended kinship group, resulted in her isolation in the nuclear family. In the marketplace the husband's compensation for his labor was money, and in an increasingly monetary and secular economy, this had the effect of increasing his status.

Theoretically, the factory system should contribute to equal status since both men and women are able to sell their labors in the marketplace. In effect, however, the system tended to make more public the lesser status of women since the women who worked outside the home were given the lower-paying jobs at the bottom of the occupational hierarchy. Husbands acquired more power over wives in capitalist economies, where men exercised the ability to

deny women sexuality or to force it upon them; to command or exploit their labor or to control their produce; to control or rob them of their children; to confine them physically and prevent their movement; to use them as objects in male transactions; to cramp their creativeness; or to withhold from them large areas of the society's knowledge and cultural attainments. (Gough 1979:58)

Thus, the gradual changes in the mode of subsistence debased the status of women in society. Eventually, laws were passed that aimed to protect women at their jobs (see Chapter 5). In fact; however, these laws comprised a public recognition of women's unequal status.

THE HOUSEWIFE IN COLONIAL AMERICA

Burden of Early Domestic Chores

Because of the shortage of females in colonial America, women married at a considerably younger age than was the norm in Europe during that time. Under the old common law, a husband had a right to his wife's body and to her domestic services. After marriage, the lot of women usually consisted of an uninterrupted series of pregnancies. The rate of infant and childhood mortality was exceedingly high, and many children who would have been helpful and comforting to a mother in later life did not live to become teenaged. Furthermore, the process of giving birth was replete with dangers for the woman because of the primitive level of scientific development at the time. However, in spite of the heavy burdens and dangers inherent in the housewife role, a sense of having done her duty motivated the wife. This was interpreted by a woman (and also the society) as a fulfillment of herself and her function in life. A letter by a husband, written in the mid–1700s to a friend, is most enlightening.

She always went through the difficulties of childbearing with a remarkable steadfastness, faith, patience, and decency.... Indeed she would sometimes say to me that bearing, tending, and burying children was hard work, and that she had done a great deal of it for one of her age (she had six children, whereof she buried four, and died in the 24th year of her age), yet would say it was the work she was made for and what God in His providence had called her to, and she could freely do it all for Him. (Calhoun 1918:90)

The individual recognition by some husbands of the enormous contributions of women to the home and to society did not lead to public and legal recognition. At a time when mere survival could not be taken for granted, many of the essential needs of the family were provided by the wife. Her activities consisted of baking bread, curing meats, picking and drying fruit, nurturing a kitchen garden and canning the vegetables, cooking, milking cows and making cheeses, churning butter, making cider and molasses beer, overseeing livestock, making candles and soap, spinning yarn, weaving, sewing clothing and bedclothes, mending, knitting, embroidering, washing clothes, and cleaning the house. Since much time and energy was absorbed in the care of the home and nurturance of the family, it was only the rare woman, usually one of means, who perceived that the lofty principles of the 1776 Revolution were promising for the full equality of women with men.

One woman who did have that vision was Abigail Adams, whose husband, John Adams, would soon help draft the U.S. Constitution. Mrs. Adams wrote her husband a letter on March 31, 1776 urging him to remember the ladies in that founding document. He felt the suggestion was amusing, as he intimated in his reply to her. Her reaction might seem to be normal human (although empty) bombast, since she could not have realized how prophetic her reply would be regarding the future change in power relationships. On May 7, 1776, she wrote back to her husband:

You insist upon retaining an absolute power over wives. But you must remember that arbitrary power is like most other things which are very hard, very liable to be broken; and, notwithstanding all your wise laws and maxims, we have it in our power, not only to free ourselves, but to subdue our masters, and, without violence, throw both your natural and legal authority at our feet. (Cary and Peratis 1981:2)

Abigail Adams's concern for the rights of women were, of course, ignored, since no mention of women appeared in the U.S. Constitution. Although equal rights for women did not exist in European cultures, and females had traditionally been seen as subordinate to males, the rhetoric for the formation of an independent country in the New World included concepts such as "equality" and "justice for all." Apparently the Founding Fathers of the nation, who were inured with ideals of liberty of thought, speech, and action, did not perceive a discrepancy when one segment of society had limited rights.

For two hundred years the creation and the application of the laws concerning the sexes were based on certain underlying assumptions, which became the prism through which decisions were filtered. These assumptions may be summarized as follows: (1) women are understood to be incompetent, childlike, and in need of protection; (2) males are protectors and financial caretakers of women; (3) husband and wife are one (the male) under the law; and (4) the double standard of morality is natural and based on biological determinism (Richardson 1988). Obviously, these assumptions worked to the legal disadvantage of women for a very long time.

The long climb upward by women toward the legal recognition of their full humanity and dignity started in the eighteenth century with the voices of a few talented women who had the wit to perceive the injustices of the status quo in spite of having been socialized into the prevailing mores. Frontier conditions in the United States are credited with leading to certain rights for married women. In the colonial states, where old English common law applied, the wife did eventually acquire some rights to previously owned property. In the middle of the nineteenth century, some states passed the Married Women's Property Acts. The first one was enacted in Mississippi in 1839; it allowed women to keep control of the property they brought with them to the marriage. In 1848 New York passed a Married Women's Property Act that prohibited a husband from disposing of a wife's previously owned property (Deckard 1983). Another act was passed in 1860 in New York which gave married women rights to their earnings as well (Schneir 1972). However, the old underlying assumption about the competence of women prevailed in the implementation of the law until it was officially changed in 1971 in *Reed v. Reed*, when the U.S. Supreme Court ruled that women were to be included as persons under the Constitution.

THE FAMILY CHANGES

A society that goes through a revolution is in ferment. Under such conditions even a basic institution like the family does not remain stable, as social change affects its internal dynamics. For example, since the Industrial Revolution resulted in the removal of production from the home to the factory, the structure of the family indelibly changed as it adapted to meet the needs of the economy. The extended family had been the basic unit, but it was too big and cumbersome to adjust to cramped urban living or the company housing that was sometimes supplied by factory owners. A chain of events was started, and the nuclear family unit and neolocal residence for newly married couples became the norm. Some broad characteristics of the concept of family that has emerged since the 1776 Revolution can be outlined. The incidence of family-arranged marriages decreased, and mutual affection became a socially recognized basis for marriage. Although the wife remained the legal and social inferior of the husband, she became perceived as his moral superior and enjoyed much autonomy within her sphere of home and children. Carl Degler (1980) referred to the latter situation as the doctrine of the two spheres. Also, family size gradually became smaller. This had a major impact on the lives of women. The role of housewife gradually became less physically demanding but more psychologically stressful as wives became more isolated in the home. Women began to feel an unease concerning their lack of self-actualization and even their alienation from the outside world.

Occupation Housewife

Role specializations in the family have usually been culturally assigned on the basis of biological characteristics. The ability of a woman to bear children, and the freedom of men from this responsibility, have influenced the cultural definitions of what it means to be a man or a woman. Informal and formal social norms are rooted in the idea that men are the breadwinners outside the home and women are dependents at home. The wife has been allocated to household tasks, which have been treated merely as an aspect of the feminine role. In spite of society's supposition that a woman acquires joy and self-fulfillment through such activity, satisfactions are dulled because the tasks are repetitive, monotonous, and even meaningless since the clean home of today is tomorrow's dirty home. Many of the chores trivialize and denigrate the wife's ability to function intellectually. This results in the consistent undervaluation of the work women do.

Jessie Bernard (1972), a sociologist who has done research on the marital relationship, has written about the reality of marriage for couples who maintain traditional sex roles. Her thesis is that there is *his* marriage and *her* marriage, and that the two parties do not derive equal benefits from the union. Data show that there are more beneficent effects on the husband. Bernard wrote: "The superiority of married men over never-married men is impressive on almost every index—demographic, psychological, or social" (1972:57). Bernard backed up her arguments with documented research evidence, including statistics that show that unmarried men have almost double the suicide rate of married men.

The wife, on the other hand, is subject to a series of shocks and discontinuities because she must lessen her attachments to her family of orientation and devote her time and energy to her husband. The structure of marriage is such that in her new status "it is the husband's role—not necessarily her own wishes, desires, or demands—that proves to be the key to the marriage and requires the wife to be accommodating" (1972:57). This adjustment is not without psychological and emotional costs for the wife. Upon marriage, the woman has a complete change in occupation while the man does not, and since her housework carries low status and no salary, his work and his needs must be met first. The structure itself contributes to a superordinate-subordinate relationship. This inequality, plus the wife's isolation within the home, can have negative psychological effects on her mental and emotional health. Bernard averred that women who suffer from the distress of the housewife syndrome receive no public empathy. Indeed, women do not themselves always realize the cause of their malaise.

Many social thinkers feel that in order to mitigate the disparity of status between husband and wife, ways must be found to upgrade work done in the home and thus permit the wife to achieve a higher level of self-esteem.

The problem is, as John Galbraith stated, that "what is not counted is often not noticed" by society (1973:33).

To date there are no laws that take account of the economic value of the work done by homemakers. Because of this, a housewife cannot obtain private disability insurance, even though her work represents clear economic contributions and the husband would have to pay for domestic services during her incapacity. Only those who earn wages are eligible, according to disability insurance policies. Even if a homemaker were to pay the required taxes, she could not be enrolled in the social security system in order to qualify for disability benefits. Furthermore, the services women perform in the home are not included in the estimation of the Gross National Product. Barbara Babcock, Ann Freedman, Eleanor Norton, and Susan Ross (1975) address themselves to the lack of official recognition of housework, and they point out that housewives are the only workers that operate under a status-based system in a wage labor economy. They quote Charlotte Perkins Gilman who, writing in 1898, stated that women were akin to slaves because of economic dependence. Gilman pointed out that:

In the closest interpretation, individual economic independence among human beings means that the individual pays for what he gets [and] . . . gives to the other an equivalent for what the other gives him. . . .

The labor of women in the house, certainly, enables men to produce more wealth than they otherwise could; and in this way women are economic factors in society. [Similarly;] . . . wives, as earners through domestic service, are entitled to the wages of cooks, housemaids, nursemaids, seamstresses, or housekeepers. . . .

[W]hatever the economic value of the domestic industry of women is, they do not get it (Gilman 1975:11–15).

The household unit is not viewed as a business even though many aspects of it are similar to one. While business people can write off for taxation purposes many business expenses such as rent, telephone bills, customer lunches, and so forth, the homemaker cannot deduct the expenses of running a home. If she supports herself by working outside the home, she does not receive adequate tax credit for her child-care expenses. Furthermore, should she become divorced, she cannot apply for unemployment insurance under the worker's compensation law since she was not part of the labor market. There is also the problem of the lack of worker's benefits, such as medical, dental, and disability insurance; retirement pensions; and social security benefits, which are often available to women who are employed in industry to do similar domestic chores. In a society where the divorce rate is high (in modern times, yearly divorces in the United States average one for every two marriages) a housewife cannot count on being included in a husband's benefits.

Housework is often disparaged and viewed as an activity for those with inferior status. Most men are reluctant to do a significant share of housework in the home. Research shows that even in dual-career households, the husband does not undertake half the household chores. One reason for the low status of this work is the low skill level required for the many tasks that must be done. The U.S. Department of Labor defines twenty-two thousand occupations and ranks them on a scale of a high of 1 to a low of 887. The rankings show that even women who do the same work outside the home (homemakers, foster mothers, child-care attendants, home health aides, nursery school teachers, and practical nurses) and are paid for it do not gain in status as the jobs are listed at a skill level of 878, only 9 points from the bottom of a very long list (Babcock et al. 1975:572). This shows that in a real sense, the professional domestic worker is competing with the unpaid work of housewives, which has the effect of keeping the salary scale low. It has been suggested that society should redefine the household as an economic unit and liberalize household expense deductions if sexual equality is to come about. Such reorientation would confer a higher status on housework and make it more attractive as an occupation for men or women.

Housework contrasts with labor market employment in its lack of salary and social recognition of the responsibilities carried by the housewife. In recent times there have been a few attempts by economists to estimate the housewife's monetary value. These have been prompted by a number of court suits concerning compensation for the loss of a wife's services. Several approaches have been tried in an effort to arrive at meaningful statistics. One method uses an opportunity approach, which looks at figures that a housewife could be earning given her level of education. For instance, if she had completed college she might have been in a particular income bracket had she worked outside instead of inside the home. Another method, a market-cost approach, evaluates the expenses of hiring substitutes to do all the tasks a housewife does, such as washing clothes, ironing, mending, cooking, washing dishes, sewing, chauffering, cleaning house, shopping, decorating, baby-sitting, nursery school teaching, catering, companionship, and so forth. Such an estimation would be based on the average wages for a particular service.

The market-cost approach has been criticized for containing a number of shortcomings. For one thing, it does not take into account the varying qualities of the work performed, and for many household tasks minimum wage would be calculated. Besides inequities concerning the quality of work, there are fluctuations in the quantity of work, in particular the unpleasant aspect concerning the housewife's gradual devaluation, since as the children grow up and leave home the tasks are lessened. This makes the comparison between full-time housework and marketplace activity somewhat unsatisfactory. That is, whereas outside employment usually brings increased salary with time and experience, the housewife's monetary worth will decline under the market-cost model as there will be less work to do as family size decreases.

Another unresolved problem concerning the elevation of housework to a paid status is the question of who would pay the housewife for her work, since room and board are hardly adequate compensations for time and energy input that could command good salaries and fringe benefits in the labor market. Solutions have been suggested. One proposal by A. C. Scott suggested that the wife should be assured a salary for her work. Scott wrote:

She could receive a percentage of her husband's salary to be paid by him or paid directly by his employer in the same way as the military sends allotment checks to the wives of servicemen who are stationed overseas. If she is paid by her husband, her salary would not be subject to tax, since it was already taxed once when the husband received it. Since the husband would in fact be the "employer," he would be expected to pay the basic household expenses for food, clothing, and shelter, allowing his wife to spend her salary as she chose, on her own perceived needs, on her family, savings, or investment. (1972:56)

Babcock and colleagues (1975), among others giving serious thought to this question, suggested that the government, the indirect beneficiary of housewives' services, could simply make payments to married women who are full-time homemakers. Still other social thinkers feel that since the wife makes a contribution to the economy by freeing her husband to concentrate on his job rather than the myriad daily chores that must be done, there should be legal recognition that half the salary the husband earns while the wife works in the home belongs to her. In case of a later divorce, her benefits would then be based on this amount, even though she had not actually received the money as her own. Thus, society would become more conscious of the value of a woman's work in the home, and women would be better off.

There are many problems, however, with any type of money transfer. Many husbands earn so little that paying even minimum wage to a wife would be impossible. If it became a government program, its high cost would depress the wages to the level of welfare payments. A fundamental argument against salaries for housewives is that getting paid for performing many menial, boring, repetitive jobs would not necessarily raise the status of women, and might actually demean "women's work" further. Nonetheless, accurate estimates of the monetary value of housework could help a wife make an informed decision as to whether to take an outside job.

Family as a Social Institution

The family has always been one of the major institutions deemed necessary for social survival. Within the home the family is a structural arrangement of statuses and roles. It rests on the differential assignment of functions, and on the overtly accepted superiority of the male as head of the family. Some social theorists feel that this is the most functional arrangement for the social good, while others feel that the system is exploitative of females, who do not have the power to change the situation.

From the social point of view, the family is an integral part of the system, as it produces and socializes children to become functioning members of society. From the individual point of view, the family provides a person with intimacy and security which are not available in an impersonal world. The family thus is seen as functional for both society and the individual. The sex-role statuses whereby men and women in the family are treated differently are viewed as normal, and arise because of the different roles men and women are called on to play in society, roles which are seen as complementary. An ideology forms to justify that order, laws are passed to reflect the ideology, and so the different statuses become reflected in the legal system. Domestic laws are thus functional acts that facilitate the smooth continuation of the social order.

Although the spousal relationship has always been asymmetrical, it has not been considered whether the wife's role might at times be dysfunctional for her and might operate to prevent personal fulfillment and the acquisition of power and resources in her own right. Today many women desire self-development and active economic, political, and social participation outside the home. In a society undergoing rapid social change, it is useful for people to understand the functionality of past sex roles but they must also acquire an awareness of the evolving social climate that is leading to changing human expectations, new power bases, and new and relevant laws.

Friedrich Engels, one of the early social analysts, felt that the family was the ultimate source of social inequality because of the institutionalized privileges of the husband in the areas of power and control of property. His view on the oppression of women was endorsed by Vladimir Lenin, who wrote that women become worn-out in the petty, monstrous household work; that their strength and time are dissipated and wasted; that their minds grow narrow and stale; and that their wills become weakened (Dunn and Klein 1970:24). Lenin's observations of more than a century ago are echoed today by modern theorists, who also argue that the U.S. family denies equal opportunities to women and that it thus contributes to social injustice.

In the family, as in society, there are elements of both consensus and conflict, of stability and change. Stereotypical gender differences, and the social interaction based on them, have long been formalized into law. One way that desired changes can come about today is through legal mandate. It is, however, necessary for the groups interested in changing laws to acquire the power to influence such change. Within the family, there is some evidence that power relationships are changing. The increased educational level of women, their occupational successes, and their financial contributions to the family are slowly eroding the stereotypes and paternalistic power relationships in many homes.

THE LAW AND CHANGE

Stereotypes and Law

The laws that have affected the status of women have been based on stereotypical images of what women are capable of undertaking. Long-standing gender stereotypes have been so pervasive in society that their validity has seldom been questioned. Trait assumptions about masculinity and femininity have been accepted as truth without empirical backing, and have been used to justify differential treatment.

One of the pervasive stereotypes is that men and women are at the opposite ends of a continuum measuring personality traits. It is assumed that the differences are innate, and that the alleged variations are extremely important. For instance, it has been an accepted presumption that women are by nature nurturant and therefore should remain in the home to give succor to its occupants. If it were necessary that a woman have a job outside the home, it was assumed that she was best suited for positions such as nursing, teaching the young, and clerical work, because of her nurturant tendencies. She was considered unqualified for leadership positions because of her monthly variations in hormone levels, since it was felt that possible personality swings could jeopardize smooth office relations. It was also assumed that men were task-oriented and therefore best involved in decision making in the marketplace and government. In short, certain qualities were attributed to all members of the class based on sex, without consideration of individual variations within the class.

Such assumptions are exaggerations that ignore the complexity of human traits and the similarities across sexual lines. They represent a narrow conception of the proclivities of human beings and the input of socialization in gender-role behavior. As such, the stereotypes can be seen as a form of long-held and deep-seated prejudice. Once stereotypes concerning alleged natural differences in temperament and abilities between men and women have become part of the culture, they not only serve to guide personal social relations, but also become the basis of legal pronouncements.

Family and Law

Traditionally, family was considered to be a cooperative arrangement of great benefit to society. Social disfavor and pressure were brought to bear on any persons who did not live up to the expectations that marriage and family were the normal course to be followed by everyone. For the wife in particular, domestic life, sexual servitude, and constant pregnancy presented severe limitations on personal autonomy in society and over her self. Through the years, the satisfying ability to give birth to babies and thus create a human life has been, in effect, a female disadvantage, since it has been used as a justification for her confinement to the home. When court decisions upheld discriminatory laws in the past, they did so on the basis of an assumption that childbearing made women unsuitable for any other occupation. Thus, the culture's presuppositions about men and women were reflected in the legal system. Changing the official rules has therefore not been simple because they have been based on long-standing stereotypes.

MARITAL DISSOLUTION: NO-FAULT DIVORCE

Marital dissolution, for whatever reason, is not something couples take lightly. Even so-called amicable divorces can leave a person with a sense of having failed. Divorce laws have often created unnecessary problems for people whose feelings are already vulnerable. The adversarial process that pits husband and wife against each other in the court can exacerbate emotional trauma. The divorce procedure has historically been based on the theory of fault whereby each spouse has to prove that the other person is culpable in the marital breakup. Proving innocence was necessary as it affected divorce settlements concerning child custody, alimony, division of property, and so forth. The fault theory of divorce is not only moralistic, the placing of blame is archaic as well. It is also unnecessarily punitive because, as humans react to each other's actions, there is seldom a clear right or wrong.

In 1970, when California introduced the first no-fault divorce law in the United States, it was considered a progressive innovation since either spouse could sue for divorce on the grounds of "irreconcilable differences." It was considered a legal reform, and by 1988 every state had adopted some form of no-fault divorce law in order to reduce hostility and acrimony and create more equity in the process of marital dissolution (Weitzman 1987). However, there emerged a gap between theory and reality. An unintended consequence of no-fault divorce was the impoverishment of many divorced women and their children. Lenore Weitzman (1987) has carried out a ten-year study, using five types of data, to assess the social and economic effects of California's no-fault divorce reforms. She found that no-fault has been devastating for most women, and that older homemakers and mothers with young children experience the greatest hardship, often ending up in poverty or near poverty.

There are many causes of the post-divorce decline in the standards of living of these women. Even if a woman could quickly enter the labor force on an economic par with her husband (which is unlikely considering her period of absence from the labor market), she must pay for child care. When marital property is divided equally, the man gets half while the other half is spread between a woman and her children (an average of three people).

In addition, the equal division of property often means selling the house, whereas under the old divorce system the house was often awarded to the mother (who was usually found to be the innocent party) so that the children's lives would not be disrupted. Another problem with the division of property is that the nature of property has changed. The new forms of property are not divided at all. These include assets such as the man's pension, health insurance, professional license, and earning capacity, which do not tend to be divided and therefore remain with the man intact even though it can be claimed that rights to this property have been acquired in the course of the marriage.

Weitzman found that "on the average, in the first year after divorce, men experience a 42% improvement in their standard of living, while women and their children experience a 73% decline" (1987:99). Thus, it would seem that a legal reform that had aimed at fairness has in fact created unfair disparities between divorced men and their former wives and children. The U.S. Census shows that in 1985, 54 percent of the children in single-parent, mother-headed families lived below the poverty line, and 80 percent of these single-parent, mother-headed families were the result of divorce or separation. Also, one-third of all poor children in this country live with parents who are divorced or separated (1987:102). One reason for the economic hardship of children of divorce is the virtual lack of institutional supports for them, as the modest court-ordered child support is fully complied with by fewer than half the fathers (1987:94). Longtime homemakers especially feel betrayed by the new divorce laws as they perceive them as penalizing the woman for having spent years as a homemaker and mother. What may be needed is a rethinking of the so-called reforms. Weitzman suggests ways to equalize divorce and limit judicial discretion. She calls for the legal assurance that the children will remain in the family home, an equalization of the husband's post-divorce income for the long-married older housewife, and the award of a greater share of the marital property to a mother who is responsible for raising the children. The problem remains a complex one, but it is undebatable that society has a vested interest in the elimination of poverty and the well-being of its children, the future society.

REPRODUCTIVE RIGHTS

Domestic Law Jurisdiction

Marriage and divorce laws have come to be a jurisdiction of the states. Although the United States Constitution does not list the reserved powers of states, the Tenth Amendment provides that the powers not delegated to the United States by the Constitution, nor prohibited by it to the states, are reserved to the states respectively. These residual powers of the states include control over education, marriage and divorce laws, and traffic, and the maintenance of the safety, health, morals, and welfare of its citizens. When an area is not specifically relegated to the federal or state powers, there has sometimes been tension concerning the proper jurisdiction. The Supreme Court's interpretive decisions have increasingly narrowed states' jurisdictions in some areas, and restrictive state domestic laws have been overruled on the basis of the infringement of fundamental freedoms inherent in the Bill of Rights of the Constitution.

One area adjudged to be a basic right to personal freedom concerns reproductive rights. Formerly, upon marriage, a wife faced a condition of constant pregnancy and, since she was mainly responsible for the rearing of children, her lot was a type of servitude to the children, husband, and home. Before reproductive autonomy would be recognized as a legal right of women, there had to be a loosening of the common concept that a woman's body was a possession of her husband. This loosening has begun, and certain laws have been passed recognizing women's rights in the areas of birth control and abortion; these laws would have been unthinkable even thirty years ago.

In order to see this issue in perspective, it must be noted that laws that discriminate against women have not been illegal. Woman's lower status has been socially justified almost since the beginnings of organized life, as discussed earlier. However, social conditions have changed somewhat.

Today in the United States about half the labor force consists of women. Working women do not want to be hampered by the discriminatory laws that had general acceptance in the past. Because of anatomy it had been felt that there was a natural connection between being able to bear children and having fewer civil rights than men. The rationale was that this was God's will. A Supreme Court case, *Bradwell v. Illinois*, which was decided in 1873, included these remarks:

The natural and proper timidity and delicacy which belongs to the female sex evidently unfits it for many of the occupations of civil life. . . . The paramount destiny and mission of woman are to fulfill the noble and benign offices of wife and mother. This is the law of the Creator. (*Bradwell v. Illinois* 1873, quoted in Cary and Peratis 1979:6)

This case was lost by Myra Blackwell, who had wanted to practice law in a state court. However, persons of vision and motivation like Myra Blackwell were not the norm in those days, as women traditionally remained in the home.

When established routines become part of the ongoing customs of a society, they usually remain unquestioned. Hence, the fact that something was always done a certain way tends to justify its continuance. Margaret Sanger, the pioneer of birth control and planned parenthood, wrote in 1920:

Woman's acceptance of her inferior status was the more real because it was unconscious. She had chained herself to her place in society and the family through the maternal functions of her nature, and only chains thus strong could have bound her to her lot as a brood animal for the masculine civilizations of the world. In accepting her role as the "weaker and gentler half," she accepted that function. In turn, the acceptance of that function fixes the more firmly her rank as an inferior. (Schneir 1972:325–334, quoted in Cary and Peratis 1979:180)

Some social scientists believe that to have women raising children and caring for the family while their husbands work to produce in the economy is functional for the society. In this way, they justify the continuation of unequal statuses and roles. However, many others realize that this is not necessarily functional for the woman today. Questions are sometimes posed concerning who had the power to make the laws restricting women and who gained by them. It is with these perspectives in mind that we discuss legislation that has gradually contributed to women having some personal autonomy over their own bodies.

Birth Control

To a greater degree than before, biology is being transcended by technology. Among other benefits, modern technology has contributed to pregnancy control, and the change in fertility has been dramatic. Since the advances in the processing of rubber in the middle of the nineteenth century, many practical uses have been found for that substance. One such product has been contraceptives.

Contraception and abortion are matters over which reasonable people can differ. However, when women are ignorant about their physical selves, biology becomes destiny, and a major consequence is unplanned pregnancies. Society has begun to accept the idea that women must have a measure of control over their own bodies, including control over fertility and reproduction. This is needed for psychological reasons as well as physical ones. In *The New Our Bodies, Ourselves*, the authors state:

Body education is core education. Our bodies are the physical bases from which we move out into the world; ignorance, uncertainty—even, at worst, shame—about our physical selves create in us an alienation from ourselves that keeps us from being the whole people that we could be. (Boston Women's Health Book Collective 1984:xix)

When Margaret Sanger opened a planned parenthood clinic to teach birth control methods in the early twentieth century, she was arrested. However, sexual freedom for women as well as men was an idea whose time had come, and women needed the means to free themselves from the anxiety of becoming pregnant. Margaret Sanger's concept of planned parenthood became accepted. She saw this as a type of woman's revolt to assert her right to voluntary motherhood—the right to decide for herself whether she would become a mother, under what conditions, and when (Schneir 1972). The means that came about for accomplishing this included not only the more widespread use of contraceptives but also the elimination of the legal restrictions concerning their availability.

Many states (including Connecticut) had prohibited the prescription, sale, and use of contraceptives on the grounds that the state had a vested interest in preserving the normal functioning of the family institution. It is estimated that about 60 percent of the states had such laws even as late as 1968. These were an institutionalized expression of early American ideas concerning women's natural sphere. These laws were challenged, and two U.S. Supreme Court decisions had overriding effects.

CASE: *Griswold v. Connecticut* (1965). Estelle Griswold was the executive director of the Planned Parenthood League of Connecticut. She was a well-educated, cultured woman, who was concerned with the global problem of overpopulation and abject poverty. She had visited some of the worst slums of the world after World War II, and had witnessed the hunger and chaos that reduces humans to a low level of existence. She was willing to fight for what she believed in, and was arrested and convicted for giving birth control advice to married couples and illegally prescribing contraceptive devices. She sued and the case reached the U.S. Supreme Court. The 1965 Court decision was in Griswold's favor, and the Connecticut statute in question, which had been on the books since the Civil War, was invalidated, as were all similar laws in other states.

This case added the right to privacy to other rights protected by the Constitution (Friendly and Elliott 1984). The Court's reasoning was that the right to privacy, although not actually stated, is implicit in many of the amendments to the Constitution. It was felt that the principle was clearly embodied in the First, Third, Fourth, Fifth, and Ninth amendments. The justices gave great weight to the sanctity of the marital relationship and the right to privacy therein. Part of the decision reads:

We deal with a right of privacy older than the Bill of Rights—older than our political parties, older than our school system. Marriage is a coming together for better or for worse, hopefully enduring, and intimate to the degree of being sacred. It is an association that promotes a way of life, not causes; a harmony in living, not political faiths; a bilateral loyalty, not commercial or social projects. (*Griswold v. Connecticut* 1965:486)

This decision dealt with contraceptives and married persons. It left the issue of contraceptive use by unmarried persons unexplored. The Supreme Court addressed that issue in the following case in 1972.

CASE: *Eisenstadt v. Baird* (1972). The state of Massachusetts had two criminal statutes prohibiting the sale or distribution of contraceptives to unmarried persons. This case concerned the apprehension of William Baird, a professor at Yale Medical School and also the medical director of a center run by the Planned Parenthood League. He gave lectures on birth control, and was convicted of giving contraceptives to an unmarried woman after one of his lectures at Boston University.

The Supreme Court decreed that a right given to a married woman but denied to an unmarried woman was an abrogation of the latter's Fourteenth Amendment rights to equal protection of the laws. The justices wrote:

If the right of privacy means anything, it is the right of the *individual*, married or single, to be free from unwarranted governmental intrusion into matters so fundamentally affecting a person as the decision whether to bear or beget a child. (Cary and Peratis 1977:183)

The Massachusetts laws were declared to violate the Constitution and were invalidated.

The right of all women to the possession and control of their own bodies free from restraint and interference from others was a revolutionary concept in view of past history. In recent years the Supreme Court has expanded this privacy notion, and it has considered the justification for state intrusion into areas of constitutionally protected freedoms in many cases. At times the principle of compelling state interest overrode private interests, but in many cases the Supreme Court has upheld the rights of individuals to the possession and control of their own persons.

Abortion

There is evidence that abortion was not unknown in the colonial United States. All through the years some women have sought to gain a measure of control over the number of children they would have, and the fact of illegality did not prevent abortions. However, pre-legal abortions were dangerous to women because the methods, whether attempts at self-inducement (such as drinking harsh chemicals or using self-made instruments) or undertaken by hack, self-styled abortionists operating under cover, were unscientific, and the conditions unsanitary and life-threatening. The accompanying secrecy posed medical and psychological problems that resulted in suffering and even death. Accurate statistics are not available, but educated guesses put the annual number of illegal abortions at about a million a year before 1973 in the United States (DePauw and Hunt 1976). It has also been estimated that over 350,000 patients every year were admitted with complications resulting from these furtive and amateurish abortions (Hall 1971).

The reasons so many women jeopardized their lives are varied. Some women must have felt there was no alternative to abortion. A pregnant woman might have been ill and incapable of coping with yet another child at the time; she may have been too poor in an era when government aid for dependent children was not available and the viability of the entire family would be problematic; she may have been too young and her education incomplete; she may have felt she already had enough children; or she may have been unmarried and unable to face the financial difficulty of raising a child herself, or the social problem of the negative labels that would have been imposed on her at that time.

In the last twenty-five years, the social environment has been changing, and there is less acceptance by females of the subjugation imposed by society or the suffering imposed by nature. The ideology of the women's movement and the rights of equal employment opportunity have contributed to the acceptance by society of the notion that women can have functions other than domestic ones; women now aspire to other modes of self-fulfillment than motherhood. The scientific environment has changed also, and technological progress has permitted greater human mastery over nature. Today the medical profession considers abortion one of its more simple techniques, and when performed by a doctor in a hospital or clinic it does not pose a physical threat to the woman. As a matter of fact, a legal abortion is statistically safer than pregnancy and childbirth among all age groups of women (Rathus 1983). Today the general public and the laws of the country tend toward the proposition that a woman's place is in the world.

Legalization of Abortion

Under English common law, the performance of abortion before *quickening* (fetal movement, which occurs after the fourth or fifth month of pregnancy) was ignored. There is some evidence that purposive termination of pregnancy was commonplace for centuries in Great Britain until 1803, when Parliament passed Lord Ellenborough's Act, making abortions illegal except to save the life of the woman. The early practice of abortion in the United States was also not unknown. In 1821, an antiabortion law was passed in Connecticut, and in 1828 one was passed in New York as well. By the time of the Civil War, abortions were generally disallowed by law (Babcock et al. 1979).

This century, activist groups formed that called for change, and public attitudes began to change in response. In the United States model abortion statutes were drafted by the Planned Parenthood Federation in 1955 and the American Law Institute in 1962 in the hope of reforming the prohibition and allowing for free choice. In 1967 both California and Colorado officially reformed their abortion statutes. The grounds for legal abortion were expanded beyond just saving the life of the woman to include such things as consideration of the pregnant woman's mental health. Several states followed this example and allowed the termination of pregnancy on lenient grounds (Geis 1975).

It can be seen, therefore, that federal legislation favoring abortion did not come about suddenly, nor is legal abortion confined to the United States. Today it is legal and widely practiced in most advanced countries of the world.

THE UNITED STATES SUPREME COURT'S 1973 ABORTION DECISION

A woman's right to control her own body was formally recognized in the landmark decision of the Supreme Court in 1973 in the *Roe v. Wade* case.

CASE: *Roe v. Wade* (1973). The Court had many complex moral and legal issues to ponder in this case. The Court's decision was rationalized on the constitutional grounds that the choice whether to bear children is based on the right of privacy implied in several amendments to the Constitution. The Court had to weigh two competing concepts—the constitutional right of privacy, and the state's interest in protecting the woman and the fetus. The Court felt the former was the overriding principle involved, since abortion during the first trimester is safer than childbirth (Ross 1983).

The Court established a sliding scale to balance the right of the woman and the right of the state at various times during the pregnancy. In its seven-to-two ruling in the *Roe v. Wade* case, the Court decided that states could not interfere with a woman's right to choose abortion during the first trimester of pregnancy; the choice rested instead with the woman and her physician. From that time until the fetus is viable (about the twenty-fourth to twenty-eighth week of pregnancy) the state may intervene only if the regulations are designed to protect the health of the mother. Also, the state could mandate that abortions take place only in hospitals. After viability (when the fetus is potentially able to survive outside the womb) the state can prohibit abortion except when it is necessary to protect the life or health of the woman (Deckard 1983, Richardson 1988, Ross 1983). Since this decision, the medically advanced D&E (dilation and evacuation) technique has made abortion twice as safe as childbirth even up to the eighteenth week of pregnancy (Rathus 1983).

CASE: *Doe v. Bolton* (1973). A second decision by the Supreme Court was also pertinent. In the *Doe v. Bolton* case the Court struck down a Georgia law that had overly restrictive provisions and treated abortion too differently from comparable medical procedures. The Supreme Court ruled that during the first trimester of pregnancy, the state could not require that abortions be performed in hospitals, that the abortion patient be a state resident, or that at least two doctors concurred in the decision. This further strengthened the privacy argument.

The Abortion Controversy

Social change is an inescapable fact of life. Along with the increasing modernization and complexity of society, social institutions change. The family, educational system, religion, the economy, and government gradually incorporate new values and norms which tend to integrate the changing social patterns. However, some social innovations jolt customary values, and some even cause confusion and disruption. Structural change is therefore often uneven.

One function of law is the coordination of ambiguous and sometimes conflicting beliefs and behavior patterns. The law thus represents the official stance of a society toward social change, and provides the authority to enforce that change. While innovations in ideology often lead to new laws, discontinuities sometimes exist between the evolving legal system and customary social values. This can cause anxiety, stress, and even hostility among some segments of the population. Abortion is an example of an issue for which this is true. The ensuing controversy has concerned the conflict between the right to life and freedom of choice concepts.

Abortion is the premature expulsion of the human fetus at any time before it is viable—that is, before the stage of development at which it would be capable of surviving outside the womb. Thus, abortion is used after conception has taken place, and on this fact rests the controversy for some groups. Legalization of abortion was not received with unanimous approval in society. Activist groups formed, with some adopting the position that the *Roe v. Wade* ruling went too far. In particular, some groups felt that the Court's decision represented an incursion into private religious beliefs. Some highly vocal groups became active in their attempts to get the Court decisions overturned, or at least rendered ineffective. Feminist groups, on the other hand, have generally been quite pleased with the Court decisions.

Public opinion remains divided concerning the right to life and freedom of choice issues. Some controversy has centered on several aspects of abortion: the alleged legal taking of human life, the perceived discrimination against poor women who could not afford the medical costs of abortions, and the usurping of parental and spousal consent to abortion.

The Fetus and Human Life

Although the 1973 Supreme Court decision specifically stated that "the word person, as used in the Fourteenth Amendment, does not include the unborn" some deep-rooted moral concerns were generated by the abortion ruling. The antiabortionists ask how abortion can be justified. Demonstrations outside clinics where abortions are performed have been commonplace, and a few clinics have been bombed in recent years.

The largest antiabortion group is the Catholic Church. As part of an organized movement, pastoral letters from Catholic bishops are read from pulpits, reaching an audience of about six and a half million parishioners (Hall 1971).

Catholic groups have not been alone in their vocal opposition to legal abortion. Protestant evangelical groups have also become active in their opposition to freedom of choice. These are affluent groups such as the Moral Majority led by Reverend Jerry Falwell. This group has a mailing list of over four hundred thousand persons and donations of over fifty million dollars a year, and so it is a formidable force. In addition, it reaches an estimated ten to fifteen million viewers through television programs, one of which is "The Gospel Hour." Reverend Falwell's religious preaching often takes on a political tone, and a stated function of his organization is "to create a moral climate in which it is easier for politicians to vote right than wrong" (Deckard 1983:426).

Activism has even become politicized. Mail campaigns have been organized by antiabortion groups and directed at officeholders, and their tactics have been criticized as amounting to harassment. National political candidates have had to take either a pro- or antiabortion stance in the hopes that their position will draw the most votes. Catholic legislators have in effect been threatened with excommunication if they supported abortion (Deckard 1983). A Right to Life political party with its candidates has also appeared on the election ballots along with traditional party listings.

It cannot be known to what extent such activism has been reflected in presidential elections. One recent presidential campaign platform held a promise of a constitutional amendment banning abortion. One candidate pledged to "work for the appointment of judges at all levels of the judiciary who respect traditional family values and the sanctity of innocent human life" (Deckard 1983:426). True to political promises, constitutional amendments banning abortion have been introduced in Congress. One Republican senator, Jesse Helms, would have liked to go further; he introduced a bill declaring that U.S. citizenship begins at conception. This bill, had it gotten the necessary majority vote (easier to obtain than the requirements of a constitutional amendment), would have had the effect of endowing on the fetus some civil rights protections under the Constitution.

The pro-abortionists, on the other hand, ask how compulsory pregnancy can be justified. This concept is argued by Garrett Hardin (1975), who speaks of the compulsion a woman feels if she is pregnant against her will. Her options are to submit to compulsion or have an abortion. Hardin's argument concerning the fetus is that there is no value in potentiality but only in actuality, just as blueprints are only potential houses and not actual buildings. Pro-abortionists feel that women must gain control over their own bodies and make their own decisions concerning whether to give birth. Of course, some women always did make this decision. The fact that millions of women may have had illegal abortions over the years in the United States and Europe shows how strong a need women have felt for some personal control over pregnancy.

The Supreme Court abortion decisions were greeted enthusiastically by feminists and civil liberties groups, who felt a great hurdle had been cleared in the fight to win reproductive freedom for women. The decisions confirmed that deciding whether and under what circumstances to have children is considered a fundamental personal right of the woman herself, and is not within the province of legislators or judges to abridge. The National Organization for Women (NOW) is one large group that espouses freedom of choice in such personal matters. NOW was organized in 1966, and the stated purpose was "to take action to bring women into full participation in the mainstream of American society *now*, exercising all the privileges and responsibilities thereof in truly equal partnership with men" (Deckard 1983:324). Members have been active nationally on issues pertaining to women's rights, and they have opposed efforts by antiabortion groups to pass legislation outlawing abortions.

The debate goes on, and reproductive rights continues to be a major moral, legal, and sociopolitical issue. Both sides remain adamant in their positions.

Abortion and Medical Costs

Aside from any personal or emotional considerations, the rights attained in the *Roe v. Wade* and *Doe v. Bolton* cases are options more available to middle- and upper-class women than to others. To date, the U.S. Supreme Court has held that states may refuse to allocate Medicaid funds for non-therapeutic abortions, leaving this power to the states. So far, only a few states have allowed Medicaid payments for most abortions.

The constitutional right to abortion has not been construed as a right to free abortions. In cases where the abortion is medically necessary or the woman's health is threatened, welfare funds are available in all states. However, in states where Medicaid cannot be used, poor women who might feel the addition of yet another child as too much of a burden have no real choice, since they may be financially unable to exercise their legitimate right to decide whether to bear the child. By funding childbirth expenses and not abortion expenses for poor women, the government in effect leaves no option open to them. Their only recourse is to resort to cheap, back-alley, self-styled abortionists, and thereby jeopardize their health or even their lives. On this point the high court has remained adamant, and in subsequent decisions it has continued to undermine the protection accorded to the poor.

The Hyde amendments are attachments that Congress has added annually since 1976 to the yearly appropriations bills for the U.S. Department of Labor and the Department of Health and Human Services (formerly Health, Education and Welfare). Each year there were different versions of the amendment, but all restricted the federal Medicaid funding for abortions.

A nationwide class-action suit challenged the Hyde amendments in June 1980, the *Harris v. McRae* case. In this case the Supreme Court ruled that it was legitimate for a state to choose to promote fetal life by funding child-birth and not abortion in spite of a threat to a woman's health. Thus, the constitutionality of the Hyde amendments was upheld.

Besides the general public, the Supreme Court itself is divided on the issue of abortion and medical costs. Although in the *Williams v. Zbaraz* (1980) case the Court again upheld the Hyde amendments, Justice William Brennan, Jr. wrote a dissenting opinion of the issue, part of which read:

By thus injecting coercive financial incentives favoring childbirth into a decision that is constitutionally guaranteed to be free from governmental intrusion, the Hyde Amendment deprives the indigent woman of her freedom to choose abortion over maternity, thereby impinging on the due process liberty right recognized in *Roe v. Wade*. By funding all of the expenses associated with childbirth and none of the expenses incurred in terminating pregnancy, the government literally makes an offer that the indigent woman cannot afford to refuse. (*Williams v. Zbaraz* 1980, quoted in Deckard 1983:150)

As of this writing, state policies on the use of Medicaid funding for abortion payment are essentially still in flux.

Consent to Abortion

As mentioned above, the 1973 abortion decision was viewed as too lenient by some groups, and attempts to circumvent or weaken it began immedi-ately. One area of contention concerned the power to consent to abortion, as some individuals felt that other interested parties besides the woman and her doctor should be included in the decision. Some states passed laws making it mandatory for the husband of a pregnant woman to give his consent before an abortion could be performed. In the instance of a pregnant minor, parental consent was necessary.

The Supreme Court declared all these provisions unconstitutional, as other people, whether husband or parents, could not prevent a woman's legal right to have an abortion. In a 1976 case, *Planned Parenthood of Central Missouri v. Danforth* (1976), the High Court invalidated the Missouri statute that allowed the husband to have veto power in the abortion decision. The Court's reasoning was: "We cannot hold that the State has the constitutional authority to give the spouse unilaterally the ability to prohibit the wife from termi-nating her pregnancy, when the State itself lacks that right" (428 U.S. 52 96 [1976]). These challenges to the rights of women to control their own bodies show clearly that the traditional outlook of male authority in the home, with nuances of ownership of the female body, has not completely died in the U.S. culture.

The aforementioned controversies have yet to be definitively resolved. A few incumbent U.S. Supreme Court justices who were elderly have recently retired. New appointments by a conservative presidency has led to a modification of the past High Court decision concerning the right to abortion, a situation desired by some and dreaded by others. To fill the vacancies, President Ronald Reagan chose three justices and elevated the incumbent William H. Rehnquist to Chief Justice in the hope of reorienting a liberal Court in the direction of conservatism. Reagan achieved his aim after he left office, and the recent Supreme Court term has had an unsettling effect on the U.S. social landscape. A restrictive 1986 Missouri abortion law, which had passed unanimously in the state legislature, had been challenged. The case reached the Supreme Court, and in a controversial five to four decision the Court gave the states the right to impose new restrictions on abortion.

CASE: *Webster v. Reproductive Health Services* (1989). William Webster was the Attorney General of Missouri, a state that sought to curtail abortions. Reproductive Health Services was a private, nonprofit clinic that performed many abortions. It reduced fees for women with low incomes, and was one of the few facilities in the area that performed abortions in the second trimester of pregnancy. Most public hospitals in Missouri had stopped performing abortions for poor women when Medicaid public funding became unavailable. Only two hospitals, the Truman Medical Center and University Hospital, continued the operations for women who could not pay, pending the appeal of the 1986 Missouri law (Wilkerson 1989).

In the decision the Court sustained Missouri's declaration that life began at conception, but felt that it did not affect abortion. Medical tests have to be performed on any fetus thought to be at least twenty weeks old to determine its viability. Public employees, including doctors, nurses, and other health-care providers, are forbidden to perform or assist with an abortion that is not necessary to save a woman's life. Even when no public funds are spent, public hospitals or other taxpayer-supported facilities may not be used for performing abortions that are unnecessary to save the woman's life. This ended abortions at two of the twelve centers performing them in Missouri.

This decision most severely affects poor women, who may have to bear children they can not afford. Such women may not be able to accumulate the money to pay for an abortion until later in the pregnancy, and also may not be able to travel to private centers. The effect of the decision will be to restrict a poor woman's right to a safe, legal abortion. The decision is also a blow to the future advancement of women's rights generally, as it opens the way for further restrictions on personal control over their bodies. The Supreme Court stopped short of overruling its *Roe v. Wade* decision legalizing abortion, but many people feel that this could eventually come about as well since three more abortion cases are scheduled to come before the Court in 1990. A complicating factor relating to the decision is that, due to medical advances since 1973, fetus viability now comes about earlier. However, this is not of much consequence for those who believe that the fetus is a person from the moment of conception, as antiabortionists do.

The *Webster* decision shows that political activism by some U.S. citizens, for whatever private or subsconscious motivation, has had its intended goal, even though inherent civil rights should not depend on political action. Justice Harry A. Blackmun (now eighty years of age), who had written the majority opinion in the *Roe v. Wade* case, rebuked the Court for showing so little respect for its own distinguished precedent. He said:

I fear for the future. I fear for the liberty and equality of the millions of women who have lived and come of age in the 16 years since *Roe* was decided. I fear for the integrity of, and public esteem for, this Court. (Greenhouse 1989:A1)

Indeed, it was the Supreme Court's decision in the *Griswold v. Connecticut* case (discussed earlier) that made specific the general constitutional principle and fundamental right to privacy, thus safeguarding the rights of women to exercise some control over their own role in procreation. In his dissenting opinion in the *Webster* case, Blackmun decried the growing insensitivity "to the fact that millions of women . . . have ordered their lives around the right to reproductive choice, and that this right has become vital to the full participation of women in the economic and political walks of American life" (*New York Times* 7/4/89:13).

The Court decision does not settle the issue for many people. It has encouraged antiabortionists who wish to have many more restrictions imposed. In many states they have mobilized protests outside of clinics in what they call Operation Rescue. Pro-abortionists, on the other hand, have realized that they must become active again, and have staged counterdemonstrations for their rights, which they fear are in jeopardy. There have been arrests for disorderly conduct on both sides (Wilkerson 1989:19).

One of the glories of the U.S. system of government—the preservation and advancement of individual rights through judicial review—could become compromised if the present campaign of conservative court-packing continues (Schwartz 1988). What is also disturbing is that an analysis of the 1977 Supreme Court decisions on sex discrimination indicated that the justices were deciding cases on the basis of their personal value systems rather than by the application of neutral legal principles (Crites and Hepperle 1987:11). In *Webster*, the justices have narrowed their previous decision but have not overturned it. They could decide that the subject of legal abortion is for the states to decide. Women who have fought long and hard for the right to have control over their own bodies are concerned.

For centuries women have been voting with vehemence for the right to abortion through the very fact of risking their lives when they resorted to dangerous illegal abortions. However, men, and not women, have traditionally had the predominant official voice in setting policies and passing laws concerning abortion. There is no specific survey comparing numbers of men to women nationally who would like the Supreme Court abortion decision rescinded. However, one small study of 212 pro-choice and pro-life activists in California showed that both movements consisted mostly of women. These activist women had differing social backgrounds. Comparisons of the two groups brought out the following information. The pro-choice women were more highly educated, and 94 percent of them were in the paid labor force, where they tended to have professional jobs. They had high incomes and a higher rate of divorce and singlehood than the other group, and typically had one or two children. The pro-life women on the other hand had lower levels of education and tended to be full-time homemakers. Only 63 percent were in the paid labor force. They had moderate family incomes and more children (Lucker 1984). Interestingly although not surprisingly, the two groups' basic views of the world differed. The pro-choice women believed that men and women are essentially similar, and opposed all forms of sex discrimination, while pro-lifers believed that men and women are fundamentally different, and that men are best suited for the marketplace while women are best suited for rearing children.

Technological Advances

In order to intimidate women seeking abortion, protests have been staged outside clinics where legal abortions are performed. Technological break-throughs may change that. In France they have developed a pill (Mifepristone, or RU 486) which chemically induces miscarriage. Abortion can thus remain a private matter. After protests from antiabortionists, who threatened to boycott all the products of Roussel-Uclaf, the pharmaceutical company producing the pill, Mifepristone was briefly taken off the market in that officially Catholic country. However, due to pressure from French feminists, the government ordered the company to recommence distribution of RU 486 in France. The French minister of health declared that the abortion pill was "the moral property of women" (Neubardt 1989:17). One can only guess whether the introduction of RU 486 will be permitted in the United States. It has been speculated that legally or illegally (smuggling pills is apparently not difficult), U.S. women will have access to the abortion pill within a few years. Pro-choice groups could use the threat of easy illegal access to RU 486 as a bargaining chip needed to counter the anti-choice threat of a boycott of any pharmaceutical company agreeing to manufacture the pill.

It is hard to imagine that long-fought-for rights of any kind for women in the United States or elsewhere could be withheld from them as in the past, even in spite of activism by some groups. Women are no longer passive concerning their rights. They realize that it is they who must control their own bodies, not legislatures.

Possible International Repercussions of the Webster Decision

The recent U.S. Supreme Court decision may have serious implications for women in Europe, where early access to abortion is legal in most countries. It remains forbidden only in Ireland, Belgium, and Malta (Simons 1989). Although abortion is legal, in Catholic Southern Europe doctors frequently refuse to perform abortions because of their moral objections or apprehensions that it could harm their prestige. The decision by the U.S. Supreme Court gives a self-justifying boost to such doctors. The onus is on poor women, who may have to travel to find abortion facilities. There are vocal minority groups in some European countries that would like to reexamine the whole abortion issue and work for earlier abortions and a reduction of the overall present abortion rate. It is understood that these groups would like restrictions rather than a return to criminalization and possible botched clandestine abortions. In any case, it is to be hoped that rationality will prevail in the long run.

5

Women and Employment

Women have always played a vital role in the U.S. economy. However, their work usually remained unacknowledged because it was generally performed within the context of the family and the home. Today, more and more women are entering the labor market. By 1985 they comprised 44 percent of the entire labor force. This represents 54 percent of all women over sixteen years of age. Public employment makes women's contributions visible, and the salaries often bring economic independence and security.

The road to equality in the workplace has been paved with obstacles for women. The early response to large numbers of women workers was an exploitative one, and women were segregated into low-paying jobs that lacked possibilities for advancement. They faced hardships and discrimination, but they persisted because of economic need. Many were active in the constant demonstrations for better working conditions that took place earlier in this century. Beginning in the 1960s, the legal system changed in order to put an end to gender discriminatory practices, and legislation was passed that aimed at workplace equality.

Women played a pioneering role in U.S. industry. Colonial women were encouraged by Alexander Hamilton, who felt that the advantage to the establishment of the new manufacturing industry was "the employment of persons who would otherwise be idle (and in many cases a burden to the community)." He stated that "women and children are rendered more useful, by the manufacturing establishments, than they would otherwise be" (Blau 1984:299). It is incredible that any man in those times would think of women as idle, for it was the rare woman who had that luxury. Under the prevalent frontier conditions, women's work at home was necessary for survival (see Chapter 4). Besides bearing numerous children, caring for them, cooking, cleaning, canning food, making cheese, tatting lace, sewing linens, and making candles, soap, and shoes, wives often also made items that were sold outside the home to increase family income. Not only did the Puritan ethic condemn idleness as a sin, the continual labor shortages led women to market activities such as trading, tavern keeping, printing, publishing, and retailing, besides domestic service and sewing (Abbott 1910).

Women thus made their contributions to the economy even before they entered the factories. With industrialization and changes in the means of production, the economy gradually changed from a family-based to a family-wage system (Andersen 1983). Families became dependent on the wages that the worker earned outside the home. As the center of labor moved from the household to the factory, an individual's worth became measured by earning ability. Thus, the wage system had the effect of devaluing the un-remunerated work done at home. Women now became financially dependent on men.

WOMEN IN INDUSTRY

Since men were required to do the labor-intensive agricultural work on their land, women and children were welcomed for jobs in the early factories. They worked because of financial need, as the exigencies of survival required an income from outside the home. In some industries, such as textile manufacturing, factories were merely a change of venue for many women, who had been doing the same type of work in the home. Those who worked in the factory system did so at lower wages than men. They became an army of cheap labor, and as such they contributed to the capitalist pursuit of greater profits. For women, working did not mean progress toward equality; it merely meant that they had two major jobs—that of homemaker and that of paid worker. Their wages were low, hours long, and working conditions often unsafe. Any difficulties they encountered in balancing two jobs were seen as their personal problems.

Although women worked in industry and comprised the overwhelming majority of industrial workers, unions refused to organize and admit them to their membership. Women did not become a part of the trade union movement until the late 1930s, even though they had been demonstrating along with men for better working conditions for a very long time. During the strikes, women picketed daily and were harassed by the police, but when they were arrested, the courts supported their bosses.

An example of blatant discrimination against women was to be found in the garment industry. The strikes of 1890 had led to an agreement between the owners and the Operators' and Contractors' unions to regulate wages and set employment standards for men only. Although 85 to 90 percent of the workers in the industry were women, the agreement specifically stated that no part of it should apply to employed females.

Women shirtwaist workers went on strike again in 1909–1910. Many women braved weeks of cold and hunger, and many were arrested, spending days and nights in the workhouse. The strike was successful in most shops but not the Triangle Shirtwaist Company, where workers had to drift back in defeat (Wertheimer 1984). For fear of being fired, they eventually compromised their demands for enforcement of more stringent safety and health regulations. Had they been successful, the tragedy of the next year might have been prevented.

The Triangle Shirtwaist Factory Fire

In 1911 the Triangle Shirtwaist Factory occupied the top three floors of a building in Greenwich Village, New York City. It was the largest such factory in the city, but it continued to violate the fire regulations even though inspectors had pointed them out. Floors were always littered with flamable materials, there were not enough staircases for the number of people employed, and the hallways were too narrow. The doors opened inward only, and they were kept locked because management was concerned with theft by employees. The fire escape, which did not reach ground level, was not designed to support much weight, and the metal shutters on the windows leading to it had rusted. Sprinklers were not required by law at that time. Although the management had been repeatedly warned of hazards, they had never held a fire drill. The stage was set for the disaster.

When the fire broke out on March 25, 1911, five hundred persons were working, most of them women. When help finally came, the ladders of the fire trucks were short and did not reach the eighth, ninth, or tenth floors. Many women jumped to their deaths, while those who could not get to the windows suffocated or burned to death. After the fire many corpses were found still bending over their sewing machines, attesting to the speed with which the fire had spread.

In all, 146 persons died, and countless others were injured and maimed for life. Most of the women were immigrants, and many were the sole supporters of families in the United States or Europe. Working women identified with the dead, and at the memorial ceremony there were eighty thousand working women who marched amid over a quarter of a million silent mourners.

This tragedy shows that women have had to pay a high price before the conscience of the public became sensitized to their working conditions. As for the owners of the Triangle Shirtwaist Factory, they collected the insurance and were acquitted of any blame (Stein 1962). One outraged reporter's article at the time stated: "Capital can commit no crime when it is in pursuit of profits" (*Literary Digest* 1912:6). The New York legislature finally passed factory safety and inspection laws.

Unionization

The fire helped swing public opinion toward unionization. However, women did not gain equally with men in the small reforms that ensued. In 1913 an agreement between labor and management, the first arbitrated by outside parties, resulted in the *Protocol in the Dress and Waist Industry*. It fixed wages but formalized discrimination. In the terms of employment, it listed individual jobs, the wages to be paid, and the sex of the jobholder. The higher-paying jobs were reserved for men only. The lowest-paid male was to earn more than the highest-paid female, and even if both did the same work they were not to be paid equally (Stein 1962). This was ironic in an industry dominated by women and where women had manned the picket lines, especially since they had been successful in getting union recognition and fixed wages.

Although the union movement was met with violence by factory owners, and both women and men suffered, women were particularly impotent in labor confrontations. In 1875 they went on strike in three textile mills, but after eight months the starving strikers had to return to work, agree to wage cuts, and promise not to join a union. After the shirtwaist strike some women did become organized, but female union membership rose only slowly. By 1920 women were 8 percent of the organized workers but 20 percent of the work force (Woloch 1984). National crafts unions did not welcome women. Women's presence in industry was seen as a temporary phenomenon, and unions refused to admit them to membership. They were also a threat to men because they represented cheap labor that could have the effect of reducing men's wages. Of course, this threat could have been eliminated if women had been paid the same wage as men. Instead, union men became great supporters of the domestic ideal of women's natural place being in the home, in order to get them out of the labor market.

Although work is significant in individuals' lives since it meets survival needs and often affords personal satisfaction, it is basically a social phenomenon. The social organization of work is hierarchical, and different jobs are differently valued and rewarded. Supposedly, job evaluation is based on importance to society or an employer, and the salary reflects the effort, skill, responsibility, knowledge, or education of the worker. In reality, through the years ascribed status has influenced pay scales (as the 1913 protocol mentioned above clearly shows). Women were paid less than men because of the common belief that women did not have to work, and that when they did work it was temporary. The facts were otherwise. The harsh reality of factory work, the fourteen- to eighteen-hour workdays, and the grossly unsafe working conditions could only be endured because of financial need. Many men's salaries were inadequate, as the concept of paying a man a "family wage" was not the norm, and factory owners paid as little as they could.

Bosses even occasionally skipped a week's salary. As a result of these practices, women were forced into the labor market.

LEGISLATION FOR WORKPLACE EQUALITY

Protective Laws

Early this century, the government passed protective legislation that limited women's exploitability and became a substitute for the unionization of women. The new laws limited women's working hours (and therefore their earnings), and mandated improved working conditions and a minimum wage. They also limited the type of work women could do, all under the guise of benevolence and the protection of women's reproductive capacity. These protective laws, passed between 1908 and 1917, set women apart from men and excluded them from high-wage jobs (Woloch 1984). In practice, they reinforced sex stereotypes and discriminated against women since they limited their earning power and were an obstacle to promotions and supervisory positions (Brown, Freedman, Katz, Price, and Greenberg 1977). Coverage of these laws varied widely from state to state, and it became obvious from the many exemptions that the employer's convenience was paramount rather than the woman's good. Thus, protective legislation was a monument both to the failure of the movement toward women's unionization and to the tenacity of the domestic ideal imposed on them.

The protective laws served to reinforce gender discrimination in the workplace by formalizing the stereotypes concerning the innate weaknesses of women in spite of the arduous work they were doing. The *Muller v. Oregon* (1908) case upheld an Oregon law that prohibited women working in a laundry more than ten hours a day. The Supreme Court decision reflected the prevalent male view by stating that women were a "special class" of citizen in need of protection from men, and that a woman's "physical structure and a proper discharge of her maternal functions—having in view not merely her own health, but the well-being of the race—justify legislation to protect her from the greed as well as the passion of man" (Kay 1988:7). The court decision makes it clear that women's main function was to provide babies for the future of the human race. One would have thought that so unique and profound a function would have given women a superior and venerated position instead of the low status and social esteem that was their lot. At any rate, the court decision ignored the fact that many women had to earn money in order to survive.

The host of legal deprivations endured by women were promulgated as a result of the inherited doctrine that the traditional notion of family unity and structure was paramount and must be preserved. Because of this belief, the government institutionalized discrimination against women. In the

United States there continue to exist on the books over a thousand state laws that discriminate on the basis of sex, resulting in cumulative deprivation in women's lives (McDougal, Lasswell, and Chen 1975). These laws are based on the old idea that the labor market is a sector reserved for men, which is part of the old man-made mythology concerning the "natural" spheres of men and women. In spite of those laws, traditionally structured families have become a minority. Rather, the reality of people's lives is leading to a redefinition of family. The traditional definition of a family—two parents living with children—accounted for only 27 percent of the country's 91.1 million households in 1988 (Gutis 1989). Included in the remaining 73 percent of households are the many single working women who are raising children alone, and who require at least the benefits afforded male breadwinners. The usual excuse for gender inequality is therefore no longer rational.

Unions did, however, finally open their doors to women. Today women comprise 30 percent of the membership of labor unions and associations, although only about 16 percent of employed women belong to a labor union. About 98 percent of all union contracts include nondiscrimination clauses. Some women have been accepted in the plumbers', electricians', and carpenters' unions. As for leadership in unions, some women are moving into regional and district-level positions of responsibility. Two women have reached the highest decision-making posts on the AFL-CIO Executive Council. About three thousand women work in mines, jobs that had been closed to them under the protective laws (Wertheimer 1984). What contributes to low female union membership is the fact that 75 percent of working women are in white-collar jobs, which are largely nonunionized sectors of the labor market.

The Equal Pay Act of 1963

A problem that needed to be addressed was the wage gap between male and female workers. The wage gap was attacked directly by the Equal Pay Act of 1963, which prohibits employers from paying different wages to men and women who work under similar conditions and perform tasks requiring equal skill, effort, and responsibility. The courts have determined that the work does not have to be identical to require equal pay; the work assignments need only be substantially equal. Employers cannot justify lower pay for women who are doing essentially the same work as men merely by creating different job classifications for it.

The Equal Pay Act has benefitted women, but it also has its limitations. It covers pay issues but does not address the problems of sex discrimination in the workplace or job segregation, the elimination of which are currently being approached through Title VII of the Civil Rights Act and through the comparable worth concept.

The Civil Rights Act of 1964

In 1964 Congress passed the Civil Rights Act which aimed at the prevention of discrimination. The protective legislation on the books in the different states has gradually been struck down by the Supreme Court through decisions in cases that have challenged sex discrimination under Title VII of this act. These decisions showed clearly that the protective laws were also exclusionary laws. Title VII of the Civil Rights Act states:

It shall be unlawful employment practice for an employer to fail or refuse to hire or discharge any individual, or otherwise to discriminate against any individual with respect to his compensation, terms, conditions, or privileges of employment, because of such individual's race, color, religion, sex, or national origin. (42 U.C.S.A. 1974 2000(e)–2a)

At the same time Congress created the Equal Employment Opportunity Commission (EEOC) and charged it with enforcement of Title VII through the promulgation of interpretive guidelines. The regulations, called the *EEOC Guidelines on Discrimination Because of Sex*, describe in detail which employment practices are sex-discriminatory and therefore illegal. The EEOC guidelines eliminating protective legislation state in part:

Many States have enacted laws or promulgated administrative regulations with respect to the employment of females. Among these laws are those which prohibit or limit the employment of females in certain occupations, e.g., in jobs requiring the lifting or carrying of weights exceeding certain prescribed limits, during certain hours of the night, for more than a specified number of hours per day or per week, and for certain periods of time before and after childbirth. The Commission has found that such laws and regulations do not take into account the capacities, preferences, and abilities of individual females, and, therefore, discriminate on the basis of sex. The Commission has concluded that such laws and regulations conflict with and are superseded by Title VII of the Civil Rights Act of 1964. (*EEOC Guidelines on Discrimination Because of Sex*, Section 1601.2[b][1])

Only those occupations where the employer can prove that sex is a bona fide occupational qualification (BFOQ) of employment are excluded from the application of the guidelines. The courts have been receiving litigation concerning discrimination in hiring, salaries, and promotions ever since, and the EEOC receives about 50,000 new charges each year (Reskin and Hartmann 1986).

The first case heard by the U.S. Supreme Court under Title VII occurred in 1971 and concerned discrimination due to motherhood. Companies often refused to hire women with preschool children, whereas such a restriction did not apply to men. In the *Phillips v. Martin-Marietta Corporation* case

(1971) the Court struck down the company's policy of using different hiring standards for men and women who had preschool children.

Some of the other early cases heard by the Supreme Court demonstrated that sex discrimination was unequivocably illegal, no matter how camouflaged it was or how generally accepted the old stereotypes were. Three cases are discussed below: One dealt with an unnecessary females-only hiring practice, the second with the alleged need to be single for some jobs, and the third with unnecessary height and weight requirements.

CASE: *Diaz v. Pan American World Airways* (1971). Only female cabin attendants were hired by Pan Am as a matter of policy, in order to maintain a particular image that was based on sexual stereotypes. The company claimed that a pleasant environment was enhanced by the cosmetic effect of female stewardesses, and that the customers preferred them. Pan Am also claimed that women handled the nonmechanical functions of the job better than men. The Court decided that the nonmechanical aspects of a job are tangential to the business, and that passenger preferences and prejudices could not be upheld. The Court stated that having male stewards would not jeopardize the business of the airline, which is to transport people. Having female flight attendants was not a business necessity and therefore was not a bona fide occupational qualification. Therefore, the policy of excluding men was ruled illegal by the Court.

A main goal of Title VII is to provide equal access to the job market for men and women, and although it might seem that only men have gained in this case, the decision also subtly weakens the old stereotype requiring women to perform a decorative function.

CASE: *Sprogis v. United Air Lines, Inc.* (1971). Mary Burke Sprogis was discharged from her stewardess job when she married. The airline did not employ males as cabin stewards, but there was no policy restricting employment to single males, or restricting the marital status of other female employees of the company. Sprogis claimed that this inconsistent policy was discriminatory.

The Court ruled that in the stewardess job description there was nothing that warranted disparate treatment on the basis of marital status. Being single did not appear to be a bona fide occupational qualification, and the situation was therefore one of sex discrimination under the guise of a seemingly neutral company policy. The airline lost its case and the no-marriage rule for stewardesses was invalidated.

CASE: *Meadows v. Ford Motor Company* (1973). Dolores M. Meadows brought a class-action suit against the Ford Motor Company. Fifty-four women had applied for employment on the production line of the Kentucky truck plant and, although 935 production workers were hired, none of them were women. Ford's employment policy required the applicant to weigh at least 150 pounds. Meadows established that 80 percent of women between the ages of eighteen and twenty-four do not meet that requirement, while

70 percent of all men in that age bracket do. It was also established that exceptions had been made for men who weighed between 135 and 150 pounds, but there were no exceptions made for women. Finally, the company could not produce any studies done to ascertain strength relative to weight for a person seeking employment.

The Court decided that such apparently neutral rules are highly discriminatory in practice as they have a disparate impact. As such, they violate Title VII of the Civil Rights Act. The Court stated that in previous cases:

The establishment of policies or practices by an employer that are neutral on their face, but discriminatory in their effect, and that have no valid relationship to the accomplishment of the particular job, have been thoroughly condemned by the Supreme Court. (6 FEP Cases 797, 802 [W. D. Ky. 1973])

Ford was prohibited from continuing the policy, and a precedent was set for litigation concerning similar requirements.

There have been many similar challenges to discriminatory practices involving obvious or subtle gender discrimination. Concerning workers' pensions, female employees must receive equal benefits, whereas in the past they had received lower benefits because of their average longer life expectancy. *Sex averaging* is illegal, and women cannot receive less pension to live on just because 15 to 20 percent of women will live longer. The courts have struck down such practices time after time, and the gradual dismantling of the superstructure, which had given legal sanction to women's separate and lower category in the work force under the guise of protection, gave women more employment equality.

The Pregnancy Discrimination Act of 1978

In the past, pregnancy was usually considered grounds for termination of employment, but there are now guarantees that pregnancy will not be punitive for the working woman. Since 1972 the EEOC Guidelines and subsequent case law have mandated that the pregnancy of a fit woman worker must be treated like any other temporary disablement, and that the woman not be fired or forced to quit. The Pregnancy Discrimination Act of 1978 amends Title VII of the Civil Rights Act of 1964. It seeks to guarantee women's right to participate fully and equally with men in the workplace without denying them fundamental rights to full participation in family life. It requires that women "affected by pregnancy ... shall be treated the same for all employment-related purposes, including receipt of benefits under fringe benefit programs, as other persons not so affected but similar in their ability or inability to work" (Kay 1988). The act is also interpreted as including a qualified right to reinstatement after an unpaid leave of absence of reasonable duration for pregnancy and childbirth disability, so that women will not be penalized for exercising their reproductive capacity. Woman may therefore have families without losing their jobs, just as men do.

Although there are now work reinstatement guarantees, women who are employed and also raising children are often unfairly burdened. Recently a controversial article by Felice Schwartz, founder and president of Catalyst, an organization that advises corporations on women's careers, appeared in the *Harvard Business Review* (January–February 1989). Entitled "Management Women and the New Facts of Life," it recommended a so-called *mommy track* versus a *fast track* for women at work. Schwartz made corporate management a suggestion that some feel would flout the equal work opportunities which women have long fought for and earned. She calls for an early identification by employers of two separate groups of female workers. One group, the top performers or career-oriented women, would be treated like talented men and rewarded. They should be recognized early, given opportunities to aspire toward leadership positions, and included in the management team, according to Schwartz. The other group of women, who want active family participation as well as a career, are supposedly willing to trade career growth and compensation for more disengagement from the office. These women opt for the mommy track. Schwartz justifies the dual treatment on the grounds that employing women costs firms more than employing men. By concentrating mostly on top women performers, companies can supposedly be more cost-effective since career interruptions and turnovers are expensive.

Needless to say, encouraging a mommy track that is separate and unequal can derail women's careers and justify second-class treatment at work. Aside from the fact that the idea rewards childlessness and penalizes family-mindedness, Schwartz seems to forget that what feminists have been urging is social and family change, and that nurturing and raising children should not be solely the mother's concern but rather should be shared by the father. A restructuring of the obsolete masculine model in the work world could lead to greater satisfaction all around, since both men and women could be given greater options and flexibility.

In a later article that appeared in the *New York Times* (3/22/89), Schwartz claimed that she was not antiwoman and that in her earlier article she had meant to help reconcile women's family and market roles and to urge employers to do more for them. The reality is that there is much pressure on many female workers to juggle these two major roles and to be "super-women." Some men in two-career families do accept nurturing responsibilities, but until it is generally accepted by the population at large that family roles are to be shared just as the breadwinning role is, women will still have to come to terms with the double burden and work it out on an ad hoc basis.

OCCUPATIONAL SEX SEGREGATION

White-Collar Women

In the twentieth century there has been a burgeoning growth of the white-collar sector of the labor market. Despite the increase in numerous types of jobs, women have been crowded into the low-salaried positions. Although they were at the bottom levels, they found white-collar work clean, less tiring, and less hazardous than factory work. Low-paying jobs suited the public image concerning women's major home responsibilities and men's breadwinning task. Besides, women's early socialization did not make them well-suited for the competitive job world and they readily accepted non-career jobs. Middle-class women extended their domestic roles to the larger society and were concentrated in the nurturing jobs. They worked as nurses, secretaries, elementary school teachers, waitresses, and social workers—occupations that became known as the female professions, and for which men did not compete. Thus, women remained segregated in low-salaried occupations.

Women entered so-called men's professions only briefly during World War II, when the government appealed to their sense of patriotism and urged them to take jobs welding, riveting, ship fitting, tool making, and other manual labor jobs. As an incentive, they were paid the same wages men would have been paid. When the war was over, the women were laid off to make room for the returning service men. The government-issued propaganda then extolled the roles of wife and mother at home. Many of these women merely switched to the traditional female-dominated and lower-paying jobs, and kept working. By 1985, 54.5 percent of the women sixteen years and older were in the paid labor force, mostly working in "female" jobs (Renzetti and Curren 1989).

Labor Market Segmentation According to Sex

Women's labor has always been necessary in the building of the U.S. economy. They entered the labor force in response to the structure of supply and demand. However, from the beginning they suffered from an under-valuation of their work and from social stereotypes concerning women's inherent nature and appropriate occupations. The resulting job segmentation according to sex was due in part to early male and female socialization, but also to rampant discrimination that prevented women's access to high-level white-collar job training. The results of the long tradition of sex segregation are apparent today; women have a lower aggregate earning power than men, in fact about 40 percent lower. In spite of the new laws and widespread education, occupational segregation is still in place, and there remain differential pay scales that were begun at a time when it was normal to exploit working women. Many social thinkers today are grappling with the complex problem of bringing men's and women's salaries more nearly into balance.

That occupational sex segregation has persisted is ascertained by the percentages of each sex in particular occupations. In 1986 females were 98.9 percent of all secretaries, 75.4 percent of elementary school teachers, 89.7 percent of bookkeepers, 88.0 percent of waitresses, 95.9 percent of registered nurses, and 87.8 percent of nursing aides. Men were 97.7 percent of all truck drivers, 85.0 percent of production supervisors, 98.4 percent of carpenters, 91.2 percent of farmers, and 98.7 percent of auto mechanics (Renzetti and Curran 1989:179). In 1984, 48 percent of all female employees held jobs in which 80 percent or more of the workers were women, while 71 percent of males were in occupations where 80 percent or more of the work force was male.

Statistics show that sex segregation persists even across educational levels. The *index of segregation*, the percentage of women who would have to change jobs so that the distribution of men and women in jobs would be equal, has remained the same since 1900 (Taeuber and Valdisera 1986). In this century, about two-thirds of all working women would have to change jobs in order to achieve an even occupational distribution (Babcock et al. 1975).

In spite of the recent phenomenon of some women entering nontraditional occupations, the U.S. labor market continues to be characterized by one set of jobs employing almost exclusively men and another set of jobs employing almost exclusively women. This latter sector of the labor market is generally lower paying than the male sector.

There are indications that occupational segregation is actually more extreme than figures indicate. Census statistics do not show a complete picture since within major occupational groups men and women tend to be concentrated differently. For example, one year the census reported that 44 percent of all assemblers were women. The category included electrical machine equipment and supply assemblers, of whom 67 percent were women, and motor vehicle and motor vehicle equipment assemblers, of whom only 16 percent were women (Babcock et al. 1975). Needless to say, the latter category is more highly paid. Since women are not doing exactly the same assembling tasks, they cannot claim unequal pay for equal work.

The Equal Pay Act of 1963 mandated equal pay for equal work. It eliminated the common practice of paying women less than men for the same work based on the dubious assumption that men needed to support families while women were being supported by their husbands. This was a disguise for sex discrimination since male bachelors were not paid less than married men for the same job. However, in spite of adherence to the Equal Pay Act, the male-female wage gap continues, and working women still earn sixty cents for every dollar men earn. It becomes obvious that the gap is due to job segregation, and that either the jobs women perform are in lower-paying fields or the jobs are lower paying because women perform them (Willborn 1986). In the latter case, sex discrimination is involved. Sex discrimination in employment is prohibited by law.

Comparable Worth Issue

The concept of comparable worth is based on the principle that jobs that are different but of equal value to the employer should command similar salaries. Value is define by such factors as skill, knowledge, education, responsibility, and working conditions required for the job. The heart of the comparable worth debate centers on the effect of sex composition on wage rates. It requires equal pay for work performed by one sex that is of value to the employer to work performed by the other sex. There are inherent comparable problems in determining the comparability of jobs since evaluation is to a large extent subjective. It is also difficult to eliminate gender stereotypes in the evaluation process, as the nurturing skills used in the predominantly female occupations (teaching, nursing, social work, etc.) are taken for granted as unpaid when done in the home.

Eliminating gender stereotypes is only part of a very complex issue. Walter Fogel (1984) has analyzed some of the difficulties inherent in the comparable worth issue. The question revolves around whether workers like secretaries are paid less because they are women than they would be if they were men, or whether the marketplace determines salaries. In the former case, it is assumed that the wage gap is caused by the historical undervaluation of women's work. In the latter case, supply and demand processes would be influential. There is much subjectivity involved in this question.

CASE: *Corning Glass Works v. Brennan* (1974). This was the only Equal Pay Act case decided by the U.S. Supreme Court. In this case, an attempt was made to justify differential payments for two jobs performed under "similar working conditions" on labor market determinants. The issue was whether night work, as opposed to day work, is a working condition that falls under the Equal Pay Act. Corning Glass Works employed inspectors for the day and night shifts at its Wellsboro, Pennsylvania plant. Since 1925 the night shift inspectors were men because of the protective laws restricting night work to men only. Initially the night shift inspectors were paid double what the day inspectors (who were mostly female) were paid, but by 1966 the differential was approximately 10 percent. Because of the Equal Pay Act, in 1964 the company eliminated lower rates for women in all jobs except those of the day inspectors. Beginning in 1966, women from the day jobs started becoming night inspectors, but they continued to be paid at the day rate. Women sued because they felt they had a right to equal wages on the grounds that the job was the same whether it was being performed during the day or at night.

The U.S. Supreme Court decided against Corning Glass Works. It said that Corning failed to prove that the day and night shifts were different. The working conditions factor for pay differences was seen by the Court as including only work hazards and surroundings, and not time of day. Corning was therefore guilty of sex discrimination. The day inspectors, most of whom were women, got an immediate wage increase plus back pay (Fogel 1984).

However, the Corning case did not solve the question of whether differential wages for men and women are based on market requirements or sex discrimination. Corning believed it had to pay more in order to hire males for a night job because of the greater market wage of men. The defense generally used by employers to justify wage differentials concerns the dictates of the labor market. Even when wages are established through collective bargaining, they are broadly consistent with market rates, especially with respect to differences in wages between predominantly male and predominantly female jobs. The Equal Pay Act aims at remedying the market influence by making the payment of a higher wage for men based on the market illegal. Wage differences for the same job must therefore be considered sex-based.

It is difficult to prove equal worth, and plaintiffs lose more Equal Pay Act cases than they win because of the difficulty of proving the similarity of different jobs. Critics of the comparable worth concept feel that there is no such thing as inherent worth to any job; a job is worth what it brings in the market. Challenges on the grounds of comparable worth have been brought under Title VII of the Civil Rights Act as well.

CASE: *Briggs v. City of Madison* (1982). Female public-health nurses employed by the city of Madison were paid less than a category of male workers called sanitarians whose jobs required the same or a lesser degree of qualification. Although both jobs required a college degree, public-health nurses, in addition, needed specialized training and certification from the state of Wisconsin. These additional qualifications were not necessary for the sanitarians.

The plaintiffs (the nurses) sought to prove wage discrimination on the basis of sex under Title VII. They claimed that the two job classifications involved work similar in skill, effort, and responsibility, which would be compensated comparably but for the employer's discriminatory treatment. The city of Madison countered that the high pay for the men was necessary to recruit and retain the sanitarians. The plaintiffs contended that market demands were not a justification for upgrading the male salaries, and that the market reflected biases that had been rejected Equal Pay Act cases.

The court agreed that the jobs were essentially similar, were performed under similar working conditions, and hence were of comparable worth. However, the court contended that employers were constrained by market forces in setting labor costs, and did not in any meaningful sense make independent judgments concerning wages. The opinion stated:

Under Title VII, an employer's liability extends only to its own acts of discrimination. Nothing in the Act indicates that the employer's liability extends to conditions of the marketplace which it did not create. Nothing indicates that it is improper for an employer to pay the wage rates necessary to compete in the marketplace for qualified job applicants. That there may be an abundance of applicants qualified for some jobs and a dearth of skilled applicants for other jobs is not a condition for which a particular employer bears responsibility. (Fogel 1986:113–114)

The plaintiffs had proven sex bias in wages but failed to convince the court that they were victims of illegal, intentional discrimination by their employer.

The Comparison of Occupations

Several methods have been suggested for the difficult task of comparing occupations. They are briefly explained here because comparable worth is one approach to the elimination of the female-male wage gap. Job evaluations are necessary to establish that any two job classifications are similar in skill, effort, working conditions, and responsibility. If the two jobs are similar and there is a pay differential in a female-dominated occupation as compared to a male-dominated one, the inference is that sex discrimination accounts for the difference. Steven Willborn (1986) describes the four basic job evaluation systems available, and the problems involved.

The Ranking Method

Jobs are simply ranked from highest to lowest in terms of worth or value to the firm. A problem with this method is its subjectivity, since there are no clearly defined objective criteria for comparing jobs.

The Classification Method

Factors such as skill, effort, and responsibility predetermine and describe job levels. Any number of job levels are decided on, and each job is placed in the most appropriate level after being evaluated. This method is simple but unreliable. Much depends on evaluator expertise, and the method is thus subject to biases and inconsistencies. Also, a job could rank high on one factor but low on another, such as when it entails no supervisory responsibilities but requires a high educational level.

The Factor Comparison Method

Several steps are required for this method. First, a number of factors are chosen, such as skill, effort, etc. Then some "benchmark" jobs are selected, such as secretary or messenger, and their worth is assessed. Each selected job is analyzed to ascertain the dollar value of each of the factors that contribute to job worth. For example, "If secretaries are paid $200 per week, it might be determined that $100 is attributable to skill, $70 to responsibility, and $30 to effort, and if messengers are paid $100 per week, it might be determined that $10 is attributable to skill, $40 to responsibility, and $50 to effort" (Willborn 1986:63). Finally, each job in the company is compared in the same way, factor by factor. The factor comparison method has limitations. It is time-consuming and difficult to explain to employees. In addition, guides are unavailable for the selection of the benchmark jobs, although this can influence the results. Finally, the assignment of money values to the factors cannot be justified theoretically or statistically.

The Point Method

First, a set of evaluation factors are selected such as skill, effort, and responsibility. Each factor is weighed and assigned points according to the importance of the factor compared with other factors, and *degrees* or relative amounts of a factor that the job requires are assigned. The job is rated on each factor separately and assigned the appropriate points, which are then totalled to arrive at the overall score for the job. The point method does exclude the effects of sex on the ultimate ranking of jobs, and is the one most widely used by state governments. However, some people have expressed concern as to the method's reliability and validity. In particular, they question whether the method yields the same results on successive trials, and whether it accurately measures the reality it is designed to assess.

Comparable worth may become the civil rights issue of the next decade. The National Committee on Pay Equity reports that as of September 1989, most state governments had taken some action on pay equity. Of the fifty states, six had put in place a broad-based pay equality plan, thirteen had made pay equity adjustments and had appropriated pay increases in female-dominated jobs, seven had conducted surveys to make salary comparisons, eighteen had researched pay equity activities of other states and held public hearings to identify job segregation and wage inequalities, and only six had taken no action at all (Simpson 1989:88).

The premise that different jobs can be compared is being increasingly accepted. It also has been the subject of some litigation. The case against the state of Washington, which used the point system to compare jobs, has been a highly publicized one.

CASE: *AFSCME v. State of Washington* (1983). In 1974 the state of Washington, which had authorized a study of wage disparities, hired a professional job evaluator. The consulting firm set *worth points* for several factors relating to jobs of the American Federation of State, County, and Municipal Employees (AFSCME), part of the AFL-CIO. The point system gave registered nurses the highest score because of knowledge and skills (280 points), mental demands (122 points), accountability (160 points), and working conditions (11 points). A laundry worker was given the same number of points as a beginning truck driver, and a senior secretary the same number as an electrician. The study revealed that significant disparities (20 percent average difference) existed between male-dominated and female-dominated jobs which were not attributable to job content (Kay 1988, Willborn 1986).

In 1983 a federal district court judge ruled that the state had indeed discriminated against women, since it paid men more for jobs comparable to those in female-dominated sectors. The state appealed the decision to a higher court and won its case in 1985. The judge who reversed the decision of the lower court reasoned that the state of Washington had taken prevailing market rates into account when setting salaries, and that the present case did not lend itself to disparate impact analysis (appropriate in cases where the same rule affects men and women differently). However, since this decision was reached, the Ninth Circuit has broadened its view of disparate impact theory (Kay 1988).

The question remains concerning whether it is best to arrive at wage equalization by one of the four methods explained above or whether more would be gained for women by encouraging and legally ensuring equal access to jobs. The latter approach would not necessarily change the aggregate salary differential between women and men since guaranteeing equal access does not necessarily result in a nonsegregated work force. Nursing is an obvious example of this. The case of the nursing profession is one that seems to refute the explanation of supply and demand in the labor market as the cause of the low wages paid to women. The United States is presently experiencing a severe nursing shortage, and in some urban areas hospitals have only about 10 percent of the needed nurses. This is attributed to the traditionally low salaries paid to nurses. Hospitals have not generally raised salaries in response to market forces, and the shortage remains. It is not known whether higher wages would attract men to nursing, or if the job would pay more if most nurses were men. At the present time many men consider being nurses as a blow to their masculinity, since nursing has always been considered woman's work. Therefore, nurses' hopes for better financial recognition rest on the comparable worth issue.

However, the general effects of wage equalization, should it become widespread, are speculative. In the Corning case mentioned above, it could have resulted in fewer women employed in favor of men since the pay was the same, or the inability to fill the night job because there was no incentive for a worker to take it. If the pay is the same and employers tend not to hire women, the problem remains; they have not overcome the gender stereotypes that have prevailed for so long.

The comparable worth issue is one that arouses heated debate, especially since it deals with the relationship between work, money, sex, and, ultimately, power. Basic human rights are involved. The concept of comparable worth is not a specific legal one, but rather a movement to raise the level of wages in traditionally sex-segregated jobs. As has been suggested, it is not an easy task to find a direct correlation between different occupations. However the issue is resolved in the future, it will affect the everyday work lives of millions of U.S. citizens.

6

Women and Power

Although power is a complex phenomenon and definitions as to its prevalence vary, it is generally agreed that to be in a position of power, whether in a small group or on a societal level, means having the potential to either control, command, or have domination, sway, jurisdiction, authority, or influence over others. It incorporates the ability, or potential ability, of having one's will done even in the face of opposition. Power is of great interest since it has never been equally allocated to all persons in a society. Power is a finite concept, and since some persons have it while others do not, those who have no power must accede to those who possess it. It is a resource that allows influence in the society and much control over one's own life.

There are different power bases from which individuals can exercise sway over others. People can have reward power (the ability to provide things that others would like to have), coercive power (the ability to provide sanctions), referent power (the possession of attractiveness, charisma, or general liking that one evokes from others), expert power (possession of skills and knowledge not possessed by another), legitimate power (due to social role position), and informational power (perceived access to useful information that others want or consider important) (French and Raven 1959, Raven 1965). Whatever the base, power always involves using some of one's resources in order to achieve a desired situation.

Men have more access to these power bases than women, although women are not entirely powerless. Instead, the power strategies used by them are different (Johnson 1976). Women may have personal resources from which to draw, such as beauty, nurturing ability, friendship, affection, or strength of personality, while men have more concrete resources such as money, skill, knowledge, or physical strength at their disposal. The latter resources afford men more autonomy, as they need not be ingratiating or rely on the benevolence of others in order to exercise some power. Our concern here is legal power, the ability to exercise legitimate rights in order to remedy wrongs. Without the legal foundation mandating equality before the law for each person regardless of sex, women can continue to be exploited as in the past.

According to historians and anthropologists, most societies have been and continue to be patriarchies wherein power is vested in men. Some male power holders have rationalized that their superior social position relative to women has divine sanction. It has been demonstrated through the years that power can corrupt. The use of power is not neutral, and the successful wielding of power often has metamorphic effects on the power holder and on the target as well. It is possible that, over time, power holders may come to feel they are above the common rules of fairness that govern others. Also, power holders may come to feel contempt for target persons and view them as nonpersons, or adopt a benevolent, paternalistic air toward them. The target persons can thus become objects of manipulation with lower claims to human rights (Kipnis 1976).

Whatever the base, power is essentially an issue of control, and it is at the heart of superordinate-subordinate relationships. Since there is a general disparity between women and men concerning access to the power bases from which they might draw, the relevant questions concern what avenues of social endeavor lead to the various forms of power, and what power bases women must pursue in order to acquire legitimate equality with men in society. There are many indications of women's powerlessness, some obvious and some subtle. My discussion will center on some of the social manifestations of women's lack of control in society: the blatant and widespread phenomena of rape and wife battering, and the more subtle issue of sexual harassment. Then I will consider reasons why such activity continues in spite of more stringent laws. Finally, I will suggest the sources of power that women must seek for meaningful sexual equality to become a reality.

THE MYTH OF THE PEDESTAL

There are women who genuinely feel that they would lose a favored status if they are treated equally in society. Perhaps those who claim they want to keep women on the pedestal are not aware of what statistics show are the real conditions of women's lives. They might not realize that in 1987 there were 47.8 divorces for every 100 marriages (National Center for Health Statistics 1988) and the rate is increasing; that after divorce the average woman's standard of living decreases by 73 percent while her ex-husband's increases by 42 percent; that the average court-ordered child support is less than the cost of day care alone (Weitzman 1985); and that in 1986, female heads of households and their children accounted for 52 percent of the country's poor (U.S. Bureau of the Census 1987). They also might not know that divorced and unmarried men are reluctant to take responsibility for children they have sired, based on the fact that ten years after divorce, 87 percent of fathers were no longer meeting court-ordered payments, and in 1981 28.2 percent paid nothing; furthermore, less than half of those who paid did not pay the full amount (Shortridge 1984). Because of the increased rate of divorce and unwed motherhood, 42 percent of white and 86 percent of black children must be raised by the mother alone for part or all of their lives (Schaefer 1989). In addition, those who believe the women-on-a-pedestal myth seem not to be aware of the amount of violence perpetrated by men (with virtual impugnity) against women, and that the FBI crime reports (which represent only the reported incidents) show that the number of wife batterings and rapes is on the increase.

Women have had to live under the burden of other socially created myths concerning their inherent nature: their alleged innate high morality, their need to nurture children and men, their inability to lead, and so forth. Laws have been enacted that ensured that women's behavior patterns would be in keeping with their natural bent, such as laws against abortion and divorce, and the restrictive work laws protecting women. Why the restrictive laws were necessary if the behavior was so natural was never the subject of enlightened debate as far as I know.

These myths served society, as they operated as a form of social control for half the population. Women generally did not question these social images or, if they did suspect that they themselves were different from the norm, they tried hard to hide their deviance. Today, women no longer have to conceal their personality characteristics or risk censure. Women are not born followers, but their weak position vis-à-vis men has assured the continuation of the myths. The ultimate goal of feminists is the social redefinition of women as neither evil temptresses nor angelic goddesses on a pedestal but simply as human creatures with the same needs and randomly distributed personality traits (good or bad, leader or follower) as any other persons, regardless of sex. They seek legal redress, more access to power, and equal economic opportunities.

SEXUAL HARASSMENT

An indication of discrimination that women have long had to endure in silence is sexual harassment. Sexual harassment is understood as power-motivated, exploitative, abusive behavior for which women pay with their jobs, their lack of deserved promotions, and the absence of job satisfaction they might otherwise have. Women have always known of the existence of the problem, but it has only recently been officially recognized. It can take various forms but is generally recognized as the "unwanted imposition of sexual requirements in the context of a relationship of unequal power" (MacKinnon 1979:1). Another definition that includes modes of behavior is that of the U.S. Office of Personnel Management, which was used for a study of sexual harassment in the federal work force: "Any deliberate or repeated unsolicited verbal comments, gestures or physical contact of a sexual nature that is considered to be unwelcome by the recipient" (U.S. House of Representatives 1980:8).

Conditions often present in sexual harassment include not only unwelcome sexual advances and the presence of intimidation resulting from the harasser's greater power, but also the suggestion of institutionally inappropriate rewards or penalties that could result from compliance or refusal (Tong 1984). Catherine MacKinnon (1979), an attorney and political scientist, identifies two types of harassment in the workplace. One she terms the quid pro quo variety, in which sexual compliance is exchanged for an employment benefit (a raise, a promotion, or simply a retention of the job). The other is the condition of work variety, whereby the woman is constantly being made aware of her body (by being touched, teased, referred to as sexy, etc.) and its uses in men's fantasies, which results in a discriminatory or hostile work environment. Whichever form it takes, it is demeaning to women, who are the main victims.

Most women work because they have to. Sexual harassment sexualizes women's work roles and often makes sexuality a condition for their economic survival. Studies, although somewhat limited as they lack a standard definition of sexual harassment and are based on women's self-reporting, reveal that harassment is a pervasive problem. One 1982 study of the federal workplace revealed that 42 percent of the female employees had experienced harassment during the previous two years on the job (Martin 1984). The women are usually vulnerable to economic consequences or psychological, physical, or social discomfort. Quitting an otherwise satisfying job has been a common way for sexually harassed individuals to deal with the degrading situation. Recently, women have sought other options to redress the unpleasant situation. In a minority of cases, litigation has been resorted to.

The early court cases were unsuccessful for the plaintiffs. In a 1975 case, *Corne v. Bausch and Lomb, Inc.*, the judge expressed concern that ruling in the plaintiff's favor might have led to "a potential federal lawsuit every time an employee made an amorous or sexually-oriented advance toward another" (p. 163). Obviously, the judge regarded sexual harassment as normal male behavior and an extension of male social prerogatives concerning male-female relationships. However, today the climate of male permissiveness is gradually changing. Later, court decisions held that the employer was culpable for maintaining a discriminatory work environment. The argument that sexual harassment is sex discrimination is based on the idea that two employment standards are created: one for men without sexual conditions, and one for women, which includes sexual requirements. Therefore, a gender-defined group is singled out for special treatment. The fact that the incidents of sexual harassment are so numerous indicates that what is involved is the female condition as a whole and not a personal or unique quality of a particular woman (MacKinnon 1979). The following sexual harassment case was one of the first to reach the U.S. Supreme Court.

CASE: *Meritor Savings Bank v. Vinson* (1986). Michelle Vinson was hired in 1974 at the Meritor Savings Bank by Sidney Taylor, a vice president and manager of one of its branches. Taylor supervised her training and in four years she was promoted to assistant branch manager. Shortly after she went to work for Taylor, he invited her to dinner and then suggested they go to a motel. Out of fear of losing her job, she agreed. Because of his demands, they had sexual relations over the next several years about forty or fifty times. She asserted that he even forcibly raped her on several occasions after following her to the woman's restroom. She said she did not use the bank's complaint procedures because she was afraid of Taylor. Sexual activity stopped in 1977 when Vinson started going with a steady boyfriend. In 1978 Vinson notified Taylor that she was taking sick leave for an indefinite period, and two months later she was discharged for excessive use of that leave. Vinson sued the bank on the grounds that for four years she had been subjected to sexual harassment in violation of Title VII of the Civil Rights Act. She sought compensatory and punitive damages against Taylor and the bank (Kay 1988).

Taylor denied all the allegations at the bench trial of *Vinson v. Taylor*. The district court ruled in favor of Taylor and the bank on the grounds that if sexual relations had indeed occurred, they were voluntary and had nothing to do with continued employment. The ruling was reversed by the court of appeals in 1985. The court of appeals also clarified the liability of the employer by ruling that whether or not the employer knew or should have known of the sexual harassment practiced by the supervisory personnel, he was absolutely liable. Unwelcome sexual advances that contribute to an offensive or hostile working environment comprise sexual discrimination and violate Title VII of the Civil Rights Act, since the wording of the act does not limit it to economic or tangible discrimination.

In 1980 the Equal Employment Opportunity Commission (EEOC), which is the agency appointed to interpret the Civil Rights Act, issued guidelines to the effect that sexual harassment is a form of sex discrimination prohibited by Title VII even if no economic injury is involved. Two types of sexual harassment were recognized—one type involving employment benefits based on sexual favors, and the other, while not affecting economic benefits, creating a hostile or offensive working environment. This latter type of harassment had not been considered in the first case (Kay 1988). When, on appeal, the *Vinson* case reached the U.S. Supreme Court, the Court clearly recognized the hostile environment type of discrimination and affirmed the judgment of the court of appeals, which had reversed the decision of the district court.

Sexual harassment has been prevalent in academic life as well. The degree of prevalence cannot be ascertained, since students' complaints have generally not been taken seriously by their institutions. Students have begun to bring litigation on the grounds that a student-faculty relationship encompasses trust and dependency, and since sexual harassment led to a deprivation of educational benefits, there had occurred a significant injury redressable by law. They charge that sexual harassment was a violation of Title IX of the Education Amendments Act, just as in the workplace it is a violation of Title VII of the Civil Rights Act.

The question remains as to whether sexual harassment is the same thing under both Title IX and Title VII. There are similarities, but the analogy is not perfect, as the student-professor relationship encompasses dependency and trust, which do not inherently exist in the workplace (Kay 1988). However, awareness of litigation has led to formal statements issued by many institutions of higher education informing the faculty and students that sexual harassment will not be tolerated and that there are grievance procedures available for victims of sexual harassment.

Sexual harassment is not an individual problem. It is part of the way women's subordinate social, economic, political, and sexual statuses are maintained. Along with wife-beating, it is one way in which a male controls a woman's sexuality and shapes her experience. Women in traditional jobs are often victims because men continue the stereotyping of women as sex objects and caterers to men. In nontraditional or men's jobs, sexual harassment is used to give the message of inequality. About the latter, Susan Martin wrote:

Men view the presence of these women as an invasion of male economic turf (i.e., as a challenge to the men's better pay and supervisory authority), an invasion of their social turf (e.g., army barracks, board rooms, and police stations), and a threat to their definition of their work and selves as "masculine." They often harass women to keep them from working effectively, thereby "proving" women's unfitness for a "man's job" and, in some instances, driving out the female "invaders." (1984:61)

Women are becoming more aware of alternatives available to them other than quitting the job or school. They are starting to understand that the sexual harassment they face is an abuse of power by a man asserting his superior status, and they are learning not to blame themselves or the attributes of their bodies as evocative. Above all, they are becoming aware that sexual harassment is against the law. This is not to say that it is quickly being eradicated. Since men still control the major institutions of society (education, business, medicine, and science) there is always the potential for males to abuse their power over females. The avenues of legal action that are now available can be a powerful educational tool for the public and an important means for women to assert and protect their rights to personal dignity in the workplace while they wait for those rights to be accepted in the general culture. Men may be forced to reconsider their assumptions about women when faced with the possibility of legal consequences (Tong 1984).

WOMAN BATTERING

There are many social indicators of the powerlessness of women, but the power elite does not seem to care. The response of the criminal justice system to crimes against women leads to an inescapable conclusion that women are not deserving of the protection afforded to men. This refutes the prevalent myth that women's relegation to a separate sphere is because of their favored status on a pedestal. There seems to be little outrage over the official statistics that tell of the high prevalence of wife battering.

According to the FBI, 50 percent of women living with a man in the United States will be battered by that man (Jones 1985). The men are seldom arrested for the crime of assault and battery. One study of nine cases in Seattle showed that assaulting men were permitted to plead guilty to a misdemeanor or causing a disturbance charge even though stabbings and broken bones were involved; they were given suspended one-month sentences and fines of up to fifty dollars (Kuhl 1985). The police stance has been that they must not interfere in domestic quarrels. This is a residue of the old English common law principle that a man is permitted to chastize his wife. If performed outside the home and with a stranger, the behavior would be a crime and the perpetrator would be apprehended.

Whether it is called chastizement, wife abuse, or a domestic quarrel with violence, it is still a beating by a husband or lover perpetrated against a weaker, dependent, and defenseless woman. The common features of battering are: (1) it results in physical or psychological harm to the woman; (2) it is a manifestation of control and domination by the man; and (3) it occurs in a context of intimacy (Tong 1984:126). The unfortunate fact is that three out of four women murdered in the United States are killed by their husbands or lovers (Jones 1985).

Battered women find little help in the courts, where woman battering is trivialized and the general attitude has been that so-called family problems are not criminal disputes. Police officers have followed an arrest-avoidance policy which only recently has undergone modification because of feminists' efforts. At times, prosecutors try mediation, a process that often allows the well-dressed, respectable-looking man to blame his violence on the victim (by alleging she said the wrong thing, failed to do what she promised, etc.). Since her wounds are often healed or inconspicuous by the time the case comes to court, the case can seem to the prosecutor like a storm in a teacup. The women is often pressured into dropping charges, and since she cannot spend time away from her child-care responsibilities, she often agrees. Restraining orders are available to women from the family court, but the maximum penalty the man faces for violation (six months imprisonment) is rarely imposed (Tong 1984). The woman still has to confront the batterer afterwards, and possibly endure worse beatings in retaliation for going public.

The inevitable conclusion appears to be that men beat their wives because they can do so with impugnity. When after years of beatings a relatively few of the terrorized wives have struck back to prevent another battering and have unintentionally killed their assailants, the courts have applied the full extent of the law for homicide or, if the woman was lucky, voluntary manslaughter, crimes that impose long prison sentences. The self-defense plea in such cases has seldom been considered valid because the woman's perceptions have not been taken into account. An insanity plea is not much better, as the woman is then involuntarily committed to a mental health institution, even though she is only a desperate, terrified person who has usually exhausted all the perceived viable alternatives for dealing with a pattern of violence that was becoming increasingly unbearable (Tong 1984). In the courts, battered women are also battered by the legal system.

Although the killing of another human being is not something that should be lightly excused, the battered woman's mental state and diminished capacity should be taken into account. What psychologists call the battered wife syndrome must be introduced at the trial. It is a recognition that after years of battering, a woman's perceptions and behavior become impaired. Expert testimony concerning the battered wife syndrome could be relevant because it explains the defendant's state of mind and shows that she honestly believed she was in imminent danger of death or serious injury. This is important in the evaluation of a self-defense plea. Kuhl (1985:200–201) has worked on cases as an expert witness for the court, has analyzed the history of abuse, and has described the battered woman syndrome defense as follows:

The battered woman syndrome delineates a population of women who are physically and psychologically battered by their spouses. Battered women are basically insecure, dependent, nonassertive, self-deprecating individuals who are often immobilized and unable to take action to change their lot. The battered woman is usually unable to share her difficulty with others and as a result of battering is socially isolated. She is ashamed, feels she has in some way been responsible for the abuse and is also afraid that her husband will beat her more if she tells. Moreover, these women may have tried on many occasions to leave the battering situation but were unable to escape from their spouses. (pp. 200–201)

In spite of the fact that battering the woman may be acknowledged, as in most cases there was a long history of summoning the police and going through other legal and informal channels to get relief, some people have taken issue with this defense and call it legalized homicide (Rittenmeyer 1981). They claim that the battered wife syndrome defense violates existing criminal law by bestowing on the abused wife the unique right to destroy her tormentor at her own discretion, that it exploits traditional stereotypes concerning women's weakness and vulnerability, and that it is a sex-based classification that violates due process and equal protection rights of male homicide defendants and victims. This is countered by facts that show that battered women have been trying hard to survive attacks by their spouses, and perceive little reason to believe the criminal justice system will protect them. The assumption that women have not been discriminated against and currently enjoy equal protection under the law is simply not reality (Kuhl 1985). This was brought out in a case decision by the Supreme Court of Washington, which stated:

Until such time as the effects of [sex discrimination] history are eradicated, care must be taken to assure that our self-defense instructions afford women the right to their conduct judged in light of the individual physical handicaps which are the product of sex discrimination. (*State v. Wanrow* 1977:558)

There is a long history of women serving as victims of men's brutality; it is a history that women would certainly like to see come to an end. Many social scientists see the hierarchical structure of the patriarchal system as having legitimized wife beating and the subordination, domination, and control of women by men. The cultural values that allow men to be socialized to be "masculine" (that is, aggressive and even violent) and which exhort women to be "feminine" (that is, passive, docile servers of men) are culpable. Until we learn better attitudes about what it means to be a total human being regardless of sex, men will attempt to assert their social power by battering their defenseless wives. In order to protect not only the rights of women but also the integrity of the law, woman battering must be dealt with "by enforcing existing laws and by making new laws tailored to the unique situation of the battered woman" (Tong 1984:150).

RAPE

Equal power can be illusive when there persist many negative social myths concerning women. One social myth that has been used as an excuse for male abusive behavior is that men are biologically endowed with such a strong sex drive (compared to women) that it is difficult for them to control it at times. This assumption of sex differentiation should rationally have vested power in those who have more control over their impulses, since lack of self-control is not a good qualification for the right to control others. Nonetheless, men have wrested power not only in society generally but over women's bodies as well—through women's sexual and reproductive activities. Rape is an extreme expression of that power.

The connection between sexuality and deviance, and the connection of both to the sociocultural context in which it arises, must be recognized. Male sexual images prevalent in the culture incorporate a "Rambo" element, whereby men take charge of situations, and a machismo element, whereby men take charge of sex. Both images are part of men's fantasies, and their self-concepts of masculinity depend on the amount of control they can exert. The most easily accessible power for a man, no matter what social class he occupies or what level of education he has attained, is power over a woman. For some men, rape is an act that fulfills both fantasy needs: It is an expression of power over a situation and control over a woman.

Rape is a serious crime in our society, and conviction carries a high penalty. Convictions are difficult to achieve, however, because unlike any other crime, the phenomenon is viewed through a series of myths. A major myth applied to rape victims that runs rampant in society is that of *victim precipitation*. This undercurrent of thinking blames the victim; she is perceived as having brought it about through her own actions, such as going out after dark, going to a bar unescorted, or wearing "sexy" clothes. In short, the victim is blamed for having dared to act as though she were free! This thinking is often the foundation on which acquittals are based when rapists are brought to trial. The common culture does not allow the same freedom of movement that men are privileged to have. Susan Brownmiller (1975) pointed out that:

The feeling persists that a virtuous woman either cannot get raped or does not get into situations that leave her open to assault. Thus the questions in the jury room become "Was she or wasn't she asking for it?", "If she had been a decent woman, wouldn't she have fought to the death to defend her treasure?", and "Is this bimbo worth the ruination of a man's career and reputation?" (1975: 435)

In view of such thinking, if the victim is not perceived as a chaste woman, chances of convicting the rapist are slim.

A major social problem that must be redressed is that rapists usually rape with impugnity. Not only is there a very low conviction rate, there is also a very low reportage rate. Women are sometimes reluctant to report a rape because they wish to avoid being exposed to the often-demeaning process of a rape trial. In court, a woman can be subject to a humiliating cross-examination about her sex life, even though her past sexual history has no bearing on her status as the victim of a crime. On the other hand, the defendant's past history of rapes cannot be introduced on the grounds that it may prejudice the jury. In addition, the accused rapist has a lawyer representing him who can play to the cultural stereotypes and prejudices of the jury. In one case the defense attorney was permitted to introduce the fact that the victim had worked as a cocktail waitress, that she was "familiar with liquor," and had worked as an attendant in a health club. He added that she was living with a man who was separated from his wife. Such questions were an invasion of her privacy, but they contributed to the acquittal of the defendant (Cary and Peratis 1977). Some people have urged the courts to outlaw questions concerning a victim's past sexual history.

However, the constitutionality of such a ban is in question, as the Sixth Amendment gives defendants the right to cross-examine witnesses against them (Tong 1984). Therefore, unless the judge intercedes, the focus at the trial will be on the victim rather than the rapist.

Another myth related to rape, and invoked in court by many rapists in many court cases, is that women enjoy forceful sex, and that although they say "no," they really mean "yes." Apparently, according to this myth, women do not know their own minds, and men must take charge. It should be noted that proof of non-consent is not required in other crimes.

If rape victims seek redress through the criminal justice system, in addition to a prejudiced jury, in many states they may face further indignity (which some have referred to as a second rape) because of the archaic rape laws in many states. Rape law has operated as a means of ensuring the protection of the accused male, rather than being an affirmation of the integrity of a woman's body. Part of the problem is the traditional definition of rape which is still prevalent in many state jurisdictions and has some necessary conditions that work in men's favor. One such condition is the corroboration requirement, which is founded on another myth concerning women, the stereotype of woman as lying temptress. The theological basis for the disdain of women was the belief that, in the form of Eve, they had precipitated the fall of the human race by introducing sin into the world (Crites 1987). In the old biblical story, Eve's wicked allurements led the unsuspecting Adam to eat the forbidden fruit, and her punishment was the pain of bearing children. This stereotype has justified unequal legal justice. Because of the alleged duplicity of women, it was believed that men had to be legally protected from scheming females who might accuse them of rape even when they had agreed to the sex act. The misogynistic image of woman as liar has skewed rape law to the extent that the onus of proof is on the woman and legitimate interests of rape victims are not always served.

In actual fact, studies of rape accusations do not show many trumped-up complaints. Furthermore, there is no indication that men are falsely convicted of rape more often than they are falsely convicted of any other crime (Tong 1984). The baseless stereotype of the mendacious woman persists, however, and it has been responsible for the corroboration rules in rape cases. These rules denegrate the testimony of rape victims. As proof that a woman has been raped, the corroboration rule prevalent in many states requires that, along with her testimony, the rape must be corroborated by other evidence before presentation of a case. What must be proven is (1) sexual penetration; (2) the use of force and the lack of consent; and (3) the identification of the assailant. The third element alone is not sufficient, even if the victim can identify the rapist in a line-up at the police station. Since there seldom are witnesses, the corroborating evidence can include traces of semen in the woman's vagina, injuries or torn clothing, strands of the rapist's hair, his skin cells under her fingernails, or a button ripped from his clothing to show that she struggled (Cary and Peratis 1977). It is incredible that the woman is expected to be rational and to accumulate evidence at such a time of extreme personal fear. The passive, inadvertent accumulation of evidence cannot always be counted on. As a result, one New York study showed that out of 2,415 rape cases, there were only 18 convictions (Tong 1984).

The corroboration rules completely ignore the view that the woman is a vulnerable human being who was the victim of an outrageous crime because of her powerlessness. The rapist's threats, his fist power, his possible possession of a lethal weapon, and the lack of imminent help from others often convince the woman to be docile and thus possibly escape with her life. In such situations, she will not have wounds to show for her ordeal. As for semen, many rapists force the victim to perform an act of oral sodomy, and thus it may be difficult for her to retain semen. The "beyond a reasonable doubt" requirement will work to the rapist's benefit should he be caught and brought to trial.

Recent Changes

Recent reform in rape law, largely due to the efforts of feminists, have altered the procedure somewhat. Most states have modified or dropped the corroboration requirements, although "in a judicial system that systematically favors defendants, juries are going to have difficulty with uncorroborated rape cases" (Tong 1984:105). Victims cannot rely on having unbiased juries, even though women are included on the panels; therefore, convictions in rape cases may still be difficult to get.

Another reform concerns jury cautionary instructions. At a rape trial, before the jury goes out to deliberate, the judge gives instructions on the law. The cautionary instruction is a practice from seventeenth-century England, and the standard version is as follows:

A charge such as that made against the defendant in this case, is one which is easily made and, once made, difficult to defend against, even if the person accused is innocent. Therefore, the law requires that you examine the testimony of the female person named in the information with caution. (Tong 1984:105)

Such instructions, which are applied at the discretion of the judge, encourage acquittal. They continue to apply in approximately thirteen states. In 1975 the California Supreme Court declared the law requiring the instruction to be unconstitutional. In a case that came to them on appeal (*People v. Rincon-Pineda* 1975) a judge in a lower court had refused over defense objection to give the cautionary instruction on the grounds that "its compulsory use had not been authoritatively reexamined for decades" (Cary and Peratis 1977:132). The Supreme Court analyzed the history and use of the cautionary instruction and concluded that it was not necessary. Part of the decision reads:

> In light of our foregoing examination of the evolution of the cautionary instruction, and with the benefit of contemporary empirical and theoretical analysis of the prosecution of sex offenses in general and rape in particular, we are of the opinion that the instruction omitted below has outworn its usefulness and in modern circumstances is no longer to be given mandatory application. (*People v. Rincon-Pineda* 1975)

An area of contention that still requires resolution in the courts is marital rape. In the past, the legal system did not recognize marital rape since the traditional definition of rape was "illicit carnal knowledge of a female by force and against her will" (Black 1968). In a legal marriage the offender is not "illicit"; the marriage contract gives him a right to sexual services. In spite of the fact that forceable rape is a violent sexual assault, most states do not allow a wife to charge her husband with rape because of the marital exemption rule, which was originally meant to protect governmental intrusion into marital privacy. The marital exemption rule is starting to be questioned, however. A 1981 New Jersey case (*State v. Smith*) brought out the fact that under certain circumstances a man can be convicted of raping his wife (Spencer 1987). A 1985 New York decision (*People v. Liberta*) concluded that raping one's wife cannot be justified under the marital exemption rule because the right of privacy only protects consensual acts, not violent assaults. That decision changed policy in New York, since it stated that "it is now the law of this State that any person who engages in sexual intercourse or deviate sexual intercourse with any other person by forceable compulsion is guilty of either rape in the first degree or sodomy in the first degree" (Kay 1988:918).

Undoubtedly a slow evolution toward justice for all is occurring as well, possibly, as the beginnings of the erosion of the patriarchal system. Blaming the female victim is one way to assure the continuation of the old social structure, which controls and subordinates women (Spencer 1987). In order to stop violence or threats of violence against women, and to ensure freedom for women to pursue personal happiness and equality in social institutions, basic attitudinal changes concerning the relationships between the sexes will have to become part of the everyday culture. The old power relationships are not conducive to legal justice. As Andrew Karmen summarized:

> Sexual harassment, wife-beating, and rape are all crimes in which male offenders try to exert control over female victims. But victim-blaming [has the effect of] depoliticizing and personalizing acts that are inherently connected to the distribution of power and legitimacy of authority, and thereby obscures the sources and consequences of crimes against women. (1982:193)

LAW ENFORCEMENT AND THE SOCIAL STRUCTURE

The effectiveness of enforcement depends ultimately on public attitudes toward the crime. After much research and a review of many cases, Laura Crites (1987) found that although there are new laws concerning domestic violence, judges are reluctant to enforce them. She noted an apparent unwillingness on the judges' part to see the behavior as a crime instead of a mere domestic dispute. This is apparent in the lenient sentences meted out, which are not commensurate with the seriousness of the crime when there is a conviction of an abusive, or even homicidal, husband. To explain a sentence that is less than the minimum required by law, the judge can cite "extraordinary mitigating circumstances" or "highly provocative acts," meaning any behavior of the wife that the judge decided to so label. Crites found an obvious double standard in the fact that battered wives are not accorded the same rights women strangers would be entitled to. She suggests a major effort be launched to educate judges about the seriousness of the crime and the complex psychosocial dynamics of wife abuse. Sensitizing male judges is necessary because they have been socialized in the syndrome of the man as leader and doer, as have other males, and may not be able to view the situation from the victim's vantage point.

Women have sought redress for sexual harassment, wife battering and rape in the courts. When one examines how women fare in the criminal justice system, it is difficult not to conclude that the interests of men are better represented in the legal system than those of women. The lack of effective recourse for women in the courts gives some credence to the novel idea that rape assaults on women carried out in the public area are activities by individual men on behalf of all men (Hammer 1978). In this view, the use of violence by some men is functional for all men. However, violence continues to be seen by society as an individual problem, and its connection with institutionalized power is seldom recognized. Rather, men are encouraged to be "assertive" and lead the family.

Since the passing of the Bill of Rights, the family has been viewed as private and free from government interference. However, government has always interfered on the grounds of the public good, and has restricted women's freedom in areas such as contraception, abortion, and divorce. The male prerogatives in marriage have seldom been interfered with, and a wife who does not acquiesce in a docile manner to her own subordination is considered deviant. The state, through its insistence on the preservation of the traditional family structure at all costs, places the wife in a position of dependence on her husband. Her lack of or limited access to outside financial resources weakens her autonomy and traps her further into dependency. Government family law and policy have made it difficult for women to deviate from the allotted territory of home and children, which opens the way for their abuse by men. The conclusion that domestic violence is institutionalized would appear to be inescapable. The social meaning of male violence will have to be clearly understood before meaningful innovations in the laws, nonsexist interpretations by the judiciary, and, ultimately, a balance of power between the sexes, become a reality.

As discussed, the state has a vested interest in stability and therefore legislation has been geared toward keeping families intact. Bearing children is a public good that ensures the future survival of and supply of labor for society. Therefore, formal mechanisms of support and protection must be set up to care for the child-bearer and her children, should she be the victim of repeated violence from her husband. These mechanisms must operate until she can reestablish her life. The type of nurturance required goes beyond welfare payments. What is needed are federally funded centers offering not only room and board but also professional help (psychiatric and labor market assistance) to assist a woman in regaining what battering has robbed from her self-esteem.

SOURCES OF POWER

In the United States power is vested in the hands of the governing elite— a minority that holds key decision-making positions in government, political parties, the labor market, the economy, and the mass media. This dominant group, composed principally of men, tends to make decisions in its own favor unless concerted activism by outside groups pressures it to do otherwise on particular issues. Today women want to place themselves in decision-making positions alongside men.

In the corporate economy women are seldom in the top executive positions. They are generally not included in the ranks of boards of directors, bank presidents, corporate lawyers, and high-level financiers who direct the wealth of the society. Similarly, they do not appear in the top levels of the oligarchical structure of labor unions even though women's union affiliation is sizeable. Women are not generally among the decision-makers in the large foundations which control billions of dollars in research grants. These foundations, through their choice of donations and philanthropies, are legitimators and reinforcers of culturally prescribed gender roles (Richardson 1988).

Although the United States is a democracy, an oligarchy controls public opinion. A sort of private ministry of information and culture results when 52 percent of the daily newspapers are controlled by twenty corporations; 50 percent of the periodical and 76 percent of records and tape sales are controlled by twenty corporations; 75 percent of movie distributions are controlled by seven corporations; and 60 percent of television and radio stations are controlled by thirteen corporations (Bagdikian 1980). Television especially is a disseminator of knowledge since people in the United States view it for many hours daily. The information it imparts is received passively and is generally unquestioned because people turn to it for entertainment. Content analyses show that television portrays women stereotypically. With few exceptions, women are dependent on men, who are in charge. The message is subtle, and is absorbed by an unsuspecting public which does not question its distortion of real life. The power differentials are thus reaffirmed.

There is no doubt that power resides in government. Since in a democracy the government represents all the people, it would be a logical place in which to find women in proportion to their numbers in the population. Such is not the case, however. From 1917 to 1980, 13 women served in the Senate, and of those, 7 were appointed to fill a vacancy. In the One-Hundredth Congress in 1987 there were 2 female senators out of 50, and 24 female representatives out of 435 (National Information Bank on Women in Public Office 1987). The major positions, such as president, vice president, speaker of the House, and party whip, have never had female incumbents, and none of the influential congressional committees have been chaired by a woman. Even if elected, the informal male social network of the inner circle wherein information is exchanged is generally closed to women. It is thus all but assured that the major decisions and policies will be determined by an exclusive sort of all-male club (Fritz 1982).

As for women's suffrage, it was a long time in coming. In the *Minor v. Happerset* (1874) case, the Supreme Court ruled that the right to vote was not among the privileges of U.S. citizens and that therefore such an important trust could be committed to men only (Kay 1988). Only after much activism by suffragists was the Nineteenth Amendment to the Constitution ratified in 1920, giving women the right to vote in national elections. However, women have never used their power to ensure a sex-balanced Congress so that their interests could be equally represented in law and public policy.

As of 1981, only 6.9 percent of all federal judges were women (Lynn 1984). The highest judicial appointees, the nine Supreme Court justices, were all male until the appointment of Sandra Day O'Connor in 1981. The next two appointments, however, were males, dampening hopes for a sexual balance in the Supreme Court at any time soon. As of 1983, only 8 percent of the 980 high-level appointments made by President Ronald Reagan were women.

Some people would like to have more women in Congress because women are perceived to value human life more than men and would be less likely to use military means to solve international problems. Recent Gallup and Harris polls show women to be "doves" concerning war (Lynn 1984). However, it cannot be assumed that women in power will be better or truer than men—a few recent exposes of improprieties at high levels have implicated women also. When it comes to ethics in government, females are not immune from corrupt practices. Even cabinet members are suspect, it seems, for in the congressional investigation of alleged wrongdoing and influence peddling of the recent HUD (Housing and Urban Development) scandal, a former female secretary of housing and urban development is included. Perhaps this is because the few women in top government posts strive too hard to be accepted by their peers; perhaps the nature of the position influences such practices; or perhaps it is because personality traits and temperament are truly randomly distributed regardless of sex. Jeane Kirkpatrick, former ambassador to the United Nations, found that women in politics had many psychological similarities to political males. Her 1975 study showed that political people of both genders had strong egos, great self-esteem, and a high sense of personal effectiveness (Kirkpatrick 1975).

How women legislators may vote and what their public service ethics may prove to be cannot be forecast, however. The personality type (hawk or dove) of a woman in politics is, in any case, beside the point. It is women's right to have representatives in government nearly proportionate in number to their presence in society.

Education

No one can dispute Ralph Waldo Emerson's assertion that knowledge is power. Schools provide the basic resources that enable students to become part of the establishment. Students receive training that will enable them to fulfill the basic requirements for positions in government, private enterprise, the media, or the corporate economy. Therefore, one must look at the educational system to ascertain the part it has played in structuring a society wherein equal opportunities have not been available to both sexes.

In the United States the public schools are formally charged with the task of educating young people. Children are required by law to attend them. The schools teach subjects that will enable students to learn not only the skills necessary for becoming viable members of society, but also the endemic value system. Besides becoming literate in many fields of endeavor, students learn the expected attitudes and associated behavior patterns. Thus, the public school system is one of the main disseminators of the basic core values of the society.

Gender Bias in Education

It has long been a practice to segregate boys and girls in same-sex schools. Those who believe in the practice feel that it offers better educational advantages. The implication is that one sex requires a different education than the other, and a segregated school can concentrate resources to that end. This pushes students into so-called appropriate fields and denies equal access to educational programs. It also ensures that there will be sex segregation and pay inequity in the work force. When the educational institution is a private one (such as a religious high school) and admission is voluntary, it will not flout equal education enactments. Those who believe in such educational segregation reason that students can more easily concentrate on studies in schools that are separate but equal, and that the special emotional problems of the adolescent years warrant it. This is an assumption with little empirical backing. *Brown v. Board of Education*, a Supreme Court case of 1954, established that separate was not equal for blacks; it is common sense that separate likewise cannot be equal for males and females. The sexes inhabit the same world, and a hiatus in interaction during adolescence is counterproductive. Alice de Rivera wrote:

A boy who has never worked with a girl in the classroom is bound to think of her as his intellectual inferior, and will not treat her as if she had capacity for understanding things other than child-care and homemaking. (1970:366)

The difference in opportunities that female adults encounter can be largely traced to the differential education they receive even when schools are coeducational. The schools have not treated males and females the same, and tracking into male and female spheres starts at a very early age, subtly giving the message of different social expectations. It often deprives women of training for future economic opportunities. This may not only leave women with limited horizons, but also may rob them of a sense that they have been deprived of motivation toward the acquisition of the available resources such as money, power, and technological knowledge.

Gender bias in education has had a long history. In the colonial era women were not considered to require formal education. Tutorial education was provided at home for some girls, but only in affluent families. Beginning in the eighteenth century, seminary schools for women began to open, offering courses like music, dancing, sewing, and fancy needlework. They also provided rudimentary training in basic English, geography, and arithmetic (Woody 1966). These schools were the beginning of the recognition that educating women could be useful for society. In the nineteenth century the normal schools were established to train teachers for the growing public education system.

Higher education remained a male domain until Oberlin College admitted women in 1837, about two hundred years after the first men's colleges were established. The course of study was intended to prepare women for intelligent homemaking and teaching, and not for the world of science or business, which were the male pursuits. The gender bias was blatant, as the women were required to serve the men at the table, wash their clothes, and care for their rooms. They were also required to remain respectfully silent in public assemblages (Flexner 1971).

Gender bias today is more subtle. The educational system exerts an early and usually lasting impact on people's lives. It is culpable because it has treated boys and girls differently, and it is therefore a formal contributor to their unequal outcomes. In the early grades children acquire a perception of the world through the stories and pictures in their primers, the toys available to them, and the attitudes of their teachers. Boys and girls are often directed into traditional courses that prepare them for different occupations. The tracking continues into high school, where girls are often not required to take mathematics, science, or mechanics courses. It can lead to female avoidance of elective subjects that they have not been conditioned to be comfortable with. The result can be a lack of adequate preparation for a modern work world where technology reigns. It is no wonder that women workers are concentrated in the service sector where the jobs, although they are as important to society as technological jobs, are generally lower paying.

This disparity is not due to lower educational levels, for today women represent 51 percent of U.S. college enrollment. Graduate school enrollment of women has increased dramatically as well, and in 1985 they represented 34 percent of graduate students and 39 percent of law school graduates (U.S. Bureau of the Census 1987:149, 151).

Title IX

Discriminatory criteria concerning admissions, standards, curricular and extracurricular programs, and student services, as well as sex-segregated classrooms and gender bias in promotions are now illegal. Title IX was added to the Education Amendments Act in 1972. It provides that "No person in the United States shall, on the basis of sex, be excluded from participation in, be denied the benefits of, or be subjected to discrimination under any educational program or activity receiving Federal financial assistance" (20 U.S.C. 1681). With some exceptions regarding athletics, any educational institution that receives federal aid must comply. Since virtually all schools— from preschools to schools of higher education—do receive such aid, they are mandated to enforce the provisions of Title IX, and are subject to prosecution for failing to do so. The U.S. Department of Health and Human Services (formerly Department of Health, Education and Welfare) is charged with interpretation and enforcement, and it can withhold funds. In spite of that, compliance has been slow. The stipulation that all institutions receiving federal contracts over fifty thousand dollars submit written affirmative action plans has largely been ignored, and federal contracts have not been terminated for noncompliance (Richardson 1988). The impact of legislation naturally depends on the level of its enforcement, which in this case has been somewhat lax.

Title IX exempts public primary and secondary schools from its ban on single-sex institutions, and therefore the potential for gender-differentiated education continues. Students can still be tracked into different curricular areas based on sex, and socialized for different occupations. As a result, when these students reach college level, the fields of study for males and females generally continue to be different. Males are nine times more likely than women to major in engineering and twice as likely to concentrate their studies in business and physical sciences. Women tend to specialize in the humanities, education, and certain health fields, which eventually lead to more poorly paying and lower-status occupations (Fox 1984).

Gains in gender equality have been made on the college level, especially in athletics. On campuses female athletes had been a rarity and facilities and funding for them had been lacking. In recent years, however, there has been some reduction in the extreme funding disparity between women's and men's sports. In 1981, five hundred schools offered athletic scholarships for women at the so-called Big Ten schools, where in 1978 the athletic budgets for women had increased to a range of $250,000 to $750,000, a direct influence of Title IX (National Advisory Council on Women's Education Programs 1981).

Title IX has come under attack by conservative politicians and sporting organizations. Since male sports in the United States attract dedicated adherents and evoke cult-like emotional responses, many males do not like what they view as female incursions into a masculine realm. The critics claim that they abhor the government interference in education, but the fact is that the hue and cry has concerned athletics only. The controversy mostly concerns funding, since Title IX suggests that allocating unequal expenditures for male and female teams constitutes noncompliance. However, the wording of Title IX is ambiguous and open to interpretation. The understanding is that scholarship funding is required to be substantially proportional to the number of male and female athletes in the recipient college's program (Kay 1988). This was supported by a 1984 Supreme Court decision that interpreted Title IX as program-specific.

CASE: *Grove City College v. Bell* (1984). Grove City College had some students who were receiving Basic Educational Opportunity Grants. The Court ruled that this subjected the school to Title IX, but that it was limited to the specific financial aid program since the athletic program did not receive government funding. The justices rejected the argument that the whole college was the covered program (Kay 1988).

This decision can potentially set back women's quest for equality in the educational system. Considering that male athletic programs in the major colleges generate revenues and do not rely on federal funding, it is obvious that only the women's athletic programs would suffer. The dissenting opinion in this case stated that the ruling could lead to practices that Congress did not intend to sanction, such as unequal treatment in college departments where no federal funds were involved. To remedy the problem, in 1988 Congress enacted the Civil Rights Restoration Act which was designed to overturn the *Grove City College* decision and apply Title IX to an institution "any part of which is extended Federal financial assistance" (Kay 1988:847).

In spite of Title IX and also many changes in the educational system, tracking persists, and it effectively ensures that sex segregation in the work force will continue and that there will be a greatly disproportionate number of women in low-paying, low-security, so-called female jobs. It is alleged that gender bias is on the decline today in the labor market since some women gravitate toward manual labor jobs upon graduation and become truck drivers, construction workers, and so on. However, the jury is still out as to whether gender bias has been substantially alleviated in the school system. A criterion for judging this could be the numbers of women graduates entering professions that society has considered male domains.

Women in Law

The most insidious insult to women is the pervasive and mindless sexism that categorizes all women as having the same inferior qualities. It has been used to justify male dominance in all aspects of life, and the legal system is no exception. The field of law as a profession is an area where one would expect gender equality since the work entails upholding the principle of justice for all, the criterion on which the legal system is based. This is not as yet the case; the difficulties that women have faced in the work force generally have also been prevalent in the profession of law. However, considerable inroads have been made on past restrictions.

When the U.S. Constitution was written, women were simply part of the household. The general societal view that women were weak and in need of protection prevailed in law as in all other fields. Women were thought to be intrinsically unfit for the practice of law because they were born to be revered by men and kept in innocence, and thus protected from the problems that must be dealt with in the courts of justice. Such ideas have been eroding gradually, but the pace of erosion has accelerated of late. What is happening throughout society can be referred to as cataclysmic social change in that more women are in the labor force than ever before and are entering professions that had barred them in the past. The legal profession is the employer of female workers as well.

Today about 20 percent of lawyers are women, compared to 3 percent a decade ago. Law school enrollment presently consists of 40 percent women, up from 4 percent two decades ago. These figures show a diminishing discrimination level, but studies indicate that the bias has not been eliminated. As in other fields of endeavor, the numbers rise but the women do not. Women have not been allowed to progress to positions of greatest power, prestige, and income, but rather have remained at middle levels in the profession (Kaye 1989). Furthermore, research in 1978 showed that women were concentrated in specialties deemed "appropriate" for them, such as family, estate, divorce, and poverty law. This research also showed a lower income for female lawyers, and fewer women than men had their own practices (Feinmen 1985).

Other statistics show that the legal profession has not been immune to the syndrome of lower status and lower pay. In a two-year study completed in 1986, the New York Task Force on Women in the Courts found pervasive discrimination against female lawyers, litigants, and court employees (Kaye 1989). There has been an underrepresentation of women in the judiciary, in tenured law professorships, and as partners in law firms.

However, there seems to be cause for optimism that the situation will change. Perhaps because of the sheer numbers of female law graduates, discrimination in hiring and the two-scale salary system (one for women lawyers and one for men) will be seriously eroded in the near future. As the public becomes sensitized, it will no longer automatically be assumed that a woman present at a gathering of lawyers is the shorthand reporter. An upbeat opinion was expressed by the Honorable Judith S. Kaye, associate judge of the New York State Court of Appeals, who wrote:

As a society and in the law, we have seen enormous development in the concept of equality—a foundation word of this great nation—and of the constitutional guarantee of equal protection. Over years of living and litigating, we have come to better understand that equal treatment does not first require that everyone be exactly the same. We have also witnessed the emergences of women visibly as women, with open recognition of differences not as disabilities in need of special protection but as positive values women have to contribute. It is not simply a different voice we are hearing, but a strong voice. (Kaye 1988:125)

Legal education has historically been biased toward males, and since law schools are conservative institutions and resistant to change, it may be surprising that feminist jurisprudence has emerged. Its emergence began when female law students realized that they faced a political structure that oppressed them as women. Their insights into the political nature of law made them realize that they could organize to challenge and change the political structure that oppressed women (Kay and Littleton 1988).

In spite of the difficulties that female law students face, it is auspicious that increasing numbers of women are entering the legal profession. Some become lawyers "who identify with the women's movement and share a set of beliefs about women's rights to equality in private and public life, and who are themselves dedicated to working towards these goals" (Epstein 1981:130). In their legal work, those within this group are primarily advocates for women's rights. Others are entering the male-dominated establishment, and their work provides access to business, government, and politics.

Law is a pivotal profession in the functioning of U.S. society since lawyers preside over property and power relationships and sometimes even enter the ranks of corporate executives and boards of directors. Regardless of male biases that make it difficult for women to rise above middle levels in this stratified profession, it is a necessary step toward female empowerment since law is an important gateway to society's decision-making positions.

A BASIS OF POWER: MOBILIZATION

Women have found that in order to gain higher status, it is necessary for them to create and maintain collective resources that can be used for political ends, such as gaining access to, influencing, and possibly controlling government. Power blocs have been effective in Washington, D.C., partly because of the perceived numbers of people backing a particular idea. The mobilization of women is not easy as they constitute a large and diverse group, do not generally possess political and bureaucratic skills, and are too individualized within the home to be unanimously unified behind a cause. The achievement of solidarity in support of common goals takes time and leadership skills. In spite of the difficulties, in group action lie the hopes for reforms.

Group action empowers the powerless. Elizabeth Janeway (1980) wrote of the two powers of the weak that become available when they have the courage to evoke their inner resources. One power is that of disbelief—the abnegation of the definition of oneself proclaimed by the strong. Janeway abjures women to question the social mythology as explanations of reality and to ask: "Is it true?" The other power is coming together—the readiness to join with others in opposition to the myths. Validation comes through sharing experiences, denying the rules of behavior, and challenging authority. "When individuals blend into a movement, individual goals become a joint purpose that would be trivialized by self-doubt" (Janeway 1980:174). Thus, the inner powers of the weak are translated into public power as common action leads to political change. Today, activist women's groups are attempting to take a hand in controlling the conditions of their lives. Some efforts are successful, while others are not.

Passage of the Equal Rights Amendment (ERA) would have mandated equal treatment for men and women in all areas of social endeavor. Although its defeat was a major setback for equality between the sexes, the vigorous campaign to get the ERA passed was worthwhile. Women came to realize that they could unify on a large scale and become effective activists for their cause. Public attention was brought to the unequal gender status that had traditionally been taken for granted, and the disadvantages women faced in the home, the work force, and the streets were highlighted. Public consciousness of women's issues—their job opportunities, their pay scales, their desire for autonomy and their need for fulfilling opportunities—became issues in the press (Mansbridge 1986). The premise on which the campaign for passage of the ERA was based was that change for women could not be effected without a legal foundation mandating complete equality for men and women. The white male superiority over the human race was so taken for granted and so ensconced a tradition socially and legally that effective change had to deal first with the overarching legal structure. Cultural change would ensue as law-abiding citizens subsequently modified their behavior patterns. Change in the laws is what can most effectively crack the old mold.

There are lessons to be learned from the failed effort to get the Equal Rights Amendment ratified; understanding them could strengthen future mobilization for equality. Jane Mansbridge's ex post facto analysis of the struggle is illuminating. She argues that, first, the struggle for the ERA was based on abstract rights that were desired for the public good. This permitted different interpretations, both pro and con, of the possible impact that an equal rights amendment would have. Each faction had a different vision of what would be accomplished. As a result, the issue became partisan and pitted one group of women against another. There existed a conservative backlash of women who reacted "against the changes in child rearing, sexual behavior, and divorce . . . that had taken place in the 1960s and 1970s" and who succeeded in mobilizing traditional homemakers who believed they had lost status during the previous two decades and were feeling the psychological effects of that loss (1986:5–6). Second, any errors in the structure of the voluntary political organization must be corrected or, as before, there will be an inability to hear or understand what others are saying. An organization sometimes can drift into oversimplified ideological stances (such as pure or impure) without realizing that a decision is being made. Institutional arrangements must promote accurate information and internal dialogue. Potentially controversial issues must be discussed at every level of the organization (Mansbridge 1986).

Because of these problems, some people feel that future activism should be focused on particular issues rather than the general interest. For instance, concerted activism could be limited to getting someone in particular elected to Congress, publishing the voting records on gender issues of members of Congress, running campaigns to dissuade voters from endorsing particular chauvinist candidates, and the like. It has been shown that women can be quite effective through activism on local issues with national repercussions. In addition, women should be heartened by the fact that largely through their efforts an Equal Rights Amendment to the Constitution was proposed and nearly passed.

The ERA effort influenced other women's rights decisions, and other means were newly employed by the legislature and the judiciary to eliminate gender bias. New laws have been passed that treat women equally. The Fourteenth Amendment has been invoked successfully, the Supreme Court decisions have struck down many state laws that discriminated against women.

Various degrees of women's mobilization have occurred in other countries as well. Many of the issues concerning the equality of women which have been paramount nationally have also been of concern internationally. Numerous international treaties ratified at the United Nations concern the same substantive areas to be addressed globally. The UN treaties relating to the status of women concern women's education, women and the family, pay equity, gender harassment, violence against women, sexual exploitation, and more, as the following section on international law and cross-cultural studies will show. As will be demonstrated, the problem of the social subordination of women is not only epidemic, it is pandemic. The symptoms are essentially the same around the world, and the cure entails enforced legislation as a beginning remedy, with the ultimate goal being permeation of gender equality throughout the system.

Part II

Global Trends: The World Community and Women's Equality

7

The United Nations and the Status of Women

As has been demonstrated, women in the United States have had to encourage changes in the laws to achieve progress toward equal status with men. In certain areas of their lives where discrimination has been prevalent, the new legal mandates are gradually correcting injustices. The fields of endeavor where overt discrimination exist are similar for women in countries around the world. Cross-culturally, women generally face a lower social status relative to men. It can be assumed that, like women in the United States, women in other countries also desire to acquire equal opportunities and equal pay in the marketplace, an easing of domestic responsibilities for working wives, opportunities for literacy and education, and dignity, respect, and appreciation for their contributions to society. In many non-Western countries, the exploitative traditional culture is reflected in laws that are repressive of women. This situation would continue in many parts of the world were it not for the United Nations. At the United Nations the different member countries are encouraged to make legal and social changes in accordance with international laws and standards that contain imperatives for gender equality.

The emphasis of modern Western societies is on individualism, and there is an increasing preoccupation with personal fulfillment. This represents basic ideational change from unquestioned group orientation. New ideas are reaching all parts of the world. People everywhere would like to maximize personal development, receive recognition, and enjoy a better life-style. International trade, the interdependence of countries, increasing urbanization around the world, more widespread education, and the pervasiveness of the mass media have all played a part in the rising expectations of women.

A major catalyst for change in the lives of women has been the world community, the United Nations. This international body has had enormous impact as member countries effect legal changes mandating nondiscrimination in accordance with the treaties that they have ratified at the United Nations. It recognizes that the continuation of modern societies and the attainment of international peace requires the development of all individuals. That is, it is recognized that the female half of the human population can be a major contributor to solving the serious political and social problems of the world which otherwise threaten to make humankind an endangered species.

THE UNITED NATIONS AND HUMAN RIGHTS

In 1945, 260 delegates from fifty governments convened in San Francisco with the expectation of creating a new world organization in the form of the United Nations. The purpose was to provide a forum to deal with political and economic matters affecting all countries, and to restore order, make a better world, and avoid misunderstandings between countries. Even before the twentieth century there had been other international conferences that had required governments to approach common problems in an organized manner and to establish international standards; consequently, the concept of an international organization was not a new one. The San Francisco Conference was preceded by the now defunct League of Nations, which was formed in 1920; however, the new United Nations was not perceived as a continuation of the league. The previous international bodies had adopted the principle of sovereign equality of countries. It is not surprising that this concept was of concern to the newly formed United Nations. Moreover, at the United Nations it was applied more broadly than ever before. From its inception the United Nations has been concerned with the rights not only of countries but of the individuals who inhabit the world.

The organization's early concentration on human rights is understandable. The brutal excesses of the Nazis and the Fascists, and the inhumanity and devastation of World War II gave impetus to the cause of human rights which earlier had been so blatantly ignored. Article 1 of the UN Charter calls for international cooperation to encourage fundamental freedoms and human rights. The United Nations Commission on Human Rights was created in 1946, and its presiding officer was Eleanor Roosevelt, the wife of the late U.S. president, Franklin D. Roosevelt. Mrs. Roosevelt brought great intelligence, ability, and prestige to the position. Prestige was important since the persuasion for reforms rested on moral authority rather than binding legal mandates. It was only later that debates and resolutions at the United Nations led to conventions (or treaties) that were legally binding on the ratifying countries.

The conventions that are approved by the deliberative bodies at the United Nations cover many aspects of government and human interaction. The focus of this book lies in the treaties that specifically call for nondiscrimination and equality between men and women. There are many such conventions and therefore my discussion will have to be limited to the salient points.

The United Nations was not the first international body to be concerned with questions relating to the status of women. In 1935 the League of Nations had issued a report plainly showing that women's status in society varied considerably according to the country. In 1937 the League had commenced a comprehensive study of the status of women as established by national laws and their applications in the various countries. The survey was to have three parts—one dealing with private law, the second with public law, and the last with penal law. By the outbreak of World War II, only the work on private law had been completed (*UN Action in the Field of Human Rights* 1980). Although the League of Nations dissolved, the concern for the status of women throughout the world continued.

The ethic of responsibility to ensure the human rights of both sexes was proclaimed in the preamble to the charter of the United Nations. The charter itself calls for the promotion of "universal respect for, and observance of, human rights and fundamental freedoms for all without distinction as to race, sex, language or religion." (Charter of the United Nations 1945:1). Member countries have formally accepted the moral and legal obligation to rectify, if necessary, inequality between men and women. Thus, nondiscrimination on the basis of sex was a major concern of the world body as early as 1945.

THE UNIVERSAL DECLARATION OF HUMAN RIGHTS

In 1948 the United Nations General Assembly adopted and proclaimed the Universal Declaration of Human Rights. At that time the world community agreed upon "a common standard of achievement for all peoples and all nations" in the area of human rights. The Declaration declared that "everyone is entitled to all the rights and freedoms set forth . . . without distinction of any kind" (Article 2), including distinction as to sex. It stands as a recognized code of conduct to measure the degree of respect for people everywhere, and is the beginning of an international bill of rights. Article 1 states: "All human beings are born free and equal in dignity and rights. They are endowed with reason and conscience and should act towards one another in a spirit of brotherhood." Article 7 states: "All are equal before the law and are entitled without any discrimination to equal protection of the law."

Since that time the declaration has served as a moral imperative and guide for countries in the safeguarding of human rights and the fundamental freedoms of its citizens. All members of the human family are included. This document provides a stimulus and inspiration, as well as standards, within the United Nations in its progressive development of methods of international accountability, and also throughout the world.

The adoption of the Universal Declaration of Human Rights has been of major importance because of the shift in emphasis it shows from concerns with countries to concerns with individuals per se. It has served as a model or standard in many member countries for the legal protection of persons in the basic aspects of their lives. The multilateral treaties that followed at the United Nations and that continued the basic ideas of the declaration have been ratified by many countries, attesting to the increasing attention being paid the rights of individual persons. These later treaties on human rights give stricter form to the basic tenets of the Universal Declaration.

Although not legally binding, this declaration has had a major influence since it became the foundation for the establishment of obligatory legal norms in later treaties concerning the rights of individuals. No country has publicly disagreed with the principles set forth therein, and many national constitutions reflect its influence as their legal systems have incorporated its standards and language. In 1966, to give the provisions of the declaration binding form, the United Nations adopted two major covenants that entered into force in 1976 and amplified the stated principles: the International Covenant on Civil and Political Rights, which (by mid–1985) had been ratified by eighty-five countries, its Optional Protocol, which had been ratified by thirty-five countries, and the International Covenant on Economic, Social and Cultural Rights, which (by mid–1985) had been ratified by eighty-four countries (*The United Nations at Forty* 1985). These two Covenants, the Optional Protocol, and the Universal Declaration of Human Rights form the International Bill of Rights.

Some countries do lag behind in the implementation of rights. The lack of economic development is sometimes used to excuse laxity on gender-equality issues by developing nations who claim that they must concentrate on providing basic survival needs and that as a result personal liberties for individuals are not a priority. Such an argument is fallacious, as it has never been demonstrated that the curtailment of human rights contributes to a country's economic development. It is true that economic development and modernization do offer a wider range of options in life for both men and women as well as a higher standard of living. However, it is questionable whether economic progress alone inevitably leads to a higher level of equality. Anthropologists attest to the fact that in societies labeled primitive, women are highly valued, and power and wealth may be equally distributed in spite of lower absolute levels of living. Wealth alone is insufficient for the equitable distribution of power and resources or the well-being of all citizens. In the more affluent developed countries there is not yet a total equality between men and women. However, more widespread education smoothens the transition to the acceptance of new gender roles in these countries.

UN RESOLUTIONS AND DECLARATIONS

When a member government takes the initiative in proposing a resolution and it is passed in the General Assembly of the United Nations or one of the UN agencies, it is with the intention of highlighting a specific issue to be applauded or condemned everywhere in the world. This brings to international public consciousness some of the pressing problems that require concerted effort by the international community in the search for solutions. Resolutions may have substantial significance as they can lead to new international programs. Resolutions also force a country to address an issue and to take into account the views of other countries on the subject. Heated debate can instigate wide attention being paid to a topic. At the very least, the debate absorbs the country's diplomats, as they attempt to get policies favorable to their countries inserted into the texts of the different resolutions.

A declaration is a type of resolution. It is an official statement of principles that will govern relations in a particular manner. It delineates the stance taken by the international community on a particular issue and accords great moral authority to it. It also provides stimulus and inspiration for future action.

These resolutions and declarations may eventually be the basis for the creation of multilateral conventions that have the force of law for the ratifying countries. The Universal Declaration of Human Rights is an example of a resolution that sought to elaborate a general principle set forth in the UN Charter. The ideological principles stated in the declaration have been the basis of many treaties detailing practical action for countries that undertake to carry out the mandates of the conventions they have ratified.

UN CONVENTIONS

In the deliberative bodies of the United Nations the international delegates have discussed many issues concerning the human condition and have formulated legally binding conventions in response. A convention is an international instrument or treaty that legally binds the ratifying countries to adhere to the provisions contained in its text. That is, when a country ratifies a convention, it agrees to abide by its terms. Ratification is voluntary. Sometimes countries will have to transform the internationally agreed rights into domestic legislation. They must adopt specific legislation and measures in order to guarantee to all persons in their jurisdictions all the rights recognized in the convention.

The UN conventions concerning the status of women have had great impact in that they have provided governments with a normative basis for the implementation of their standards. While the objectives of some treaties concern the rectification of adverse social and economic conditions of men and women both, other treaties concern women in particular. The public attention these conventions receive encourages countries to respond to the obligations that they have undertaken in adhering to the treaty. For instance, the Convention on the Elimination of All Forms of Discrimination against Women, which entered into force in 1981, was the result of many years of work. It has been particularly effective and its ratification by many countries has been rapid. Within a short time span it has become a legal basis for equality in many countries. The convention creates a supervisory body at the United Nations, the Committee on the Elimination of the Discrimination against Women, as well as a procedure of compulsory reporting by the ratifying countries. These periodic reports are examined by the committee to determine how the obligations are being undertaken, and there is a constant mutual exchange of experience and information.

What follows is a brief explanation of some of the UN conventions that address themselves to particular areas of women's lives. (For a comprehensive explanation of the deliberations, see the official UN publications on the various topics. Especially recommended is United Nations, *Compendium of International Conventions Concerning the Status of Women*, 1988.)

Some of the conventions mentioned were adopted by the General Assembly of the United Nations, while others were adopted by the specialized agencies of the United Nations. Some concern specific rights of women, and some have provisions bearing on women's status. Some of the rights concern the spiritual integrity of the human person, some deal with political rights and personal freedoms, and some discuss economic, social, and cultural rights. The treaties all represent international law, suggest guidelines for implementation, and usually call for a monitoring system to assist the countries in their progress toward each treaty's aim. They will be presented here in chronological order to show the progression of the ideals discussed at the United Nations in regard to women.

It should be noted that many years pass between the initiation of open discussion and debate of a topic, its formalization into a treaty, the presentation of the treaty for signature and ratification, and the time that it comes into force. It should be noted that a treaty cannot be ratified by a country unless it has signed the treaty within the specified time period. However, if a country has not signed within the time specified, it may accede to the treaty. When a country accedes, it expresses a willingness to comply with the treaty provisions. This has the same effect as ratification, and the legal provisions are equally binding. In addition, the submission by a ratifying or acceding country of reservations, declarations, notifications, or objections relating to specific provisions of a convention is an accepted practice, and has the effect of altering the application of these provisions in respect to that country.

UN TREATIES AFFECTING THE STATUS OF WOMEN

Convention for the Suppression of the Traffic in Persons and of the Exploitation of the Prostitution of Others. Adopted by the General Assembly in 1949; entered into force in 1951.

The preamble of this treaty states that prostitution is incompatible with the dignity and worth of the human person, and that it endangers the welfare of the individual, the family, and the community. The treaty specifically deplores the traffic in women and the exploitation of prostitution, and calls for effective measures to curb the practice. It reflects the then-prevalent view that prostitutes are victims and procurers are culpable. The treaty also covers those who gain financially from running a brothel.

Ratifying countries agree to the punishment of offenders and the provision of rehabilitation for the victims of prostitution. They undertake to report to the secretary-general of the United Nations on measures that they adopt to the end.

Convention Concerning Equal Remuneration for Men and Women Workers for Work of Equal Value. Adopted by the International Labor Organization in 1951; entered into force in 1953.

The purpose of this treaty is to eliminate sex-based wage discrimination and to promote the principle of equal remuneration for work of equal value. Adoption of the principle of rate for the job rather than rate based on sex was urged. Article 1 defines the term *remuneration* as "the ordinary, basic or minimum wage or salary and any additional emoluments whatsoever payable directly or indirectly, whether in cash or kind, by the employer to the worker," and defines "equal remuneration for men and women workers for work of equal value" as "rates of remuneration established without discrimination based on sex." Article 2 suggests ways to apply the principle, such as by national laws or regulations, legally established or recognized machinery for wage determination, or collective agreements between employers and workers.

To carry out the aims of this treaty, ratifying countries must undertake the objective appraisal of jobs and wage discrimination. Action is called for in the areas of vocational guidance, training, placement, and equality regarding access to employment and occupation of women workers.

As of the end of 1987, 108 member nations have ratified this convention and are therefore bound by its mandates.

Convention on the Political Rights of Women. Adopted by the General Assembly in 1952; entered into force in 1954.

This was the first legal instrument dealing exclusively with women's rights. The aim of this convention is to ensure equality for men and women in their participation in public life. Equal voice in government and full political rights in the areas of voting and holding public office are not to be denied to women, and they have the right to exercise all public functions on equal terms with men without incurring discrimination. It is the first worldwide treaty in which a charter principle of equal rights for men and women has been applied to a concrete problem. It recognizes that everyone has the right to serve as a freely chosen representative in his or her country's government regardless of sex.

The countries that ratify this treaty undertake legal obligations concerning equal rights. Periodic reports are to be submitted so that the United Nations can follow the implementation progress of the treaty's provisions. By the end of 1987, ninety-four countries had ratified or acceded to this treaty and had thereby undertaken its obligations.

Convention on the Nationality of Married Women. Adopted by the General Assembly in 1957; entered into force in 1958.

Many women face difficulties when they are married to men whose nationalities are different from their own since national laws will then deprive them of their own nationality. Upon divorce, a woman may be left stateless. This treaty aims to rectify government laws that impose on the woman the nationality of the husband. The underlying principle of this convention is that the nationality of the wife should be independent from that of the husband—that is, men and women are to have equal right in the acquisition or retention of their nationality. Article 1 of this convention reads:

Each Contracting State agrees that neither the celebration nor the dissolution of a marriage between one of its nationals and an alien, nor the change of nationality by the husband during marriage, shall automatically affect the nationality of the wife.

Special reporting procedures were established so that the implementation of the convention could be supervised.

Convention Concerning Discrimination in Respect of Employment and Occupation. Adopted by the General Conference of the International Labor Organization in 1958; entered into force in 1960.

The purpose of this treaty is to promote equality of opportunity and treatment in the workplace, with a view to eliminating any discrimination. Article 1 clarifies the meaning of discrimination by defining it as "Any distinction, exclusion or preference made on the basis of race, color, sex, religion, political opinion, national extraction or social origin, which has the effect of nullifying or impairing equality of opportunity or treatment in employment or occupation." Article 5 states that member countries may, after consultation with workers' and employers' organizations, determine that other special measures might be "designed to meet the particular requirements of persons who, for reasons such as sex . . . are generally recognized to require special protection or assistance" without it being deemed to be discrimination.

Ratifying countries oblige themselves to establish the requisite rights, to encourage organizations to promote the policies, and to bring laws and administrative practices into compliance with these objectives of the treaty. As of the end of 1987, the convention had been ratified by 108 countries.

Convention against Discrimination in Education. Adopted by the United Nations Educational, Scientific and Cultural Organization in 1960; entered into force in 1962.

The purpose of this convention is to promote equal opportunity and treatment for all persons in education. Discrimination is clearly defined in Article 1, which reads:

For the purpose of this Convention, the term "discrimination" includes any distinction, exclusion, limitation or preference which, being based on race, color, sex, language, religion, political or other opinion, national or social origin, economic condition or birth, has the purpose or effect of nullifying or impairing equality of treatment in education.

Equal access to educational institutions is called for, as is nondiscrimination in various phases of the educational system such as administration of schools, admissions, financial aid, facilities, and teacher qualifications. The convention does permit sexual separation in schools provided the institutions have equal staff and the same quality equipment and premises.

Countries are to submit periodic reports concerning actions taken by them for the application of this convention. By the end of 1987, 94 countries had ratified or acceded to this treaty.

Convention on Consent to Marriage, Minimum Age for Marriage and Registration of Marriages. Adopted by the General Assembly in 1962; entered into force in 1964.

By national legislation both spouses are to be assured equal rights in connection with marriage. There should be free and full consent to the marriage by both spouses, and the responsible authorities should ascertain that this is the case. To avoid exploitation of girls, a minimum age of marriage should be established. Countries are urged to abolish any customs, ancient laws, and practices that condone child marriages or the betrothal of young girls before the age of puberty. Appropriate penalties are to be applied where necessary. Also, all marriages have to be registered so that practices similar to slavery will be abolished.

The Economic and Social Council of the United Nations is entrusted with the supervision of the implementation of this convention.

Convention on the Elimination of All Forms of Discrimination against Women. Adopted by the General Assembly in 1979; entered into force in 1981.

This is the most comprehensive of the conventions concerning women. In the preamble of this convention, the United Nations acknowledged that discrimination against women still exists in spite of the numerous international resolutions adopted in the past. The preamble reiterates the assault on human dignity to which discrimination has led. The reasons stated are:

Discrimination against women violates the principles of equality of rights and respect for human dignity, is an obstacle to the participation of women on equal terms with men, in the political, social, economic and cultural life of their countries, hampers the growth of the prosperity of society and the family and makes more difficult the full development of the potentialities of women in the service of their countries and of humanity.

The preamble also specifically states that "the welfare of the world and the cause of peace require the maximum participation of women on equal terms with men in all fields."

This treaty covers many topics included in past treaties, reiterates the norm of nondiscrimination in education and employment, and proscribes traffic in women. New topics include obligations of member countries to encourage joint-parental responsibilities within the family, as well as efforts to eliminate gender stereotyping. Article 5 of this treaty obligates countries "to ensure that family education includes a proper understanding of maternity as a social function and the recognition of the common responsibility of men and women in the upbringing and development of their children." Article 11 concerns the elimination of discrimination in the field of employment. There is a prohibition against job dismissal on the grounds of pregnancy, and countries are urged to introduce maternity leave with pay and without loss of seniority. Provision of the necessary supporting services, such as child-care facilities, is required to enable parents to combine family and employment. Part (d) of Article 11 concerns "the right to equal treatment in respect of work of equal value."

A reporting procedure is established by the convention. It consists of a committee of persons elected from different geographic locations and serving fixed terms of office. The aim of the committee is to promote cooperation, exchange of experiences, and the making of general recommendations to assist countries in their progress toward the implementation of the convention.

Ratification of this convention continues at a rapid pace, and, on average, twelve countries a year ratify this treaty compared with an average of two or three per year for other treaties. As of April 13, 1989, ninety-nine countries had ratified or acceded to it.

Convention Concerning Equal Opportunities and Equal Treatment for Men and Women Workers: Workers with Family Responsibilities. Adopted by the International Labor Organization in 1981; entered into force in 1983.

The general purpose of this treaty is the extension of nondiscrimination in respect to employment, and the assurance of equal opportunity for all workers even if they are responsible for dependent members of their family. The ratifying countries agree to develop community services for working parents and also to educate the public regarding equal treatment of men and women. Part of the underpinning of this treaty is the recognition that "all human beings, irrespective of race, creed, or sex, have the right to pursue their material well-being and their spiritual development in conditions of freedom and dignity, of economic security and equal opportunity." Article 8 of this treaty provides that "family responsibilities shall not, as such, constitute a valid reason for termination of employment."

In effect, the mandate is for countries to make it possible for women with family responsibilities to work outside the home by developing services to enable them to do so. One such arrangement is the provision of day-care centers, a service U.S. working women have desired for a long time. This treaty is extremely important in that it shows the trends in international legislation. It recognizes the need for social services for married women with families (a major segment of the world's women) if there is to be true equality and if women are to be enabled to take their places in government and industry alongside men. Lacking such provisions, even in countries where an equal legal status for women is specified in the judicial system, there can be wide discrepancies between law and everyday practice due to women's family responsibilities.

By the end of 1987 only nine countries had ratified this treaty, Sweden being one of them. The slow ratification rate may be due to the fact that, since the commitments that countries make often require basic and even expensive innovations at home, deliberations can be protracted. Feasibility studies may be undertaken and dissention overcome, especially when the provisions of the treaty are not easily incorporated into the local culture.

Through these conventions, and others not discussed here, the United Nations has given the world standards to which to aspire in the abolition of discrimination and the promotion of equality of men and women. Since women have borne the major brunt of institutional discrimination in countries around the world, they have the potential of great gains through the efforts of the United Nations. The public attention that some conventions generate encourages countries to respond more rapidly to their obligations to remedy legal deficiencies on the national level and proceed toward the goals of the international instruments. Women who are citizens of the many countries that have ratified the treaties and thereby have undertaken to implement their principles have gained and are moving toward equal rights with men legally, politically, economically, and, hopefully, toward equal status culturally.

In some countries progress has been slow and women's advancement is still constrained. More effort is called for to eliminate economic exploitation, marginality, and chronic inequalities. In recognition of this, the United

Nations proclaimed 1975–1985 as a decade for vigorous action by countries to promote gender equality.

THE UN DECADE FOR WOMEN

International Woman's Year: Mexico City, 1975

The UN General Assembly proclaimed the year 1975 International Woman's Year, and called for intensified action to promote equality between the sexes and to integrate women in their societies with the full realization of their rights. To this end, the World Conference of the International Woman's Year was held in Mexico City during the summer of 1975. More than one thousand delegates from 133 countries attended. Reports on the agenda concerned current trends and changes in the status of women, the major obstacles to be overcome in the achievement of equal rights, and many other substantive items. Many declarations and resolutions resulted from this conference. One was the World Plan of Action for the Implementation of the Objectives of the International Woman's Year, which defines a 'society in which women participate completely in economic, social, and political life.

The UN General Assembly endorsed the proposals that emanated from the World Conference and proclaimed the Decade for Women: Equality, Development and Peace. The ten-year period was to be devoted to effective and sustained action to implement the World Plan of Action and its related resolutions. Periodic reports were to be submitted in order to appraise the progress achieved toward the full equality of women with men in all spheres of life. A midterm conference was planned for 1980 in order to evaluate the progress made.

World Conference on Women: Copenhagen, Denmark, July 1980

At this conference, which marked the completion of the first half of the Decade for Women, targets were set for national and international action to enable the integration of women in political, social, and economic life. For the achievement of these basic objectives, special attention was to be paid to education and training for employment. In addition, the special needs of rural and urban poor women were to be addressed.

The program that was adopted at the Copenhagen Conference called for specific action that would be required for the realization of sexual parity, including such things as reward for unpaid work in the household. It was recognized that government policies have profound implications for women, not only with regard to employment, wage levels, and job security, but also with respect to the status of individuals in the family. It was acknowledged that women could be called invisible as they were making vast but unacknowledged contributions to the wealth and welfare of their communities in the form of unpaid domestic work or small-scale trading activities.

World Conference to Review and Appraise the Achievements of the United Nations Decade for Women: Nairobi, Kenya, July 15–27, 1985

The Decade for Women was concluded with the World Conference to Review and Appraise the Achievements of the United Nations Decade for Women. Some 157 governments and 163 nongovernmental organizations participated and were represented by about 2,000 delegates. The opening remarks of Letitia Shahani, the secretary-general of the conference, stressed that substantial and visible legal progress had been made during the decade. She also referred to the need to go beyond advocacy and consciousness raising and to focus on concrete action for change in the post–Decade for Women period. She believed that the full participation of women was necessary in shaping the future of society and contributing to international peace and security, and stated that "the values, aspirations, and ideals of women could re-orient a troubled and violent world" (United Nations 1986:106). She concluded that women represent new hope for the world as it prepares for the coming century. Shahani spoke of the global force of the women's movement and praised the significance of the conference and the dynamic impact that such a widely represented gathering would have on the practical efforts to elevate the status of women in the various countries.

The conference agenda included the assessment of the many steps taken by countries on behalf of women during the decade. Maureen Reagan, the U.S. representative and daughter of President Ronald Reagan, urged the conference to focus on four issues that are of concern to the United States: women refugees, women in development, literacy, and domestic violence.

The decade's themes of equality, development, and peace, and its sub-themes of education, health, and employment, formed the bases of the many workshops at the conference. Strategies were to be devised for further advancement during the rest of the century (United Nations Chronicle 1985).

As the conference progressed, much of the work revolved around the three main foci—equality, development, and peace. An abbreviated account of the content of discussions gives some indication of matters of concern to the delegations.

Equality

Concerning equality, most delegates cited extensive legislative progress. The required legal framework had been put in place in their countries to guarantee women full civil and political rights. It was reported that in many countries women had achieved de facto equality in many spheres of life. In some countries women accounted for almost one-third of the members of the legislature. In many developing countries, however, de facto equality was still lagging behind de jure equality with respect to women's access to resources. Among the obstacles cited were persistent sexual stereotyping and the deep-seated traditional attitudes of male superiority rooted in the sociocultural norms.

Development

Concerning development, many countries reported significant progress in women's actual contributions to national development, and also in the realization of women's potential input toward overall socioeconomic development of their countries. Some delegates lauded the income-generating activities of women, and others recognized women's important role in food production and food security. Many of the disparities that still exist between men and women were highlighted, such as in earnings, job segregation, and the double burden borne by female workers with family responsibilities. It was suggested that the present international economic crisis has mostly affected women in many countries, especially in employment, education, and health. A lack of an adequate data base has perpetuated women's so-called invisibility; indicators for measuring women's economic contributions to the gross national product are unavailable in many countries. However, the consensus was that progress was being made in the recognition of women's importance in national development.

Peace

Concerning peace, some countries emphasized the necessary role of women in preparing societies for life in peace. On the grass-roots level, women have been active in peace efforts ranging from activism in peace movements to disarmament campaigns and opposition to military conflict. On the higher government levels, it was felt necessary to have women in decision-making capacities as the most important requisite for a just and lasting peace (United Nations 1986). Peace was understood as the absence of conditions that produce violence in the family and on the local, national, and international levels.

The final document that came out of the conference was the *Nairobi Forward-Looking Strategies for the Advancement of Women*. The text of this document (372 paragraphs long) had to be adopted one paragraph at a time (United Nations Chronicle 1985). Besides careful deliberations concerning the basic themes at issue, the text acknowledged the existence of challenging political and economic conditions and identified some of the emerging issues for women such as power, technology, being without men, violence against women and other abuses, and family planning. One paragraph of the final document dealt with the elimination of racism, a concept that includes the suppression and often the forced dislocation of women and children.

The activities of the Decade for Women have allowed the invisible majority of humankind—the women—to become more visible on the global scene. It is generally agreed that an irresistible momentum was generated at the Nairobi Conference, creating a global force that will continue and will evoke positive changes for women all over the world.

THE UNITED STATES AND UN TREATIES

The United States has not ratified the Convention on the Elimination of All Forms of Discrimination against Women. It has to date ratified only three of the UN treaties that bear on the status of women. This will surprise many people as the United States has from its inception proclaimed its belief in human rights and has done much to implement such rights in practice. Those opposing ratification take the position that constitutional authority to ratify such treaties is lacking in the United States; such a premise is based on what some view as limitations on the treaty-making power of Congress. Malvina Halberstam and Elizabeth Defeis (1987) have summed up the three basic arguments that have been used to prevent U.S. ratification, and they analyze the relevant Supreme Court decisions that make it clear that no constitutional impediment exists to ratification of the UN conventions for the elimination of gender-based discrimination. A brief summary of their main points follows.

The Domestic Jurisdiction Argument

According to this argument, the United States cannot ratify a treaty if the subject matter dealt with would be within the domestic jurisdiction of the U.S. government. The past secretary of state Dean Rusk stated that the UN Convention on the Political Rights of Women involved no legal restrictions and was in compliance with the Constitution. He therefore recommended ratification, and the United States did later ratify it. The American Bar Association, on the other hand, opposed ratification on the grounds that the convention concerned matters within U.S. domestic jurisdiction, such as the right to vote. Since the Nineteenth Amendment to the Constitution already guaranteed women the right to vote, their argument could not have been based on questions relating to the possibility of a convention mandating the change of existing internal laws.

As for the domestic jurisdiction argument, many people argue that there is nothing in the U.S. Constitution limiting treaties to matters not covered by it. As treaties are a major means of creating international law, and hence of enforcing global understanding and unity, this argument would appear to misconceive the structure of international law and the function of treaties.

The States Rights Argument

The basis of this argument is that ratification of human rights conventions would be an infringement by the federal government of matters constitutionally within the reserved powers of the states. This argument loses cogency in connection with conventions providing for equality of women, however, when one recalls that the topic is already governed by federal law to a large extent.

Legal scholars have asserted that "there is practically nothing that is dealt with by treaty that could not also be the subject of legislation by Congress" (Henkin 1972:146). This principle was established in the *Missouri v. Holland* case (1920), which dealt with a treaty with Canada that Missouri had challenged concerning the hunting of migratory birds. U.S. Supreme Court Justice Oliver Wendell Holmes's majority decision included the words: "No doubt the great body of private relations usually fall within the control of the State, but a treaty may override its power." The principle involved was that states rights did not constitute a limitation on the scope of federal treaty power. The only limitations of treaty power are the guarantees provided for by the Bill of Rights.

The International Concern Argument

Thomas Jefferson noted several limitations on treaty-making power in his *Manual of Parliamentary Practice*. Jefferson's contention that the United States could not enter into treaties on matters within the reserved powers of the states has already been rejected by the Supreme Court in the *Missouri v. Holland* decision, which was mentioned above. However, Jefferson's position that a treaty must be of "international concern" has found support in other court decisions.

It may be argued that treaties of international scope and laws of internal concern are not mutually exclusive. A country's treatment of its own citizens has often aroused great international concern and international consequences (i.e., apartheid in South Africa, or the USSR's treatment of Jewish citizens). In addition, the United States has often ratified treaties that have affected its relations with other countries but which, at the same time, have also affected internal affairs. One category does not automatically exclude the other. The Restatement of the Foreign Relations Law of 1965 (1980 draft) makes clear that international treaties with domestic effects are not excluded; the only limitation is that a treaty not contravene the provisions of the Constitution (Halberstam and Defeis 1987).

The rights of women have been discussed at great length at the United Nations. When treaties are the result of long and serious deliberation, and are ratified by up to one hundred countries who commit themselves to its stipulations, it cannot be said that the subject matter is not of international concern and cannot be entered into by the United States. In 1968 a president's commission was appointed and chaired by Supreme Court Justice Tom C. Clark to study the constitutionality of the ratification of human rights treaties by the United States. The commission's conclusion was that such treaties fall within the preview of treaty-making powers. Justice Clark stated:

I would like to reiterate here, however, our finding, after a thorough view of judicial, congressional, and diplomatic precedents, that humans are matters of international concern and that the President, with the U.S. Senate concurring, may, on behalf of the United States under the treaty power of the Constitution ratify or adhere to any human rights convention that does not contravene a specific constitutional prohibition. (United States 1968:339–340)

In view of the above statement there would seem to be no restrictions on the ratification of the United Nations conventions concerning the rights of women.

The decision whether to ratify a particular convention would appear to be largely a question of public and foreign policy. Many federal and state enactments, court decisions, and executive orders in the United States have the common goal of eliminating gender-based inequality and are in accord with conventions dealing with the elimination of discrimination. In fact, the conventions in question concern the same guarantees that are provided in the Bill of Rights. In any case, if any specific provision of a UN convention infringed upon an amendment (for example, the First Amendment guarantee of freedom of association) the treaty could be ratified with a few formal reservations that would mean the ratification does not obligate the country for that particular article of the treaty.

President Jimmy Carter recommended ratification of the Convention on the Elimination of All Forms of Discrimination against Women in his letter of transmittal to the Senate in 1980. He emphasized that it would show the commitment of the United States in the area of gender equality. Part of Carter's letter read:

Ratification of the Convention on the Political Rights of Women in 1976 was a recent express affirmation by the Executive and Legislative branches of the U.S. Government that human rights in general and women's rights in particular are matters of legitimate concern to the international community and are not subjects with exclusively domestic ramifications. U.S. ratification of the Convention at hand, the newest of the international human rights instruments, would be consistent with this affirmation and would make clear at home and abroad the commitment of the United States to eliminate discrimination against women. (Carter 1980)

This convention has not as yet been ratified by the United States. However, it has been argued that if it were, women seeking equal rights on the national level would no longer have to rely on the Fourteenth Amendment to the U.S. Constitution. Ratification of the Convention on the Elimination of All Forms of Discrimination against Women would, when executed, have the effect of superseding the inconsistent federal and state laws and would become the supreme law of the land (Halberstam and Defeis 1987). When the United States ratifies a UN convention, the convention is legally binding and overrides past laws on the subject. This is because Article 6 of the U.S. Constitution provides that "all treaties made or which shall be made, under the authority of the United States, shall be the Supreme Law of the Land." However, it has been pointed out that feminist activism has not been directed toward urging the United States to ratify the many international treaties that bar gender-based discrimination. Women's efforts aimed at ratification of this convention would render unnecessary many small campaigns on various issues concerning gender injustices. Furthermore, ratification of the convention would obviate the need for an equal rights amendment (Halberstam and Defeis 1987). The mandates of the treaty specify the elimination of discrimination in various aspects of social endeavor and require that countries "modify or abolish existing laws, regulations, customs and practices" that discriminate against women.

On the international level, ratification of human rights instruments would enhance the image and credibility of the United States as a world leader in human rights. There is hope that perhaps the barrier to ratification of human rights conventions may have finally been broken with the U.S. ratification of the Genocide Convention in 1986 (Halberstam and Defeis 1987). Possibly, ratification of the conventions eliminating discrimination against women will soon follow.

8

Cross-Cultural Studies

This chapter probes the extent to which new national laws benefitting women have been a catalyst for change. In spite of international law and the ratification of treaties relating to women by many countries, there still remains a gap between the de jure and the de facto situation in regard to discrimination in many areas of the world. Ingrained cultural attitudes can take longer to change than laws. Often widespread education and reeducation are needed to change prejudices and customary attitudes concerning the so-called inferiority of women. Five countries—Argentina, Sweden, Egypt, India, and China—have been selected as typical of the different global areas.

The case studies of these countries will give an indication of the status of women throughout the world. The discussion will center on the historical conditions that have influenced the legal status of women, the limitations imposed on women because of their sex, and the gains toward gender equality that have occurred in recent years. The subthemes include women and family, women and employment, and women and power. The last category will include coverage of reports to the United Nations by the different countries, in which it is stated what steps have been and are being taken on behalf of the elimination of gender bias in the country in response to the mandates of the ratified UN treaties.

ARGENTINA

Argentina is the second largest country in South America. As of 1980, it had a population of 27,085,000 persons, of which women numbered 14,191,463. Of the women, 61.2 percent were women between the ages of fifteen and sixty-four (Argentina 1987).

Argentina is a republic with a federal constitution and a representative government, although this has at times been suspended. The constitution provides that Catholicism is the state religion (Page 1983). One eligibility requirement for the presidency and vice presidency is adherence to Roman Catholicism. Voting is required of all citizens eighteen years or older, and since 1947 the suffrage has included women. As the literacy rate is high (in 1977, 92 percent of the women and 94 percent of the men were literate), one might be tempted to believe that women were in an advantaged position. However, two social elements dealing with public ideology and private mysticism are ingrained in the traditional culture and are so accepted a part of everyday life that social change of any kind is interpreted as contributing to system collapse. These elements—the unity of church and state and the twin concepts of *machismo* and *marianismo*—strongly influence the status of women.

Religion and Government

Argentinians are mostly Roman Catholics (94 percent of the population), and there is a close connection between church and state. Argentina retains national patronage over the church, a residue from the old Spanish royal patronage system. The appointment of bishops is a function of the president of the Republic. The president also affirms papal bulls and decrees, which sometimes must be incorporated in an act of the Congress.

The relations between church and state have been amicable and close in Argentina. The Partido Democrata Christiano (Christian Democratic Party) places heavy emphasis on the teachings of the papal encyclicals. It is estimated to be the third or fourth largest political party, depending on the basis of calculation, and is predominantly Catholic (Worldmark Encyclopedia 1976). The various political parties often unite along socioeconomic and religious lines. Alliances are commonly formed to preserve the traditional order through defense of the church and the status quo. This constitutes a formidable barrier to the acquisition of basic freedoms that women seek, such as the rights to divorce and remarriage, equality within the family, and access to contraceptive devices and legal abortion.

Machismo/Marianismo

The other ingrained cultural element in Argentina is the machismo/marianismo dichotomy. In most countries the long-held patterns of expectations concerning the distribution of the basic tasks are influenced by the assumed natural attributes of men and women. Over time, gender positions take on a validity that is socially constructed and not necessarily related to human potential. In Latin America the form of gender assignment is particularly extreme, and is justified under the twin phenomena of machismo and marianismo. These concepts represent opposite poles that philosophically justify gender positions based on ascribed characteristics of the sexes. There is a dynamic interplay between the two positions, as they are seen as reciprocal and as part of the natural order of things.

Machismo is the historical orientation of men, which can be described as the cult of virility. The chief characteristic is a strong sense of pride in being male. Historically it has represented the masculine ideal, embodying concepts like personal honor, courage, respect for others, and provision for the well-being of one's family. The male is oriented to proving his virility and shouldering his responsibilities. The bullring illustrates the epitome of masculinity as the *torero* (bullfighter) defies death in his brave struggle. The concept of machismo came to the New World with the Spanish conquistadores, who treated indigenous women as sexual and domestic servants. Local women were treated as property and used to bolster men's status as property holders (Almquist 1984).

For women, the allotted pattern of attitudes and behavior is subsumed under the cult of marianismo. It embodies the expectation of the acceptance of suffering because of moral superiority and spiritual strength, the characteristics of the ideal woman. This female strength carries with it the notion of women's infinite capacity for humility, submissiveness, self-denial, patience, and sacrifice. There is a complete acceptance of men's foibles, since men are inherently intemperate, obstinate, and unable to control themselves. Marianismo is not a religious concept, but its similarities to the purity and veneration of the Virgin Mary in the Catholic Church are unavoidable (Stevens 1973). Marianismo stresses that the ideal wife's most important function is the bearing and rearing of children, as this symbolizes not only her maturity but also the virility of her husband (Almquist 1984). In actual practice, the similarities with the Virgin Mary are limited, as women are neither held in high esteem socially nor venerated for their roles as sacrificers.

The concepts of machismo and marianismo today continue to influence the lives of men and women, although in a somewhat modified form. Men still seek satisfactory evidence of maleness for themselves and society. One way they seek validation is through attachment to male peers through whom their values are reinforced. Machismo has often been degraded to mean sexual prowess over women as men conquer and exploit them. Both sexes consider men's infidelities normal, but not those of women. For women, marianismo means not straying because even minor deviations can cast them as self-serving temptresses like Eve. The ideal includes premarital chastity and postnuptial frigidity, as sex is reserved for married women who thus serve their husbands. Many women endure their prescribed limitations and fatalistically contain their sorrow without rebelliousness. Many still follow the customary dictates upon the death of a family member that call for a long period of mourning (which includes giving up most forms of entertainment) and the wearing of black clothing only. The death of a husband requires a lifetime of mourning, no matter how young the wife may be at the time.

Even those who deviate from the marianismo patterns hide behind the mythology of their ideal womanhood as they present the facade to the public. It is not clear to what extent women are contributing to the perpetuation of the concepts of machismo and marianismo by their acceptance of the necessity to put up a front and their seeming acquiescence to the sexual exploits of men.

Residues of these concepts are still governing forces in Argentina today. The long-standing legitimation of different spheres for women and men continues to keep women in a socially inferior position.

Women and the Family

The common theme in many magazines that appeal to intellectuals and deal with social and economic problems is the declining influence of family in Argentine life as a result of the presence of women in the labor force. As evidence of family decline, statistics are given showing the smaller size of the average family and even the growing incidence of childless families. The general tenor of such articles is that women are working in order to indulge in profligate expenditures, and are thus rejecting motherhood, their most noble function, thus endangering the defense of the country against aggressive nations (Hollander 1973). These criticisms do not address themselves to the real problems of women's exploitation and the impact on them of oppressive conditions. They also disregard entirely the right of women to develop their human potentialities aside from the housewife and mother role.

Laws and attitudes in Argentina are based on strict interpretation of Roman Catholic doctrine. For men, a cultural characteristic that has been referred to as excessive individualism stemming from the obsession with personal dignity fosters a predisposition toward authoritarianism in general. In the family, the concept of *patria potestad* gives complete authority within the family to the husband. It means that the father has total rights regarding the children, while the mother has the obligation for their care (Calvera 1984). For the wife, it means that finances and property are in the control of her husband, whose signature she must obtain for most legal matters of interest to her. She is expected to assume a passive role, and she is, in effect, treated like a minor.

The government has an official policy that is called pro-family and interpreted as pro-natal. It gives special stipends to government employees who have big families. Employed women get paid maternity leave for six weeks after childbirth, and, for a year, are entitled to two free hours a day for nursing. In actual practice, not all women receive these benefits, and many get fired when they become pregnant (Morgan 1984).

The distribution and sale of contraceptives has not been openly permitted following a 1971 government decree. Recent amendments to that decree specifically forbid doctors to prescribe contraceptives to single women. The result of such tight control is that information concerning modern methods of birth control does not reach rural women. As for abortion, it is generally illegal and only available in extreme circumstances such as rape or incest. In spite of the laws, however, it is estimated that one of four women will have an illegal abortion, in spite of possible imprisonment of one to four years for the woman and one to ten years for the practitioner. It is estimated that in 1970 the number of abortions almost equaled the number of live births (Morgan 1984). Whether from attempts at self-induced abortion or improperly performed illegal ones, the number of maternal deaths due to resulting complications is high. Although women do seem to be attempting to have some control over their own bodies, it is only at great expense to themselves.

Cohabitation by unmarried couples is not rare, especially among the poor and rural population. Although an unwed mother is regarded as having committed a sexual crime and the government does not sanction common-law unions, there are many illegitimate children. The law states that children born in or out of wedlock are to receive equal treatment, although out-of-wedlock children legally inherit only one-quarter of the amount of property that in-wedlock children receive (Morgan 1984).

As for wife beating, since *patria potestad* legally gives husbands complete authority over their wives, it is not surprising that there are no laws against beating them. Wife battery is a commonly tolerated practice and is viewed as a husband's prerogative. A woman's only recourse is divorce, which functions as a legal separation since the wife does not have the right to remarry. During his presidency in 1954, Juan Peron introduced a new family code that included the right to marital dissolution, but with his ouster in 1955 the country reverted to previous Catholic taboos concerning divorce (Hollander 1973). The more affluent women go to other countries to obtain divorces, but these actions are not recognized under Argentine law (Morgan 1984).

Eva Peron, who was vice president under her husband Juan Peron, has been given the credit for changing the status of women because of her consciousness-raising and mobilization efforts for women's political autonomy and her establishment of the Peronist Feminist Party in 1949. She publicly stated that her name was a battle cry for all the women of the world. However, during her tenure she gave what some feel are conflicting messages. In her speeches she constantly alluded to her subserviance to her husband and to woman's role in the home. She publicly stated "the home is the sanctuary of motherhood and the pivot of society," adding that the home is the "appropriate sphere in which a woman, for the good of the country and of her own children, fulfills her patriotic duty daily" (Hollander 1973:156).

In spite of Eva Peron's ambivalence concerning women's social role, women were an important political constituency for Peronism. Eva Peron was instrumental in getting women the right to vote in 1947, although it had been alleged that she merely did so because she realized the useful effect for her husband that lower-class women would have at the polls. She was a charismatic leader who stimulated Argentine working-class women, provided them with a coherent revolutionary ideology, and gave the feminist party equal standing with the men's parties.

Women and Work

As elsewhere, women in Argentina have contributed to the nation's growth and industrialists' profits by providing a cheap labor source. Major forces in Argentine life have been the rapid pace of urbanization from 1860 to 1926 and the high level of immigration from rural to urban areas and from other countries. The pressures from these forces and the contact with new ideas affected the roles of women, allowing some to break away from the Spanish tradition of sheltered womanhood to become active participants, albeit second-class ones, in the nation's growth. Since 1860, Buenos Aires has been expanding as the principal city of Argentina, and it stimulated an increased demand for clerical workers. In response to the need, professional schools for women added classes in typing, accounting, stenography, and general clerical work. The lower echelons of office workers and sales clerks became identified as female occupations, with minimal pay and few benefits (Hollander 1973).

After 1870 vocational schools also sprang up in response to the need for labor. Many of these had special training programs for women, although the skills taught were traditional ones that did not assure a future of steady employment in industry. The schools taught needlework subjects such as embroidery, lace making, hem stitching, millinery, corsetry, and such. It was hoped that women could become independent home craftsworkers instead of servile factory workers. Mothers could earn an income while spending time with their families (Hollander 1973). While the idea had merit on the surface, in actual practice piecework by women at home had an extremely low remuneration rate for the long hours put in at the expense of other household activities. Pieceworkers are not entitled to the fringe benefits that formally employed workers get. Home piecework has now become recognized as a crass exploitation of poor women whose families need the meagre added income that such tiring informal labor can provide.

As business expanded, women began to fill the factories and sweatshops as they formed a source of super-exploitable labor. They worked in hazardous, unhealthy conditions for long hours at low wages, which were on the average half those paid to men. By 1887, 39 percent of the paid labor force in Buenos Aires were women. Employers interviewed in 1904 often explained that their preference for women workers was based on women's servility, better attendance, and cheaper cost. This situation contributed to the super-profits of the industrialists.

By the early twentieth century, a struggle in Congress led to Law 5291. This law regulated working conditions for women and minors, and it helped conditions slightly. Another protective law was passed in 1924 (Law 11.317), which limited working hours for women to eight hours a day and forty-eight hours a week. Night work and dangerous jobs were forbidden. The law established special rules regarding maternity, and factories with more than fifty female workers had to provide rooms in which women could nurse their infants (Hollander 1973, Little 1978).

The 1924 law was a step forward, but it had its limitations as well. For one thing, it did not affect agricultural workers at all. For this work, families were usually hired as a unit (husband, wife, and children), although the salary was paid to the husband. The law also did not address itself to the unequal wages paid to men and women for the same work, nor did it affect the large numbers of domestic workers whose jobs depended on the benevolence of their employers. In the economic depression of the 1930s, all workers suffered, but women lost their jobs disproportionately. In 1932, 61.3 percent of women workers became unemployed. A demographic shift in internal migrations to Buenos Aires started occurring, and females outnumbered male migrants in search of jobs. This added to the supply of cheap labor. By 1947, 31.2 percent of women in Buenos Aires worked outside the home, the middle classes in low-paying traditional women's jobs, and the poor classes in industrial settings (Hollander 1973).

Women and Power

The following information is from a documentary by Susana Munoz, which was made in 1986. It is included here to show the special circumstances prevalent in Argentina, and to show that women are not passive in political affairs even though their help has seldom been acknowledged and rewarded. It also demonstrates how the struggle for the equality of women comes to a standstill in a country when neither men nor women are afforded basic human rights. In 1976 a new military junta took power in Argentina. All constitutional rights were suspended and a campaign of daily kidnapping, torture, and murder was implemented. About 30,000 young people disappeared. The military leaders justified their actions by stating their belief that they were saving the country from the subversive actions of the young people who, they alleged, were Marxist-influenced. It seems that when President Juan Peron won a landslide victory at the polls in 1973, the disgruntled military blamed left-wingers. When Peron died a year later, and his second wife, Isabel, who succeeded him was deposed, military leaders claimed it was civil war and that secret operations were justified. Their target was the young women and men who, in their idealism for a better society with equality for everyone, had joined the Peronista Youth Organization. These young people were systematically kidnapped from their homes at gunpoint or from the streets, and no one saw them again. No reason was ever given for their arrest. Occasionally, dead bodies were left on streets to terrorize the population.

In spite of the general climate of fear and repression, in 1977 several mothers of kidnapped young people defied the law to protest the disappearance of their children. They began to meet in the Plaza de Mayo every week. It was a dangerous thing to do. Other mothers were inspired by their defiant act and gained courage. Before long there were many female protesters demanding human rights and information about their children. They also wanted to claim their grandchildren, who were generally put up for adoption when their incarcerated pregnant daughters gave birth before being killed. They tried to enlist the help of many agencies but no one would listen, not even the Church. Out of eighty-three bishops, only three supported the mothers. The police harassed them with the claim that they were continuing the subversive activities started by their children, and made them move on. In December 1977 the mothers put an advertisement in the newspapers with the names of the missing.

Through their activism the mothers gradually succeeded in making the public aware of the situation, including residents of other countries. President Carter stopped supplying arms to Argentina in 1977 because of the abrogation of human rights. By 1982 the Argentine government was on the verge of bankruptcy due to corruption and the Falklands war. The defeat of Argentina in the war encouraged people to call for elections.

In 1983 a new government was elected. The mothers' cause was now acknowledged in their own country. However, the bill they tried to have passed to bring the murderers to justice was defeated. They were told it could subvert the government. As for the generals, the military tribunals refused to pass judgment. Civilian courts took up the case, and of all the murderers of 30,000 young women and men, only nine came to trial. Four of the nine were vindicated. Of the five condemned, two were given life sentences and three only light sentences (Munoz 1989).

The mothers still march every week in Plaza de Mayo because they feel they have not received justice. The new government has not sought nor made public the records on their missing children. One can only speculate what the outcome would have been if women had decision-making positions in the legislative, judicial, and military arenas in proportion to their numbers in the population.

Argentine Report to the United Nations

At the United Nations, Argentina ratified the Convention on the Elimination of All Forms of Discrimination against Women in 1985, and on December 7, 1987, presented its initial report to the monitoring agency, the

Committee on the Elimination of Discrimination against Women. The report had the aura of sincerity in that it frankly admitted the obstacles women encounter in Argentina. It mentioned that bad patriarchal habits are in many cases legitimized in Argentine culture, and that their impact within society holds back the development of women by handicapping their access to food, health, training, and employment.

The Argentine delegate indicated that a new beginning for Argentina meant a new beginning for women. After the ousting of the dictatorship, illiteracy rates dropped and many innovations occurred. New legislation has been adopted, the objective of which is to:

Promote those reforms necessary for the suppression of all forms of legal discrimination and to place the woman on a footing of equality with the man on the legal level, a necessary, although not sufficient, condition for the attainment of her full participation in society. (Argentina 1987:8)

Ratification of the convention prompted numerous institutional reforms in the country, at both the national and provincial levels. An Under-Secretariat for Women has been created by the Health and Social Action Ministry. Its main objective is to promote women's rights in all spheres of life. The following information is from Argentina's report to the committee and the General Assembly official records of the committee's forty-third session (Argentina Report 1987, United Nations *Commission* 1988).

A recent legislative reform in Argentina is *patria potestad compartida*, which is co-parental sharing. Any juridical discriminatory measures against children born out of wedlock have been eliminated. There is a new marriage law that affirms unity and democracy in family relationships. Some of its directives concerning marriage and divorce are summarized as follows.

Concerning matrimony:

• Husband and wife share equal rights and obligations;
• They jointly elect the conjugal domicile; and
• The wife is not obliged to use the surname of the husband.

Concerning separation and divorce:

• The incorporation of new causes such as prolonged de facto separation and disturbances that cause behavioral distortions, making a shared life impossible (alcoholism, drug addiction, and serious mental changes); and
• It concedes a new ability to marry after divorce.

The following are some of the innovations that Argentina has recently adopted in order to remedy the conditions of women that have been prevalent under their patriarchal system (Argentina Report 1987).

Battered Wives

A Center for Assistance for Battered Wives has been created. It understands that "the battered wife is one who is the victim of physical, psychological and/or sexual violence on the part of the husband, violence to which the wife does not consent" (Argentina Report 1987:125). Its interdisciplinary team gives legal and psychological advice to victims, and clarifies their possibilities of finding work, seeking accommodations, and getting health care. Victims are also aided in lodging complaints with the appropriate legal or police authorities. They inform wives that the law punishes a violent husband, and also that:

- Violence is grounds for divorce against the violent person;
- Violence is a cause for the exclusion of the husband from the conjugal home;
- Violence may be a cause for loss of parental rights;
- Violence influences judgments on the custody of children;
- The battered wife may be granted a divorce and continue to receive maintenance; and
- The battered wife who obtains a divorce for this reason has the right to inherit from her former husband.

It was asserted that violence against women was not considered a virile or masculine trait by Argentine society in general, and that the propensity was only found at the lower sociocultural level.

Work Force

Argentina is becoming aware of what they call the femininity index—the total number of posts held by women as a ratio of the total number of posts held by men. In 1977, women held 9.9 percent of the positions in banking, 16.8 percent of positions in state companies, and 19.4 percent of positions in what they refer to as decentralized bodies. Although safeguards for domestic workers have not been addressed as yet, and protective laws regulating women's night work have not been revised, the Labor Contract Law provides that there is to be no differences in remuneration between men and women for equal work. Courts accept complaints of pay discrimination, and rule through principles outlined by the convention and by the national legislation. Retirement pensions can be collected after thirty years of service, and the allowable retirement age is sixty for men and fifty-five for women. Although statistics are not available of women's participation in trade unions, it is acknowledged that lack of participation is due to prevailing machismo attitudes in the organizations.

A campaign aimed at modification of social and cultural patterns, and including support for working women, is under way. It includes public discussions and mass media publicity programs. Some of the specific steps being taken include the following.

Mass Media

Some programs that exploited women as sex objects in the mass media have been banned as a result of court action.

Family Planning

Family-planning services are available on request, but birth control devices are not distributed free of charge. Concerning abortion, it is illegal, but it is not considered infanticide.

Rural Women

There is a concerted effort to encourage women to attend agricultural technical schools. Women's labor on small-scale and livestock farms and in the home has not in the past been considered productive work, and there is therefore a lack of statistics concerning it. The introduction of new technologies has been detrimental to women. Agricultural technical schools are available, but not many women attend because of the incompatibility with family duties.

Education

In the state schools coeducation is the norm and primary education is compulsory and free of charge. As for higher education, in 1986 females were only 11.9 percent of the students initially registered in higher studies. The government is implementing a national literacy plan to eliminate functional illiteracy. "Courses at a distance" (a distancia) have been introduced which offer education in remote areas by television videotapes. Students gather at centrally located municipal centers and follow the lessons, which include primary and secondary levels of education. After successful completion, the students are evaluated and awarded certificates.

At the committee meeting the representative from Argentina listed the laws and decrees adopted since 1983 for the benefit of women, summarized as follows:

(1) ratification of the Convention on the Elimination of all Forms of Discrimination against Women,

(2) adoption of the American Human Rights Convention, the International Covenant on Civil and Political Rights and its Optional Protocol, and other international instruments,

(3) law on joint parental authority,

(4) law on marriage and divorce,

(5) law on equal rights between children born in and out of wedlock,

(6) right to pension in case of cohabitation in *de facto* marriages,

(7) law on the elimination of discrimination in the trade unions,

(8) decree on family planning,

(9) decrees creating governmental organs in charge of the status of women, and

(10) decree on cancer-screening tests (UN General Assembly Official Records 1988:61).

The questioning period following the Argentina presentation gives an indication of how the monitoring system works at the United Nations. The members of the Committee on the Elimination of Discrimination against Women are experts in the various areas of rights that are covered in the Convention. Their task is to guide countries in the implementation of the treaty directives. Clarification was sought by some of the experts on issues raised in Argentina's report. In particular, the experts requested statistics on wage differentials between men and women, and pointed out the difference between equal pay for equal work and equal pay for work of equal value (which is the language of the treaty). Criteria have to be established to allow comparison of female-dominated with male-dominated jobs to get a gender-neutral job evaluation. This could allow the upgrading of female-dominated jobs, and the wage gap could thus be eliminated.

Other questions on which clarification was sought concerned sexual harassment at work, minimum wages, plans to introduce paternity leave, and whether the income tax system discouraged women from outside employment. Argentina was commended on its new family law, and additional information was requested on the revised grounds for divorce. The Argentine delegate gave comprehensive replies in clarification of the topics queried.

SWEDEN

In the international thrust toward the improvement of the status of women, Sweden can be seen as the paragon since its legislation on behalf of women's equality is the most advanced in the world. The new structures that have been put in place go beyond giving women rights equal to men's. The new laws aim at redefining what it means to be a man or a woman. Sweden has backed new social arrangements that affect gender-linked behavior, since it was reasoned that to provide for women's equality only in the political and economic arenas, given the inequality of traditional arrangements in the private sphere, would put an unfair burden on women resulting in inequality of outcome. Therefore, men's roles had to change as well.

Sweden was not always what some would call a feminist country. In the nineteenth century, Sweden, along with most other countries, was a patriarchal society that afforded few legitimate opportunities for women to compete with men. It was not until 1920 that the law that committed women to the guardianship of their husbands was changed. The interest in the status of women developed in the larger context of the ideology of the social welfare orientation that emerged in the 1930s (Davidson and Gordon 1979). The disruptions that were caused as Sweden was transformed from an agricultural country to an industrial one influenced the establishment of the Social Democratic Party, which ushered in the welfare state. A basic belief of the party was that social ills could be cured and that society could be transformed through legislation and welfare measures. Gender equality has been an integral part of the party platform, and many types of laws prohibiting discrimination have been enacted. Since Sweden was not only a culturally, religiously, and racially homogeneous society but a prosperous one as well, there were profits to support social welfare legislation. These laws were aimed at gender parity and reduction of the gap between the affluent and the poor. An ideological underpinning was the Swedish belief in reason as a force that can prevail in righting the wrongs of a troubled world (Childs 1980). The egalitarian socialist philosophy of the government has been responsible for the high status that women enjoy in Sweden.

Swedish policy is centered on the notion that each individual can achieve economic independence through gainful employment. Economic prosperity has led to a demand for labor, and thus women have become a necessary and integral part of the labor force. Special efforts were made to improve conditions for women in the labor market. Part of the strategy concerned encouraging men to take a more active part in caring for the home and children, since the new patterns of living presuppose changes in the roles of both sexes. In 1983 the government appointed a Working Group to study the male role. An important element of the group's 1985 report concerned the need to encourage more men to utilize their parental benefits to a greater extent to improve their contacts with and sense of responsibility for home and family. Various projects were launched to research men's attitudes and their expectations of parenthood in an effort to encourage them to use parental benefits (FSS 1987).

After passing many measures mandating equality in various spheres of endeavor, Sweden did not rest on its laurels but rather has implemented a policy of constant surveillance to ensure that equality will be the norm within certain time periods. In 1988 the Swedish Parliament passed the Government Bill on Equality Policy to the Mid-Nineties. A large amount of money was set aside, and concrete goals were specified. In this bill the four goals for equality policy were defined as:

1. Women and men are to have the same rights, obligations, and opportunities in all the main fields of life;

2. Every individual should have a job paying sufficiently to enable her or him to earn a living;

3. Men and women should share responsibility for their children and the work of the home; and

4. Both sexes should to the same extent devote themselves to political, trade union, and other matters of common interest both at work and in the community. (Ministry of Labour 1988:4)

The Family

Swedish families have a very low fertility rate. Some families choose not to have children at all. This is of concern to the government, and a policy was adopted of granting higher child-support payments for each subsequent child after the first two.

As a social norm, the value of *familism* (the importance of identification, loyalty, and mutual assistance among family members) appears to be weak and declining. Replacing familism is the value of social equality and individual rights, and family law reflects this by focusing not on the family unit but on the individual and the individual's rights (Popenoe 1988).

In Sweden about 80 percent of all cohabiting couples are married (FSS 1987). Before women and men in the community could participate in work life on equal terms, there had to be changes in the traditional family arrangements. Reforms within the social welfare system have aimed toward giving both men and women the opportunity to combine work and family responsibility. The parental insurance scheme, a predominant element in the welfare state, pays benefits to parents in connection with bearing and rearing children. In 1974 maternity leave became paternity leave as well. Both parents receive benefits upon the birth of a child, since the care of children is viewed as the responsibility of both. The scheme presently allows nine months parental leave at 90 percent compensation and a further fixed daily rate for the next three months. A new Marriage Code, passed by the Swedish Parliament in 1987, strengthens government policy. Effective 1988, the Plan of Action for Equality extended the covered period to eighteen months at approximately 90 percent of income (the equivalent of a sick benefit). The leave of absence can be taken by either parent, or both can divide the time between them. In addition, all fathers are entitled to a ten-day leave of absence with parental benefits when a child is born. Furthermore, either parent can take up to sixty days per year to care for a sick child.

Most fathers do take advantage of the sick-child benefit, while only 20 percent take paternity leave. Since the Swedish government feels it is important that fathers have early and close contact with their children, as previously mentioned, the government-appointed Working Party on the Male Role has stressed the importance of stimulating more men to take parental leave. To that end, the recommended measures concern not only more intensive dissemination of information to parents to encourage more even sharing of parental leave, but also research into the process of early male-role formation in order to learn more about male attitudes. The rationale of the Working Party was stated by its chairman, Stig Ahs:

The point could perhaps be put by saying that we men are the prisoners of a system for which we ourselves are primarily responsible—a system that is not only detrimental to us as men but also postulates a role for women that renders any equality between the sexes impossible. Our male role makes us both oppressors and oppressed. (Ahs 1986:2)

Some of the measures in force in Sweden today include the following:

Day-Care Facilities

Most women work, and in 1985 only 10 percent of women between the ages of twenty and sixty-four were full-time housewives. When both parents are gainfully employed, good child-care amenities are a necessity. Since the 1970s such facilities have been expanding in Sweden. In 1986, 47 percent of all preschool children were cared for in various types of public child-care facilities. All children have the entitlement of such facilities from age one and a half to six years (FSS 1987).

Family Planning

Premarital sex has long been an accepted practice for an engaged couple, and brides have often been pregnant. Marriage did not always follow, however, and the illegitimacy rate was high compared to the rest of Europe from the 1800s to the 1930s. By the early 1900s the illegitimacy rate in Sweden included every seventh child (Popenoe 1988).

Family planning is based on the principle of choice in the spacing of children. The emphasis is on prevention of conception by birth control. Contraceptive information is disseminated widely in Sweden. Prenatal care is free, and prospective fathers are encouraged to attend classes on child birth along with the women. In 1975 restrictions concerning abortions were abolished. The average birth rate in Sweden is 1.6 children. Only 10 percent of all women remain childless in spite of the fact that eight out of ten women are gainfully employed outside the home (Swedish Act on Equality: 1985).

Teenage Pregnancy

Because of Sweden's aggressive sex education program, the teenage fertility rate is half that of the United States. Human sexual anatomy instruction has been compulsory in all schools since 1956. Since 1977 the information provided has come under the heading "Education in Life Together," because the stress is not only on physical sex but also on the social and emotional aspects of intimacy. Many junior high and high schools are connected with gynecological clinics that youngsters can consult free of charge. The trained personnel at the clinics have the right to prescribe contraceptive pills to girls and condoms to boys, at no cost. They can be consulted also when young people experience personal concerns such as relationship problems, self-doubts about sexuality, and pressures toward conformity.

Swedish television also directs informative programs about sex and life together to young people. Altogether, there is a massive and multifaceted campaign to inform and influence teenagers in what is called *family-planning matters* (Trost 1985). All this contributes to a female's sense of control over her own body.

Divorce

In the early 1970s Sweden instituted a policy that incorporated the concept of no fault and made divorce quicker and easier. It has been estimated that about 70 percent of divorce actions are initiated by women (Trost 1985). The divorce law is based on what is best for the child. Couples are entitled to divorce if both agree to it. Otherwise, there has to be a six-month deliberation period. Joint custody of children is automatic. The parent who does not live with the child, whether the mother or the father, is required to pay maintenance in proportion to financial status. The great majority of children under eighteen years of age (81 percent) live with both parents.

Children born out of wedlock are in most legal respects placed on a par with children born to married couples. Since the early 1980s, if no name is reported at the time of birth, the child automatically assumes the mother's name (Popenoe 1988).

Cohabitation

Unmarried cohabitation is becoming increasingly common. In many respects the cohabitees are regarded socially as forming a family unit. The tax laws do not discriminate between married or unmarried cohabiting couples. Recently, the Swedish Parliament addressed some of the problems concerning the dissolution of such unions. The 1987 Marriage Code contains legislation concerning the property of unmarried cohabiting couples and how it should be shared upon separation. If property is not shared, a corresponding sum of money has to be paid by one cohabitee to the other (Sweden, Ministry of Justice 1988). There have also been modifications in the code of succession and inheritance to provide rights to cohabitees (FSS 1987).

Women and Employment

The Tax Reform Law of 1971 eliminated joint income tax returns for married couples in favor of purely individual taxation. Husbands could no longer claim wives as dependents, and so had to pay the full rate. This tax reform was a turning point in the gender-equality issue as it discouraged women from being full-time housewives. As a result, today almost 85 percent of Swedish women with children under seven years of age are in the labor force (although a majority work only part-time) (Popenoe 1988).

The government is committed to breaking down traditional barriers between the sexes in the labor market, and has passed legislation to that end. Sweden has a population of 8.4 million, of which almost half (just over 4 million) are gainfully employed. Of these, almost one-half are women. Of all women, 82 percent are employed, while 90 percent of all men are employed (FSS 1987). Although women have the legal right to employment in all occupations, they are overrepresented in lower-paid sectors of the marketplace.

In spite of employment, women still have most of the responsibility for housework and child care. Therefore, 44 percent of the women work part time, compared with 6 percent of the men. This accounts for a great deal of the pay differential. As can be seen, several decades of formal laws defining men and women as equal have not completely nullified informal practices.

Women predominate (more than 60 percent) in 56 occupations while men predominate in 161. In the 1982–1983 fiscal year, funds were earmarked for a campaign called More Women in Industry. Programs were designed to encourage and train girls and women for nontraditional jobs. In 1985 more money was allocated by the government for wide-ranging action programs to strengthen the labor market position of women. The recommended policy measures concern not only work but also the fields of education, family, and politics (FSS 1987). This is a recognition that changes in one sector are insufficient if the enabling conditions are not present in other sectors of a woman's life.

The Equal Opportunities Act, which came into force in July 1980, forbids discrimination in the workplace on sexual grounds. It requires employers to work actively to effect equality. An Equal Opportunities Ombudsman ensures that the act is complied with and fair treatment is given to both men and women. The Swedish view of fairness is based on equality of outcome rather than equality of opportunity alone. Therefore a *positive special treatment*, as it is termed, is sanctioned by law. Women get preference for jobs where men have traditionally predominated, and vice versa. Section 6 of the Equal Opportunities Act reads:

Where the distribution between women and men at a place of work is generally uneven in a certain type of work or within a certain staff category, the employer shall make special efforts when recruiting new staff to attract applications from the underrepresented sex and seek to ensure that the proportion of employees of that sex is gradually increased. (JämO 1984:17)

A five-year Plan of Action for Equality, starting in the 1988–1989 fiscal year, sets higher goals than previous bills. It addresses the shortcomings still prevalent and seeks ways to remedy them. It states that equality ultimately depends on decisions taken by individuals, and therefore political endeavors must be designed to determine the framework within which individuals make their own decisions and then remove all barriers impeding equal opportunities (Equality Between Men and Women in Sweden 1988). This suggests that possibly the socialization process could act as a brake that keeps women from fully participating in society. In other words, cultural rather than legal constraints are preventing complete equality in Sweden, as is the case elsewhere in the world.

Entrepreneurs

In Sweden, a prosperous country, there is a great interest in individual enterprise. Manpower studies are carried out each year, and according to statistics in 1982, about one hundred thousand women were involved in running their own businesses. Women represented 30 percent of the total number of entrepreneurs. They are usually in industries that have the largest number of female employees—the catering and hotel business, personal and similar services, the retail trade, education, and health care (Brantingson 1983). These women are mostly in the twenty-five to forty-four age group, and the government sees this as an indication that they will remain active for at least another twenty years. According to one entrepreneur who is also a housewife, women are suited as managers and business leaders because of the skills acquired running a home, such as planning, organization, caring for others, household economy, conflict solving, and engaging family members in domestic activities (Stern 1983:31). The obvious and important skills that women acquire in managing their homes have seldom been publicly articulated or formally appreciated by social planners in the global community.

Women and Power

According to many analysts, Sweden is one of the most egalitarian societies in the Western world. The historical circumstances, such as a weak hold on the people by an organized religion and a type of agrarian economy that kept men away from home much of the time, were conducive to empowering women. Swedish society and relative female equality have been synonymous for a long time (Popenoe 1988). Swedish women have had a relatively easy progress in their mobilization efforts to achieve social status parity with men. The goal of the feminist movement became gender equalization—the sharing of all roles by women and men in both the occupational sector and public life. This has been largely achieved. Sweden has ratified the major UN treaties that concern the rights of women, and has been reporting to the appropriate agency on its progress in implementing the mandates of those treaties.

First Periodic Report to the United Nations, 1982

Sweden ratified the Convention on the Elimination of All forms of Discrimination against Women. In accordance with its terms, Sweden submitted its first periodic report to the Committee on the Elimination of Discrimination against Women (CEDAW) on December 15, 1982. In its report Sweden outlined its National Plan of Action for Equality in support of the program of action for the second half of the UN Decade for Women. The following are some of the highlights of the broad-based activities included in the report.

Sports

Sweden has a wide approach to gender equality and feels that changes must include measures affecting men also. Many avenues of approach have been explored. A survey of men was conducted with questionnaires and interviews to elucidate men's condition and ascertain their attitudes concerning equality. The feasibility of legislation against sexually discriminatory advertising was probed. A Committee on Equality between Men and Women was formed; one of its interests concerns equal sporting opportunities. The sports movement is one of the largest mass movements in Sweden.

Female Prisoners

There has been a discrepancy in the imprisonment of women and men. There was only one penal institution for women in the whole country. Therefore, more local prisons that can admit women are being built. Local prisons allow for the application of the *proximity principle* so that women can have better opportunities for contact with next of kin and local welfare authorities.

Health

The National Board of Health and Welfare has embarked on an education campaign directed toward parents. One topic that is of concern for maternal health is alcoholism or drug abuse during pregnancy. Health-care personnel are being trained to help.

Pornography

Amendments to the Public Order Statute in 1982 prohibit public performances of a pornographic nature. The prohibition carries penal sanctions. Accordingly, the prostitution that is facilitated by sex club activities is expected to diminish. Reports of the National Board of Health and Welfare show that intimidation, sexual oppression, and contempt and hostility toward the opposite sex are common among alcoholics and drug abusers. Personnel are being better equipped to handle such problems.

Education

Sweden realizes the importance of education for future equality of opportunity. Amendments to the Education Act and the Education Ordinance

underline the duty of those in authoritative positions to promote equal opportunities for males and females in the schools so that the result will be
equal responsibilities in family and society and genuine choice of occupation
in the family, the labor force, and public life.

Educational courses must not be allowed to incur a heavy sexual bias. To
that end, child-care and home economics courses are compulsory for both
sexes, and the science/technology courses are also mandatory for both sexes.
All senior-level pupils, regardless of sex, are to gain some experience in each
of three occupational sectors: (1) technology and manufacturing; (2) trade,
communication, services, agriculture, and forestry; and (3) clerical and administrative work, health care, and education. Both boys and girls are expected to acquire knowledge and skills that were formerly reserved mainly
for one sex. This includes typing and handicrafts. Throughout elementary
school, boys and girls are to share sports lessons; there are no provisions for
separate sports groups.

During the school year students are subject to an information drive drawing attention to the negative effects of sexually biased course choices on
their later employment prospects. Girls are encouraged to broaden their
range of educational choices to include vocational/technical courses. The
Swedish National Board of Universities and Colleges is conducting a project
to coordinate various measures promoting equal opportunities in research
and research training in higher education. Documentation is being compiled
so that further measures can be taken to extend activities to promote equality.

Adult education is available for those whose previous education has been
inadequate. Immigrant women especially are encouraged to attend. Municipal authorities have set up child-care facilities, and a special hourly benefit
for students is provided as incentive for women to attend classes. Initially
the immigrant women are mainly given literacy training, which can then be
followed by vocational training.

Work Force

Since 1980 Sweden has had a policy of affirmative action in connection
with hiring, promotion, and training in order to promote sexual equality in
the work force. The Equal Opportunities Act of 1980 prohibits discrimination
on the grounds of sex, and encourages the active promotion of equality in
the private and public sectors. An equal opportunities ombudsman and an
Equal Opportunities Commission were appointed to ensure compliance with
the act. As a result, many instances of discrimination have been reported,
and solutions have been reached.

Other legislation has aimed at specific areas of employment. For instance,
in 1981 a government bill was passed eliminating sexual bias in the recruitment of officers for the armed forces. A Labor Market Ordinance provides
guidelines to firms and labor market training to help those who are disad-
vantaged in the labor market. Equal Opportunities training grants are avail-

able to introduce job applicants to nontraditional vocational courses. This has proved a good way to introduce women to training in engineering, for example.

Since 1982 a new rule has been in force recognizing that a parent should be able to refrain from gainful employment to raise children for a time without losing benefits. A parent caring for a child under three years of age for the greater part of a calendar year can be credited for that period as gainfully employed under supplementary pension insurance. A year of this kind is equated with work years for which the person concerned earns pension credits.

Choice of Surnames

A new Names Act, coming into force in 1983, reflects the contemporary attitudes between the sexes. The couple can agree to share either the husband's or the wife's surname, or can opt to retain separate surnames. Their children can bear either name or a hyphenated compound, or a parent's name ending with "son" or "dotter" (son or daughter); however, all siblings must share the same surname.

Second Periodic Report to the United Nations, 1987

The fulfillment of its commitment to the Nairobi Forward-Looking Strategies is a priority in Sweden. In its second periodic report to CEDAW (March 26, 1987), Sweden showed that considerable progress has been made, especially in the labor market. The report quoted specific subparagraphs of the articles of the Convention on the Elimination of All Forms of Discrimination against Women, and then explained the progress Sweden had made in those areas. Due to the length of the report and the limitations of space, only topics dealing with violence against women will be highlighted here.

Sexual Harassment

There is in Sweden an increasing awareness of the problem of sexual harassment because the equal opportunities ombudsman has been receiving many reports of it. Procedures have been started to investigate this important and difficult question. The Equal Opportunities Act is not directly applicable to sexual harassment in Sweden. However, the Swedish Work Environment Act stipulates that the working environment must be physically and psychologically sufficient. Sexual harassment is being approached in the same manner as other work-environment problems. An investigation is being undertaken of the industrial sectors, where men tend to predominate, and the results will be included in the next periodic report to the Committee on the Elimination of Discrimination against Women (CEDAW).

Battering

Battering is defined as maltreatment of a woman that occurs indoors and in which the woman is known to the offender. Statistics show that over

10,000 cases of battering are reported to the police every year in Sweden, although it is believed that the incidence is probably even greater since records by the helping organizations are not always kept. Voluntary women's reception centers exist in about a hundred Swedish towns, and offer support and protection. These centers receive government grants. The social welfare service at the municipal level offers financial assistance, housing, and baby-sitters. More personnel are being trained to assist maltreated women.

Rape

After intense debate in Parliament and in the press, and after extensive preparatory work, new provisions concerning rape came into force in 1984. A main point in the new provisions of the Penal Code reflects the basic view that court decisions are not to be influenced by the raped woman's way of life, morals, or behavior prior to an assault. The offense covers not only sexual intercourse but intercourse comparable thereto, and not only violence but the threat of violence involving imminent danger. Penal sanctions in the form of prison sentences are specified. A section of the Penal Code inflicts culpability on a person who induces another person to have sexual inter-course by gross abuse of his or her dependent position. This could be in-terpreted to include marital rape.

In 1984 there were 955 cases of rape reported to the police. This is not considered a large amount, although the figure shows an 8 percent increase over the preceding year. It is felt that this may merely reflect a growing readiness to report the offense. A parliamentary committee appointed by the government has proposed that a victim of sexual offenses should be entitled to a personal counsel to help plead the complaint. Plaintiffs need such support during court interrogations and in the matter of damages.

The CEDAW considered Sweden's second periodic report at meetings held on March 1 and 2, 1988. At this time the Swedish delegate was asked to clarify certain points, and the following facts were put forth to show Sweden's progress. Concerning women and power, with the recent appoint-ment of a female minister of justice, the Swedish Cabinet was composed of six women and fifteen men. The target for women's representation in all government decision-making bodies was 30 percent, which would represent a 14 percent increase over the current level. Women represented 31 percent of Parliament. In addition, 23 percent of the judges, 30 percent of the lawyers in the legal aid offices, and 45 percent of the legal trainees were women. Larger numbers of women vote than men. The delegate further explained, concerning the equal opportunities policy, that Sweden had a five-year plan of action concerning women in the economy, labor market, education, and family, and concerning representation in government. In 1987, 90 percent of women aged twenty-five to fifty-five years were in the labor force, com-pared to 93 percent of men (CEDAW 1988).

At the meeting of the committee, the Swedish representative indicated that while much progress had been made, more remained to be done in some areas. For instance, in the labor force a wage gap persisted because of the segregated labor market wherein some sectors still had unequal proportions of men and women. In all, 38 professions were mostly occupied by women and 134 mostly by men. Technical careers such as engineering had a low number of women. Teaching accounted for 88 percent of the active female population; however, only 5 percent of the professors were women. One of the problems with comparing work statistics of men and women is that some women work part-time. However, a person working seventeen hours a week had the same rights as a full-time worker. The representative explained that the availability of child-care facilities was for all in the near future, whereas at that time only 80 percent of preschool children currently had access. In the home there was still an uneven sharing of responsibility for unremunerated housework.

The goal of equal pay for equal work had almost been achieved, but the concept of equal pay for work of equal value had not been addressed. Comparable worth is seen as a new instrument for equality, and is still under discussion in Sweden.

At the end of the CEDAW meeting, the delegates from other countries complimented Sweden's achievements, which they felt could become a model for many countries. The reader should keep in mind when considering other countries that they do not all have the same circumstances. It must be noted that although the example of Sweden in its concerted efforts at gender equality is exemplary, Sweden is an advanced industrial nation with jobs available for anyone willing to work. Unemployment is a very low 1.9 percent. In many Third World countries, paying jobs outside the home for women are unavailable.

EGYPT

The Islamic religion is one of the most widespread belief systems in the world today. Large numbers of Muslims can be found in all the Arab countries of the Middle East, in North Africa, and in most countries of Asia. The religion is followed by about one-fifth of the total global population. One must view the historically lower status of women in Egypt from the perspective of the belief system.

Islam was founded around the year 610 A.D. in Mecca, which is now the capital of Saudi Arabia. It spread rapidly through the military conquests of its leader, Mohammed, who was hailed as its prophet. For adherents the religion provides not only a belief system and structure but also rules of behavior for even mundane daily activities. The prescribed rituals and code of ethics are set forth in the *Quran* (also spelled *Koran*). Since Muslims believe it to be the literal word of God, they strive to adhere to its specific injunctions. The Prophet Mohammed's teachings are seen as revelations from God, and they are recorded in the collection of traditions called the *Hadith*. The Quran and the Hadith provide the common bond for worshipers and are the basis of the Islamic law called the *Shariah* (Renzetti and Curran 1989).

The three sources of religious lore, the Quran, the Hadith, and the Shariah, form the framework that governs every aspect of Muslims' daily lives. In a discussion of law it is important to realize that Islamic law is felt by many to supercede civic law, which is why some practices continue even though they have been outlawed by the State. The Islamic law is intended to apply at all times and to all situations, although in practice not all countries adopt the legal formulations in their pristine form (Haddad and Lummis 1987).

About 80 percent of the verses in the Quran relate to what is considered proper behavior between men and women. Islamic leaders (who are all men) maintain that men and women have equal status that derives from the complementarity of their roles, and they apparently do not see a contradiction when they say that different roles of men and women bring different rights and responsibilities (Renzetti and Curran 1989). Although Islamic men deny this, women do seem to hold an inferior position in the religion. The simple explanation in the Quran is: "Men are in charge of women because God has made one to excel over the other" (Haddad 1985:294). There can be no equivocation with divinely ordained pronouncements.

The Veil

Women are enjoined in the Quran to dress modestly (S.24:30–31), and this has come to be understood in most parts of the Islamic world as requiring that, when outdoors, women must be completely covered except for eyes and hands. Such curtailment of freedom for women is deemed necessary so that they cannot engender sexual thoughts in men (Haddad and Lummis 1987). This is one of the major themes in the Quran. The premise is that the powers of temptation and seduction of women are a danger and a source of destruction, and thus men must be protected from these seductive powers. To ensure the protection of men from alluring women, the latter must be confined to the home. If a woman must go out, "she must cover her body completely and not expose her attractions or anything that is liable to seduce a man. Her ornaments should be hidden and her external genital organs preserved intact" (El Saadawi 1982:144–145). Although an outsider may well wonder at the implied lack of self-control of Muslim men, it is the women who must be accountable for their alleged irresistible sexual allure and who must pay the price of curtailed freedom. The black, foot-length veils prescribed for women in the streets of Egypt make them appear to be moving shadows, an unexaggerated analogy, as women seem symbolically to be the shadows of men.

Strict adherence to the veiling norm varies according to country and individuals. Some Muslims believe that strict adherence to praxis is essential, while others have adopted a more flexible interpretation of the religious writings. However, on the global scene there are signs of a return to fundamentalism and a literal interpretation of the Quran in matters concerning behavior and the seclusion of women. For women who had previously been freer; it has meant adopting the veil in public for the first time.

The Cult of Virginity

The cult of virginity takes an extreme form in some countries; among them is Egypt. A woman's virginity has to be vouched for on the wedding night. This is especially true among the ultraconservative Muslims in rural areas. While family and friends wait outside the nuptual chamber, the groom has to consummate the relationship. He has to produce a bloodied cloth resulting from the penetration of the bride's hymen to prove that it was her first intercourse.

The hymen is at the entrance of the vagina, and is a vulnerable, fragile, and thin membrane that tears easily during exercise; even if it remains intact, it is often elastic enough that there is no bleeding on the wedding night. When El Saadawi summarized data of young women from Baghdad's Institute of Forensic Medicine over a thirty-year period, she found that only 41.3 percent had so-called normal hymens that might have bled noticeably at the first intercourse (El Saadawi 1982). Since many women no longer have a naturally intact hymen by the age of puberty, the ritual becomes a charade that is indulged in to continue the tradition of male prowess and conquest.

In extreme cases, if the male decides that the new wife was not a virgin, he may kill her with impugnity to defend his honor. Public sympathy sides with men who "wipe out the shame in blood" and save the family honor; as a result, if they are arrested at all, the sentence is minimal and the men are treated royally in prison (Minai 1981). It is therefore not surprising that some women have a surgical procedure performed wherein a small piece of skin is sewn at the base of the vagina. This plastic surgery has been called the hypocritical operation which only some affluent women can afford. The poor often insert a pouch of chicken blood in the vagina to ensure the desired result (Minai 1981). Women, who are denied the right to their own sexuality, seem to go to great lengths so that the men can glory in their masculine mystique.

Genital Mutilation

An extreme manifestation of the cult of virginity has been, and still is, practiced in some parts of Egypt. Aside from the psychological degradation due to the inescapable conclusion that a woman's merit depends on the condition of her hymen, there are physical abuses women must endure concerning sex. Genital mutilation of women is one such practice, although the custom is not suggested in the Quran. The practice has been euphemistically referred to as female circumcision, but it is often an actual amputation. When the girl is very young a clitoridectomy is performed "to abort sexual awakening of a young girl to assure her chastity until marriage and her fidelity thereafter" (Minai 1981:96). Records show that the operation has been practiced since the time of the pharaohs. Muhammed disapproved of it but apparently could not eradicate it. The operation varies from removing the tip of the female clitoris to radical clitoridectomy, which is the excision of the entire clitoris and labia minora. At times infibulation is practiced whereby, the labia majora are sewn together after the radical clitoridectomy has been performed. In the latter case, the area is cut open again to allow intercourse when the girl gets married. For the mutilated female there can be many medical complications such as infections, urinary retention, obstetric complications, and fetal abnormality, to mention a few (El Saadawi 1982, Minai 1981). It also renders a woman nonorgasmic for life. In spite of such problems, infibulation is still practiced in the hinterlands of Egypt today, although the laws forbid it.

Modern Fundamentalist Influences

The new fundamentalism emerging in some parts of the world is a complex movement, an aspect of which concerns women. In Egypt a countervailing force to the laws emancipating women is the new movement calling for a return to so-called pure Islam. For example, women have started using the veil, in spite of their education and past life-style. Although for Westerners veiling is a symbol of female degradation, some Muslim women have voluntarily returned to it. The Egyptian career woman, who twenty years ago was well-dressed and chic, today sometimes chooses a modest Islamic attire, which involves wearing a scarf to cover the hair and a loose-fitting, long-sleeved, long-skirted dress (Hoffman-Ladd 1987). The veil has become symbolic of a woman's determination to lead an integrated Islamic life-style, since some feel that the embrace of Western modernity simply exchanged one form of exploitation for another. Use of the veil today broadcasts a woman's respectability and helps her avoid incidents of harassment that males direct at women in Western clothing, who are often suspected of being susceptible to sexual immorality. The notion is that public display of the body symbolizes degradation of women; hence, modesty requires her segregation from the world of men and the male-dominated public sphere.

From the male viewpoint, the major argument for strict female seclusion is that when women leave their natural place (the home) for work or school, they lose their femininity and also neglect the role God created them for—to serve their husbands and children. Such reasoning is specious since it ignores the fact that at least 80 percent of Egyptian women are peasants who never wear the veil and who do leave their homes every day to work in the fields or carry loads of dung or pails of water on their heads (El Saadawi 1982). Men's concern with female femininity seems, therefore, to be an urban phenomenon and an exploitative class position.

Some female students at the University of Cairo demanded segregated classes (Minai 1981). Cairo University is a seat of the struggle to rid the Quran and Hadith of the influence of interpretations by past Western orientalists who had tried to make them compatible with Western thought. The aim is the achievement of a modern national identity for Muslims based on a return to the pure and timeless precepts of Islamic belief and law. This is deemed necessary by some for Islamic survival. Cairo University is thus a fertile field for conservative religious activism (Reid 1987). Some women feel that they are not giving up their freedom but rather are redefining it. They want to avoid commercialized Western culture since they feel it makes sex objects of women's bodies. Some young Islamic women want to be more in touch with their cultural heritage.

When the late President Anwar Sadat liberalized marriage and divorce laws, he received protests from young women. Through militant protests in the streets, Egyptian women helped block the passage of liberal divorce laws for five years (Minai 1981:237). This is startling to the outsider because for the male divorce was always quite liberal: Islamic law gave them access to the *repudiation* formula. That is, under Islamic law, men are allowed to divorce their wives by merely repeating the words "I repudiate thee" three times in succession in front of witnesses.

Apparently ethnocentrism is so strong in Egypt, and accurate knowledge of the situation in developed countries is so weak, that for some women their own oppression is preferable to perceived Western exploitation of women's bodies to sell products. It is possible that women abroad have been made scapegoats in order to promote an ideology of anticolonialism and new religious nationalism. The equal education of women in the future may be contingent on the resolution of opposing ideologies concerning a conservative or liberal interpretation of Islamic law.

Women and Family

While the unifying force that confers a common identity on all Muslims is religion, for the individual the basic unit is the extended family network. For women it means confinement within the family's realm and a very strict limitation on the types of interaction possible between the sexes outside the family. A wife has to adapt to a type of sexual apartheid. The restrictions often preclude women from consulting male doctors for illnesses and, more important for their development, from entering the paid labor force. The marriage and divorce laws are mainly drawn from Islamic law, which accords a women some rights, such as keeping her name after marriage and the ability of disposing of her own money without requiring permission from her husband. However, the husband has complete control of his wife's destiny.

The Egyptian marriage law was passed in 1929, and many consider it archaic, as it allows the continuation of the oppression and exploitation of women. Men still have the privilege of divorcing at will, and also of having several wives. The tradition is a legal remnant of feudalism and the patriarchal system whereby the "woman becomes like a piece of land owned by the man, who is permitted to do as he wishes, to exploit her, to beat her, to sell her at any time via divorce, or to buy over her head, a second, third, or fourth wife" (El Saadawi 1982:202). The frequent wars and battles between tribes in the Middle Ages took a heavy toll on men's lives and led to an extreme imbalance in the sex ratio. The victors brought back women as the spoils of war. They became wives when suitable, or else were made concubines or slaves. The superfluity of women helped devalue their status. The Quran permits polygyny (plural wives for men), and the only restriction is the injunction that each wife must be treated perfectly equally. It has been suggested that this is not possible in reality since there is often a preference for a new wife over the preceding ones. The judgment of fairness is left entirely to the husband. Polygyny has long been the custom, and a 1979 law (Decree Law 44) reaffirms it. It states that a wife's duty is to obey her husband or else be in a state of "infringement." Article 345 forces her to submit to her husband's demands. For instance, if he beats her and she leaves him, he has a legal right to force her return (Morgan 1984). A wife's major satisfaction is bearing a son for her husband. It is ironic that in the villages a married woman sometimes encourages her husband to seek another wife in order to keep him happy, assuage the degree of cruelty toward her (wife beating is not rare), and ensure that he will have a son if she has borne only girls (El Saadawi 1982).

Concerning divorce, it is extremely easy for the husband, as stated earlier. Much depends on male benevolence, as by law a husband is permitted a good deal of irresponsibility with wives and children, even though he legally owns them. He need not provide for them at all upon divorce. If the father dies, his daughters have the right to inherit only one-half of what the sons get of the estate (Morgan 1984).

Egypt has an extremely high birth rate, and in 1975–1980 the average rate was thirty-eight per thousand live births in the population. By comparison, the rate in the United States in 1982 was sixteen per thousand, and in Sweden in 1977–1978 it was eleven per thousand. The infant mortality rate is high as well, and in the period 1975–1980 it was eighty-five per thousand for females and ninety-five per thousand for males (Morgan 1984). Family planning was made a government priority in 1962 by the National Charter. The Ministry of Public Health and the Ministry of Social Affairs operate family-planning centers (in 1977 there were 3,030 such centers). In 1970–1980 only 20 percent of married women aged fifteen through forty-nine used contraception. Abortion has been outlawed, and punishment has been specified for illegal abortions by the 1937 Penal Code (Articles 260, 261, 262, and 263), except in cases to save a woman's life or if it has been proven that the fetus will be deformed. In actual practice, it has been estimated that in 1980 one out of four pregnancies ended in illegal abortions performed under the usual unsanitary and dangerous conditions for such procedures (Morgan 1984).

Women and Employment

The following information is from a report presented at the United Nations at the 1987 meeting of the Convention on the Elimination of Discrimination against Women (CEDAW) (Egypt Report 1987). The Egyptian government reports that, in varying degrees, women are entering many fields of work, including the judiciary. They have filled positions in juvenile courts and the administrative prosecutor's office. At the time of the report, the first group of women law graduates had enrolled at the Police Academy and would soon become police officers. Female law graduates were already employed in such police work as the morals bureau and juvenile care. Most working women in government service (80 percent) are employed in the health and educational services, including a high percentage in scientific research. In 1983–1984 they were 46.9 percent of all teachers in primary education, 44 percent of the teachers in teacher training institutes, and 40.3 percent of the teaching staff in general secondary education.

The 1984 research undertaken by Egypt in collaboration with the United Nations Educational, Scientific, and Cultural Organization (UNESCO) showed that women were 32 percent of the personnel engaged in scientific and technological activities. The breakdown was as follows: women constituted 29.1 percent of the scientists, 32.2 percent of the technical staff, and 35 percent of the supporting personnel. In these activities, 20.48 percent of all individuals with a Ph.D. were women. The field of pharmacy attracts women, and their numbers in this field have been increasing rapidly. In 1984, 73.2 percent of pharmacists were women.

Recent changes in the structure and membership of the trade unions added about 100,000 female workers to the movement. Voting for worker's representatives on company boards resulted in twenty-two women obtaining seats and six women being admitted to the executive committees of the general trade unions. The number of Egyptian women in industry has been increasing in the past ten years; they work in such industries as dyeing plants and fertilizer and chemical companies. Women share the task of advancing industrial effort, and have "proved their excellence and capability in mastering various kinds of work in this domain, a fact which is highly appreciated at the supervisory levels of most factories in which women are employed" (Egypt Report 1987:19).

In 1979 the Labor Law was amended to the benefit of women. Women have the right to equal remuneration and benefits from all jobs on an equal footing with men. However, they are prohibited from certain jobs. This was explained as being "for reasons of health, or morals, or because the work is too hard" (Egypt Report 1987:5). Also, the law stipulates that women may not be employed at night, except in certain situations. The exceptions are for work in hospitals, medical centers, tourist industry, and airports, and in hotels, restaurants, and cafeterias that are under the supervision of the Ministry of Tourism.

This prohibition against certain occupations is in stark contrast to the situation of women in the Egyptian countryside, where rural women have always worked alongside men in the fields. It has always been felt that rural prosperity could only be achieved through the common effort of men and women, and that "it would be unacceptable for half of the available human resources to remain idle while the other half bore the entire burden of the overall development effort" (p. 19). Therefore, rural women have proved invalid any claim that a woman's feminine nature makes her unable to undertake strenuous work.

Women and Power

First Periodic Report to the United Nations, 1982

The UN Convention on the Elimination of All Forms of Discrimination against Women was signed in 1980 and ratified by the Egyptian Parliament on September 11, 1982. In conformity with its mandates, the Egyptian government sent its initial report to the Commission on the Elimination of Discrimination against Women (CEDAW) in 1983. It stated that Article 11 of the Egyptian Constitution guarantees harmony between women's family duties and their equality with men in political, economic, social, and cultural fields of life without prejudice to the prescriptions of Islamic religious law. Concerning equality in political life, the Law 114 (1983) amends previous laws and states that "all lists in 31 constituencies must include one female member in addition to the male members assigned to it" (Egypt Report 1983:2). Women have thus been able to accede to the higher positions in the government.

Egypt has a reservation concerning Article 16 of the UN convention which concerns marital equality between men and women. In order to achieve a fair and just balance, the rights guaranteed by Islamic law must be observed. The reservation is explained thusly:

This is made in consideration of the sacred character of marital relations in Egypt which is derived from firmly established religious tenets that cannot be violated, because it is considered that a complementarity between rights and duties which achieves real equality between the spouses is one of the most important foundations for marital relations, rather than the manifestations of formal equality which do not give the wife any useful interest to be obtained from the husband so much as they burden her with restrictions. This is so because the Islamic religious law obligates the husband to fully support his wife from his own money. (Egypt Report 1983:3)

Second Periodic Report to the United Nations, 1987

A second periodic report was submitted by Egypt in 1987. It gave facts and figures concerning constitutional and administrative measures taken relevant to the provisions of the Convention on the Elimination of All Forms of Discrimination against Women (Egypt Report 1987). Some of the facts covered in the report follow.

Of the thirty-one government ministers, two are women—the minister of social affairs and the minister of social insurance. The minister of social affairs heads the newly established National Commission for Women in Egypt, which is concerned with formulating policy and enforcing treaty recommendations concerning women, subject to the conditions of Egyptian society. Projects have been set up to assist women workers to fulfill their multiple roles as mothers, housewives, and workers participating with men in the development of Egyptian society. There are seventy-one family guidance and counselling offices that are concerned with family problems, thus preserving family cohesion and stability and preventing divorce and family breakup. The ministry has set up projects to train women in certain productive skills in order to increase family income. Raw materials are provided, and help in marketing the productions is provided. The number of child-care nurseries has increased to 2,341, of which 176 are for girls. In addition, the ministry supports 651 family-planning centers to assist women in birth control, and twenty-three institutions to care for girls exposed to delinquency.

In response to Article 5 of the convention, which calls for the elimination of the notions of the inferiority or superiority of either sex, the National Commission for Women has alerted the mass media that the use of any expression that would represent women as inferior is forbidden.

Regarding Article 10 of the convention, the Egyptian constitution stipulates the right of both sexes to education, which is free at all levels of state schools. In spite of this, at the primary-school level there is a lower female student enrollment than the male enrollment. In 1983–1984, girls were only 42.1 percent of total enrollment. This is mostly because of the low enrollment of girls in rural areas. Both sexes receive identical education. Pupils are free to choose between agricultural education and home economics. The latter course of study includes needlework, home management, child rearing, and general hygiene.

Egypt encourages young women to enroll in technical secondary schools, of which there are three types—industrial, commercial, and agricultural. In 1983–1984, females were 10.5 percent of the total enrollment at the industrial schools and 57.2 percent of enrollment at the commercial schools. According to the report, the higher enrollment at commercial schools provided "an indication that this type of education is more appropriate to women" (Egypt Report 1987:13). An agricultural technical school report in 1983–1984 showed that 14.8 percent of those enrolled were female. This report indicated that women have been successful in this area, particularly in "those subjects that are more appropriate to their nature, such as food processing, poultry raising, dairy work, and floriculture" (1987:14).

At the level of higher education, forty-seven thousand females graduate annually. In 1982–1983, 33.8 percent of students enrolled for master's and doctoral degrees were women. Their major fields of endeavor at the university level were home economics, language, tourism, mass media, arts, economics, and political science. Concerning equal opportunity:

the only criteria for acceptance at a university are the overall grades obtained by the student in the General Secondary Certificate examination and the student's choice of enrollment in a particular faculty, without any distinction on the basis of sex. (Egypt Report 1987:16)

For the academic year 1983–1984, female enrollment in theoretical colleges was 37 percent of the total, and in practical colleges was 28 percent.

Women have an important role in health care. In 1984, female doctors were 30.8 percent of all doctors registered by the Ministry of Health. Most choose specializations in pediatrics, gynecology, and internal medicine, and rarely surgery, osteology, or urology. Concerning dentistry, of the yearly graduates from dental schools, 55 percent are women.

The official census of 1976, the latest taken by Egypt, showed the illiteracy rate for women was 70 percent while for men it was 43 percent. The problem of illiteracy is being addressed aggressively. The efforts go beyond reading and writing to "the eradication of functional illiteracy through effective adult education curricula closely related to the real educational needs of women and related to the performance of her important functions as a mother, housewife, citizen and worker" (Egypt Report 1987:18). Future plans for Egypt include compulsory education for all girls and boys, expansion of technical education, and emphasis on the importance of higher studies. The policy will be to encourage and reward persons who undertake research that can contribute to solving economic, social, health, and population problems.

Women have recently acquired a modicum of power in marriage dissolution. Under Personal Law No. 100 of 1985, polygyny is still legal, but women have gained a few small advantages, as follows:

The authenticating official must notify the wife/wives regarding the new marriage by registered letter with delivery return. A wife whose husband marries another woman may request a divorce if she suffers material or moral damage which would render continued cohabitation with him impossible, even if she had not made it a precondition that he would not marry another woman while legally married to her. (Egypt Report 1987:33)

The law also now stipulates a wife's grounds for divorce, such as if her husband renegs on his obligation to pay his wife maintenance from the date of the valid contract. Also, she can ask for a separation if experts verify that her husband has an ingrained physical defect.

INDIA

India is a tradition-bound Hindu-Islamic society (84 percent Hindu and 10 percent Islamic). It has a population of about 800 million people, which makes it second only to China in size. A reading of the demographic statistics of India leads one to the conclusion that the status of women is extremely low compared to any other country of comparable size. For instance, in 1971, 81.3 percent of the total population were female illiterates (Liddle and Joshi 1986). Also in 1971, 81 percent of all voters in India were male, in spite of women having legal voting rights. Politics is seen as a sphere for men exclusively (Mukhopadhyay 1982). Whereas acceptance of modern ideas tends to be an urban phenomenon worldwide, India remains rural. About 80 percent of Indians reside in villages and are subject to village-level politics (Morgan 1984). Women are virtually excluded from traditional village-wide councils.

To convey the status of women in India, mention must be made of the caste system, *purdah*, *sati*, and dowry system, which are practices of long-standing tradition that continue today in varying degrees.

Gender division and women's subordination have been related to the caste system, which has survived for 2,000 years. It is both a structural and a cultural system. Structurally there is a hierarchy of four layers, with *Brahmins* at the top and *Sudra* (the untouchables) at the bottom. Certain professions and occupations are permitted to each individual, depending on caste. Culturally, there is the belief in *karma*, the idea that one's birth placement is due to previous actions. Both systems contribute to an acceptance of one's fate as rightful, since they are sanctioned by the Hindu religion. For men, passivity is not required, as mobility of the male group can be achieved over time through ritual purity. The signs of ritual purity are vegetarianism, teetotalism, and the exercise of tight constraints on women. There are two forms that control over women takes—disinheritance of real property, and removal from public life to the domestic sphere of the home in the form of seclusion or purdah (Liddle and Joshi 1986). The purity of the male group seems to depend on the purity of female sexuality, and men benefit from higher caste status at the expense of women.

Purdah

Purdah remains an integral part of Indian society today and represents a core of underlying principles concerned with status, ownership of property, arranged marriages, impulse control, and division of labor in the home and the wider society. For women it means being confined to the home, veiling their bodies and faces while outside, and not talking to males as a rule. This is viewed as protection and an important embodiment of the family's honor. It is a sign of social standing and prestige, since only the upper-caste Brahmins could afford to seclude the wife within the home rather than have her work outside to enhance family income. Sylvia Hale wrote: "To the extent that sheltered women embody family honor, unsheltered women symbolize prostitutes. They are defenseless, and if raped, they will be disowned by their families" (Hale 1988:280). It has been alleged that in general women are proud of their status of seclusion and contribution to family honor.

Sati

Sati (also called *sutee* in Europe) is the religiously sanctioned sacrifice of widows on their husband's funeral pyre. It was widespread mostly among the upper castes, and was emulated among the upwardly mobile groups. The number of women that the princes burned was considered an index of success. History has it that one raja of Bundi took eighty-four satis with him on the pyre upon cremation. Hindu widow burning is not abhored. According to the religion, the physical world, including the body, is an illusion, a mere garment to be discarded in the funeral pyre. Women's power comes through sacrifice and transcendence of the material world through devotion, subordination, and total submission (Mukhopadhyay 1982). Women who participate in sati are admired for their willingness to transcend the world of illusion.

The religious ideals of asceticism, sacrifice, and transcendence seem not to apply to men in such a destructive way. Only women are expected to cleanse themselves so radically of the material world. Hindu misogynism is apparent in many sacred works and creation myths, where women are said to be sensual seducers of men. They are tricky, fickle-minded, greedy, impure, thoughtless, inconsistent, cruel, and represent the root of all evil (Mukherjee 1978, O'Flaherty 1976). If Hindus believe this about women's nature, it seems that women bear the burden of a type of original sin and so have to try extremely hard to prove their virtue and loyalty. Nothing in a woman's upbringing teaches her to refute the ancient myths and value her own life. Assuming that it is completely voluntary when women throw themselves on the dead husband's funeral pyre, and not the result of having been drugged or of unavoidable cultural pressure, then the low status of women in the Hindu religion helps explain the tradition. That is, the ideology of sacrifice is a means whereby the constant negation of the woman can be justified.

Sati was outlawed in British India in 1829 by the governor-general. Although it has been suppressed, the practice has not entirely disappeared. Since 1981 there has been a revival of sati (Morgan 1984). As long as it is felt that through sati the dead husband gains attonement for his sins, and that the entire state gains because of the perception of his elevation to sainthood, it is seen as a good. Women still seem to bear the added burden of men's spiritual glorification.

Women and Family

The ideology of *Pativratya*, or husband worship, holds that a woman's spiritual salvation depends on her total devotion, service, and complete subordination to her husband. The ideology stresses complete docility, meekness, and selflessness for women. If they succeed at that, they may avoid the worst fate of all, which is being born a woman again in another life. The ideal of sacrifice is based on the mythological Hindu woman-goddess Sita, who was abducted by her husband Rama, patiently endured all the privations he inflicted, and then undertook without complaint the ordeal by fire to prove her fidelity and innocence (Liddle and Joshi 1986). The early myth embodies the traits of silence, subservience, and self-effacement, which are seen as ideal for women in Indian patriarchal society. This double standard in gender behavior remains in actual practice in modern times.

Family Structure

There are two main types of family structure in India, the joint family and the nuclear family. The most common in northern Indian villages is the joint family type, which consists of a group of patrilineally related males sharing a common residence, budget, and rights to property. Women are segregated and subordinate. In the joint family the wife is considered a man's property in the same way as land. In such a family the primary relationship for a wife is with her mother-in-law, not her husband, since she has, in a real sense, married the family (Liddle and Joshi 1986). She carries on all domestic duties under the supervision of her mother-in-law. Even if she works outside, she is expected to do all the housework. Traditionally a man does not help with household chores and would be ridiculed by other family members if he did.

A modified joint family structure can be found in urban areas, where it is less autocratic. The more mature age of the urban bride and her job outside the home have ameliorated the relationship with the mother-in-law.

There is a more democratic sharing of child-care and household tasks among women, and this encourages taking outside jobs.

In the nuclear family the entire liability of the housework and child care fall on the wife, although she does not have to take care of in-laws. When she is employed outside the home, she bears the burden of overwork and also guilt over the perceived neglect of her children. Even if she is a professional, her husband expects her to be a good housewife first and anything else secondarily. Many such women report being under great strain (Liddle and Joshi 1986).

In both types of family, men do not look after themselves or others but rather are looked after by women. However, they do benefit financially when the women have outside jobs. It seems that the thought of doing domestic work undermines their masculinity, but having wives in the paid labor force does not.

Dowry

The dowry is the sum that millions of fathers feel compelled to pay to the families of the bridegrooms to enhance their daughters' marriageability. This material reason for anxiety over the birth of daughters is one cause of the Indian practice of female infanticide, murders that are made to look like accidents.

According to tradition, only males could inherit immovable property, but when females married a significant portion of the other property was removed from the patrilineal line of inheritance and given to the daughter's marital family as her dowry. Many feel that this practice has gone out of control, and although it began as a middle-class practice in the north, it is now a phenomenon of all the Hindu castes. It has also crossed religious boundaries, and Muslim and Christian men have started demanding dowry as a condition of marriage (Crossette 1989).

Many people in India feel the dowry system is extremely demeaning to a woman as it symbolizes her inferior status. She is used as a kind of commodity to enhance the wealth of the male's family when he marries. Problems can arise at the woman's expense. Sometimes the bride's family is unable to pay as much dowry as promised. The husband can then intimidate her family to pay up by beating her. Many cases of abuse have been reported. In addition, if the wife dies, the husband can remarry and acquire another dowry. The increasing number of wife burnings within the home is causing alarm. Although they are made to look like kitchen accidents or suicides, murder is often suspected. Although the authorities want to investigate such cases, the wife is usually cremated immediately, eliminating evidence of foul play. Although the authorities are aware of the phenomenon and would prosecute, the husband usually goes unapprehended. Burning women, whether the traditional widow burning or the modern bride burning, seems to be a thriving phenomenon in spite of laws passed to protect women. These fatalities are often referred to as dowry deaths. Each year they increase in number; 1,786 were recorded in 1987 (Crossette 1989).

This social evil, which has been practiced for several centuries, has been illegal since the Prohibition of Dowry Act of 1961. As is the case with the reform acts called Personal Laws which have been passed since India achieved independence in 1947 and which were designed to prohibit abuses of women and raise their status, the law is enforced neither by the government nor by the women themselves. A case in Kerala, India, in November 1988 is particularly poignant. Four sisters hanged themselves and left the following note:

Our parents are not yet to pay fully for the dowry of our sister who was married some time ago. Having sold their gold and land, we are not sure that they will be able to provide anything for our marriages. Hence the decision to end our lives. (Crossette 1989:10)

The implementation of laws passed to ensure equality is hampered by caste and patriarchal family structures. If these remain unchanged, the new laws will remain weak and will attack only the symptoms and not the causes of the unequal status of women. For example, although paying dowry is against the law, evasion of the Dowry Prohibition Act of 1961 is possible because a broad definition of dowry is applied by the courts. "Presents" made by the bride's father at the time of marriage are considered legal. The tradition reduces women to the level of property, and property that is not satisfactory can be destroyed. In the cases of burnings, the dowry victims are scarcely recognized by the courts as citizens with rights, and even when a witness or the dying wife accuses the husband, he is rarely sanctioned.

Abortion

The Medical Termination of Pregnancy Act was passed in 1972. Although the act was envisaged by the government partly as a family-planning measure to alleviate the overpopulation problem, the limitation of the number of unwanted children was also presumed to relieve the anguish of overburdened wives. However, the reform of social values trailed behind those of the laws. When Indira Gandhi was prime minister, she stated, "Unless the girl's life is in danger, there should be no abortion" (Minattur 1975:108). Such an attitude does not enlighten illiterate village women concerning their options and rights. However, the Pregnancy Act was liberalized in 1975, and women may now obtain an abortion even if their husbands object.

Female Infanticide and Female Mortality

Female infanticide has long been a practice in India. It has been outlawed, but continues. In fact, a modern innovation of the practice comes from advanced medical technology. Amniocentesis, a method of sampling the amniotic fluid of the pregnant woman to detect the sex of the fetus, is practiced in all but one state, where it has been outlawed. The determination of the sex of the fetus is sometimes followed by female feticide. In the family of one prominent politician, no girls have been recorded as having been born in forty years (Crossette 1989).

Even in childhood there are sex differentials in mortality. In industrialized countries statistics show that the survival rate is higher for female children than male children. Also, life expectancy at birth is usually higher for females than males. An exception to this pattern is India, where male life expectancy is higher, and the gap between male and female life expectancy has increased for the last five decades (Leonard 1979). T. Paul Schultz (1982) relates this to the low status of women, a conclusion derived from census statistics. While his figures have some limitations, as all areas in India are not included and some available figures lump female and male deaths together, they do show a trend. In 1969 in the villages, where 80 percent of the people live, there was a differential in childhood mortality from the second month of life to the tenth year of age.

Schultz's research showed that the illness of a girl is treated by local "wise women," whereas more strenuous efforts are made to cure boys, with parents going miles or standing in long lines at city hospitals to ensure proper treatment. In terms of feeding, fathers and sons get fed first, while mothers and girls eat what is left, possibly placing females at a nutritional disadvantage (Schultz 1982). The childhood survival indicators can be related to gender status, as the birth of a girl represents a calamity assessed by the family in monetary terms.

In 1978, infant mortality for every 1,000 live births was 131 for females and 120 for males. Two-thirds of the children who die before age four are girls. Compared to males, females have a higher death rate from ages twenty to thirty-nine as well, probably owing to neglect and lower food allotment at a time when their work is most intense and pregnancies most frequent. Pregnant women consume only 60 percent of their nutritional requirements (Morgan 1984). Complications from iron and calcium deficiencies, along with pre- and postpartum hemorrhages due to lack of proper care, are major causes of deaths at this time. About 90 percent of pregnant women have no prenatal care. The average maternal mortality rate in 1981 was 370 per 10,000 births, a rate that is extremely high.

The fact that in India females have a shorter life expectancy than males is evident in the overall population demographics. In 1981, the female life expectancy was 51.6 years, while for males it was 52.6 years. In 1982, females comprised 46.7 percent of the total population, a figure at least 3 to 4 percent lower than in most other countries (Morgan 1984).

Child Marriage

Child marriage for women is another abuse that is difficult to stop. The orthodox ideal for Brahmins was marriage to a girl before she reached the age of ten years, and the practice became widespread in all the castes and classes. The Age of Consent Act raised the legal age for the consummation of a marriage for women from ten to twelve years as long ago as 1891. The minimum marriage age for girls was then raised to fourteen by the Child Marriage Restraint Act of 1929. In spite of the laws, however, child marriage persists. According to census data of 1970–1978, 17.5 percent of girls ten to fourteen years of age were married, and 56 percent of females fifteen to nineteen years of age were married. Violation of the laws carries a small prison term penalty, but it is rarely enforced (Morgan 1984). One of the many problems arising from this exploitative practice is early widowhood for women. Sometimes a widow may still be in her twenties. The cultural ban on remarriage by widows and the imposition of a life of austerity largely persists in spite of favorable laws (the Widow Remarriage Act of 1856) because of the belief that the woman is the exclusive sexual property of the husband even after his death.

Women and Employment

In 1981, 80 percent of all employed women were in agriculture, which is not surprising in a largely agrarian society. However, only 32 percent received wages for the work (Morgan 1984). Women's input in the production of the world's food has gone largely unrecognized in all Third World countries. With the increasing mechanization of agriculture in India, women's traditional occupations are being eliminated, but women have not been included in the new technologies.

Outside jobs do not exist for all women in rural areas. For those who do have jobs, equal pay for equal work is not the norm. Sex discrimination in wages exists in the workplace. Although complete national data are unobtainable, in 1975 women in the mining industry earned 33 percent of men's minimum pay and 20 percent of their maximum pay. India has an equal pay policy which is mandated by the Constitution (Article 39.d) and also by the Equal Remuneration Act of 1975. However, employers exempt themselves from this labor legislation by hiring women as perpetually temporary workers (Morgan 1984). The government itself is not consistent since it has a set of sex-differential pay scales for male and female sowers in different states. Also, in spite of illegal discrimination, when women get married or become pregnant they are often fired. As of 1981, only 2 percent of women laborers were organized.

Women and Power

In view of the foregoing, Indian women can be said to be relatively powerless. During India's struggle for independence from the British government, a women's group was formed that was active and effective in the struggle, but today women's citizen rights are fragile. As a group, women lack political clout. This results from the secondary and politically invisible place to which they have been assigned by long-standing attitudes and customs of their society, and which their gender-role socialization conditions them to accept as the natural order of things. Any change in the political order will necessitate the effective use of the political process and entail women holding powerful decision-making positions in numbers that approximately reflect their percentage in the total population. Although India is a democracy and women have the franchise, women do not seem to realize that they have so much potential power. Organizational difficulties are exacerbated by the fact that India is 80 percent rural and has a high illiteracy rate among women.

Because of judicial nonenforcement, law has not succeeded in playing its role of social engineering and influencing deeply rooted social attitudes. That is, traditional attitudes grounded in the concept of inherent inferiority of women have superceded the equality principle of the Constitution. For instance, although the Indian constitution (Article 15) asserts the principle of equality for all citizens and prohibits discrimination on the grounds of sex, the guarantee of equality has not been sufficient as judicial attitudes have justified discriminatory treatment in many cases in spite of legislative intent. There remains an enormous gap between what the law has mandated and what has been achieved.

Many Indians realize that social inequities do exist, but they rely on legislation to bring about change. There is an absence of concerted political activism to enforce the laws concerning women's rights. The Uniform Civil Code written into the Indian constitution remains a guide but does not have much clout. There is also a general reluctance to give up some of the myths and ideals that are used to defend ancient Indian civilization. The joint family, "with its complementary roles for members of differing age and sex, is still defended and proposed as the basis of a modern society which accords equality to women and men" (Leonard 1979:106).

Political activism could lead to the ratification of one of the major UN treaties that is helpful to women, the Convention on the Elimination of all Forms of Discrimination against Women. Although ninety-nine countries have so far ratified or acceded to this treaty, India has not. India has ratified some of the earlier treaties dealing specifically with women, including the Convention for the Suppression of the Traffic in Persons and of the Exploitation of the Prostitution of Others in 1949, the Convention Concerning Equal Remuneration for Men and Women Workers for Work of Equal Value in 1951, and the Convention on the Political Rights of Women in 1952, with the formal reservation that in India the last treaty will not apply to recruitment to and service in the armed forces or the forces charged with the maintenance of public order (United Nations *Compendium* 1988:128).

The achievement of equality for women in India would appear to be an undertaking that as a prerequisite requires insight as to what needs changing. The necessary political activism might be aimed at government enforcement of laws concerning dowry and age of marriage, as well as the passage of new legal mandates guaranteeing equal status in the workplace, in health and educational opportunities, in inheritance and divorce, and in other matters that affect a woman's status in her husband's family.

CHINA

According to the 1982 census, the total population of China at that time was 1,008,180,738, which is roughly one-fifth of the world's inhabitants. Females account for 48.5 percent of the population. About 60 percent of China's people live in the countryside (Waddle 1988).

The status of women in modern countries often depends on their level of education. In China, the differential between males and females in schools increases with age. For example, in 1981 females comprised 43.9 percent of primary school students, 36.6 percent of middle school students, and 24.4 percent of university students. The government figure for the Chinese literacy rate was 76.5 percent in 1982, and of the illiterate and semiliterate group, 70 percent were women.

In spite of the illiteracy rate for women, the Chinese Revolution, which culminated in 1949 with the formation of the People's Republic of China, brought gratifying improvements in women's lives. Modern China is a testimonial to the fact that swift and dramatic social change concerning the status of women can become a reality. During the first half of this century, the Chinese family was an extreme example of patriarchy. The status of a woman was so low that her name was not recorded in her father's geneology. After marriage, even her given name was discarded, as her new family often renamed her. Her lot was slave-like obedience among strangers in her husband's household.

Confucian Patriarchy and the Status of Women

The Confucian patriarchal system was shockingly brutal to women. Common practices included female infanticide, sale of child brides, arranged marriages, polygyny, wife beating, and the mutilation of women's feet. In the name of beauty, women's feet were bound tightly at an early age so that the toes turned under and the feet remained small and deformed. Women could take only short, painful, hobbling steps. This ensured that they would remain close to home. Foot binding was common up until the 1940s. For men, a common practice to ensure their pleasure was concubinage. It was accepted practice to bring another woman into the household for sexual reasons, and children born from the relationship were considered legitimate.

A wife's lot was one of complete subservience. Even in the upper classes, women prepared the meals but ate separately. They tended to the house but could never own one, as laws prohibited inheritance by women. A woman was subordinate under the law and was not recognized as an independent entity. If she was forced to marry before puberty or without her consent, if she was sold to a man, or if her husband beat her, she had no legal recourse. Her only escape was through suicide. A woman was conditioned for obedience to a man—to her father during childhood, to her husband during marriage, and to her son during widowhood. She had a subordinate status that was almost subhuman (Stacey 1975).

The Confucian patriarchal order lasted 2,000 years. When communism started gaining ascendancy in some areas before the war, women embraced the new ideology as its policies toward women and the family accorded them a dignity and importance they had never had before, and even promised them equality. The young communist party passed marriage laws in 1931 and 1934, patterned on those of the Soviet Union. Among other reforms, these laws gave women the right to divorce and to retain custody of their children. The demise of the Confucian patriarchal order was complete in 1949 when the People's Republic of China came into being.

Women and Family

In traditional China, family life was the basis of the social system to a greater extent than in most other preindustrial countries. It was within the patriarchal family that male supremacy had its most extreme manifestation, and where it went unchallenged. In order to ensure rights for women, attempts were made to change the old family system. The Marriage Law of 1950 liberated women from some of the many abuses they had previously had to endure and provided them with a measure of autonomy. It outlawed infanticide, child marriage, wife buying, polygyny, concubines, and foot binding. It also made divorce possible for women, and allowed widows to remarry without the permission of the first husband's family. Women were permitted joint ownership and management of family property, and could inherit property. Article I of the Marriage Law reads:

The arbitrary and compulsory feudal marriage system, which is based on the superiority of man over women . . . is hereby abolished. The new "Democratic Marriage System," which is based on free choice of partners, on monogamy, on equal rights for both sexes, and on the protection of the lawful interests of women and children, shall be put into effect. (Kristeva 1974:130)

The 1952 constitution prohibits any curtailment of the freedom of marriage. Married women are also empowered to use their own family names if they wish (Article 11). This rule was meant to strike a blow at patrilineal descent and elevate women to symbolic power.

The Chinese leadership believed that women had to become actively involved in society in order to overcome resistance. One technique used was the "speak-bitterness" sessions, a type of consciousness-raising meeting. Women were encouraged to speak publicly about the mistreatments that they had endured in the family before communism. It was a release of anger and also an education for younger women.

The Chinese also believed that, to further effect societal change, kinship could no longer be the central organizational fact in the system. Communes were therefore formed. Resources and land were redistributed, and agricultural work was organized communally. Commune membership became the central fact for the individual, supplanting the extended family and the clan in importance. The work unit members would become a kind of extended family. The aim was to infuse collective goals rather than kin-based ones. The communes were made up of the combined social endeavors of industry, agriculture, commerce, education, and the army.

The commune system is still a central fact of Chinese life. Communes are broken down into work units to which a person usually belongs for life. Workers are allotted housing, and members join each other in the communal recreational facilities and get together for political study. Communal kitchens and other structures are supplied, which relieve wives of housework and child-rearing functions. The family is submerged by the commune system, which has control over the work and social lives of its members. This is by design, as the aim is to free women for work and also to redirect loyalties to the state. Child care is far from universal, however, and about as many young children are cared for by grandparents as are enrolled in work unit nurseries or kindergartens. Healthy elderly women are thus an asset in a family (deGlopper 1988).

The legal marriage age was raised as a means of limiting fertility. The minimum marriage age for women is twenty years and for men is twenty-two years. Late marriage contributes to the emancipation of women and their participation in the work force. Eroticism is generally suppressed. Women often do not wear makeup or jewelry, and clothing is often masculine in style and similar to what men wear. It has been alleged that premarital sex and illegitimacy are virtually unknown.

Women have rights to free prenatal and postnatal care and free delivery of babies. Since 1980 the government has instituted strong incentives for married couples to have no more than one child. Public government posters extolling the glories of small families show the happy mother and father with a single female child. Abortion on request has been legal and free since 1955. Contraception and sterilization are also readily available. Incentives for having no more than one child include preferential housing, employment, child care, free child education and health services, and also, in some districts, a monthly cash bonus for a period of time. The penalties for having a second child include increased family taxes of up to 15 percent from the time the woman becomes pregnant until the child is seven years of age. Penalties become harsher with additional pregnancies (Morgan 1984).

One outcome of the one-child policy has been the growing recurrence of female infanticide, which is outlawed. A couple can then have another baby with impugnity in the hopes that it will be a boy. Also, in rural areas, women are blamed for bearing girls. It seems that the higher evaluation of males has not been eradicated by legislation.

The policy of government favoritism and economic benefits for families that have only one child could inadvertently perpetuate inequality since it is often the couples who have girls who defy the authorities and have a second child. This leaves the family more economically deprived than families that have an only boy.

There also has been some defiance of the policy among peasant couples in rural areas where labor is needed. Additional exceptions to the policy have been made in provincial regulations, according to Peng Peiyun, head of the National Family Planning Commission. She explained that should the first child be a girl (about 50 percent of first births), rural couples will now be allowed a second chance to have a boy (Tien 1988).

There are emerging signs of an increasing fertility rate in China, although it is still extremely low. Population trends show an increase in the birth rate to twenty-one per thousand citizens in 1986, compared to eighteen per thousand in the 1983–1985 period. Wang Wei, head of China's Family Planning Commission, explains this as an "echo boom," since in 1986 there were more persons of reproductive age because of a baby boom twenty years earlier. He acknowledges, however, that because rural couples desire sons, there was an underreporting of female births in 1983–1985. He also mentions an immediate problem of the reemergence of early marriage and early reproduction, and also a rise in premarital sexual activities, especially in the cities (Tien 1988).

The parent-child relationship in Chinese society is a reciprocal one, and parents are obliged to give their children as favorable a place in the world as they can while children are obliged to care for parents in old age (de-Glopper 1988). The 1980 Marriage Law may perhaps increase perceptions of daughters as economic assets, for it makes daughters as well as sons legally responsible for old age support. Also, the development of the economic potential of handicrafts and sideline occupations, in which women have traditionally excelled, may also change perceptions (Tien 1988).

The 1980 Marriage Law also had the effect of relaxing the late-marriage strictures of the 1970s. This resulted in a boom in early marriages, and statistics show that 4 percent of people are married by age 15–19, 25 percent by age 20, and 88 percent by age 25 (Tien 1988). Although the Marriage Law of 1950 and the later law of 1980 call for free marriage choice, in actual practice according to some studies, many marriages are the result of a go-between's service.

Child-care services are in demand in China but are expensive (only 25 percent of eligible children were enrolled in 1982). This activity is therefore still left in the realm of "women's work" (Morgan 1984). Although Chinese women have indeed moved into paying jobs, Chinese men have not been given incentives to participate in so-called women's activities. Most women consequently bear the double burden of domestic work and outside work.

Women and Employment

The 1982 census showed that approximately 54 percent of the total population was in the labor force, with 22 percent in the nonagricultural sector. Males accounted for slightly more than half the work force. The labor-force participation rates for persons fifteen years of age and over were among the highest in the world. There was also a general unemployment rate of 5 percent in 1982. Women accounted for a little more than half of this rate, as 13 million women and 12 million men were unemployed.

As a rule, almost all women of working age have jobs outside the home. This has been one of the major indications of change in the status of women in China. According to standard Marxist ideology, the communist party views the liberation of women as dependent on their participation in the labor force. Chinese women have full legal equality, and equality of the sexes appears to be socially accepted as well. Women have access to the same services as men, and may also serve in the People's Liberation Army and become party members. Most jobs have a lifetime tenure. However, many of the jobs held by women are less desirable and lower-paying than those of men. A mid–1980s sample of 10 percent of the working population revealed that men occupied the great majority of leadership positions. Also, women retain the double burden of domestic chores while having full-time jobs (Waddle 1988). Although women's opportunities and rewards are not entirely equal with men's, on the whole women are far better off than they have been historically.

Women and Power

The United Nations admitted the People's Republic of China to membership in 1979. In 1980 China ratified the Convention on the Elimination of All Forms of Discrimination against Women. In compliance with the terms of the treaty, China submitted its initial report to the Committee on the Elimination of Discrimination against Women (CEDAW) (China 1983). The report states the government's agreement with the principles of the convention and indicates that China already has many legal measures that are in conformity with it and are aimed at the elevation of the status of women. A few salient points of China's report follow.

Under the law, women enjoy equality in all spheres of life—political, economic, cultural, and social. The principles of equality are embodied in the Marriage Law, the Criminal Code, and the Labor Insurance Regulations. The state applies the principle of equal pay for equal work stated in the Chinese constitution, and selects men and women equally for training.

Concerning political life, 95 percent of women eligible to vote did so in 1981. There is an increasing percentage of women deputies at people's congresses, and some women have leading posts in governmental organs. There is also an All-China Women's Federation which actively participates in the formulation of the constitution and government policies.

Concerning education, both sexes have equal opportunities. Coeducation has been universally introduced, and 93 percent of all school-age children are in school. According to the report, half of all the graduates from training and adult educational institutes over the last thirty-three years have been women. In the universities, one-fourth of the faculty are women. In the Sixth Five-Year Plan for the Development of the National Economy (1981–1985) it was specified that in the countryside

women will not only receive general education but also training in scientific farming, breeding domestic fowls and animals, braiding, weaving, embroidery and other specialized skills suitable to women to help them improve their techniques in productive activities geared to local resources. (China 1983:7)

Concerning employment, women constitute an important force in the nation's economic construction. They are to be found particularly in many so-called nontraditional professions. In urban areas, 39 percent of the work force are women, and in rural areas they account for over half the labor force. Women workers are entitled to pay, benefits, awards, and labor protection equal to those of men. After retirement, urban working women receive lifelong pensions amounting to 60 to 90 percent of their former salaries, depending on length of service.

Women workers are given special attention during four specific periods—menstruation, pregnancy, confinement, and breastfeeding. For the first year after giving birth, two thirty-minute paid feeding breaks are provided for working women. According to the report, in recent years there has been a rapid growth of child-care services which offer educational facilities and also relieve working mothers of their household responsibilities.

Concerning marriage, the report states that the 1980 Marriage Law was necessitated because of "practical experiences." It stipulates that, depending on the couple's wishes, the woman may become a member of the man's family or the man may become a member of the woman's family. Both have a right to use his or her family name after marriage, and children may adopt either the mother's or father's family name.

Concerning fertility, the report explains that the government encourages the birth of only one child per couple, and that it provides contraceptives and sterilization surgery free of charge. The benefits to the complying couple include health subsidies, longer paid maternity leave, and priority in housing, medical care, and nursery enrollment.

Concerning divorce, the husband may not apply for one when his wife is pregnant or within one year after the birth of a child. The restriction does not apply if a wife seeks a divorce. The law stipulates that any property acquired during the marriage is the joint possession of the two parties. Both have the right to inherit each other's property.

The Chinese government's report frankly acknowledges that problems still remain for some women. Discrimination, maltreatment, and abuse of women do still occur, attesting to the continuation of the feudal idea of male superiority. The turmoil of the decade 1966 to 1976 has not been fully overcome in the legal system. In rural areas some parents are still reluctant to send daughters to school, and the female dropout rate in the primary schools is high. Some institutions of higher learning have also raised the admission scores for female candidates, in spite of the illegality of doing so. In employment, various excuses are still used for not promoting or even hiring women in spite of equal achievements and qualifications. As for marriage, there are still occurrences in some places of arranged or mercenary marriages.

To combat these problems, the government has launched a nationwide education campaign to eliminate feudal ideas and customs that uphold male superiority. Women are being informed of their legal rights, and the public is being informed of the sanctions for their infringement. The campaign is viewed by the Chinese government as a positive approach to raising the status of women in all aspects of life—political, economic, cultural, and domestic. The report pledges that the People's Republic of China will continue to strive for the elimination of all forms of discrimination against women and will use law as a weapon to assist in redressing the wrongs done to them.

9

The Global Community

Through UN efforts, human rights violations are investigated and publicized in the hopes of building an effective long-range system for the protection of such rights through an elaboration of international standards. UN activity also brings to international public consciousness some of the pressing problems that require concerted effort to achieve solutions. If the problems being addressed by the international body on a global scale sound familiar to women in the United States, it is because they are not alone, as women all over the world have been exploited and have had to endure lower social status in relation to men. Today there is very little real isolation of societies, and ideas spread readily and to virtually everyone. The concept of equality has taken on an energy and urgency never seen before, and even men who have benefitted in the past from discrimination and are in positions of power have become incensed with the need for equal access to leadership and decision making in the hope of tapping all human potential in the service of a better world in the future.

The six countries focused on herein have all been influenced to bring about an equalization of opportunities for women with men, although they have had varying degrees of success. However, there is no denying that much progress has been made, and women are gradually realizing an improvement in social status.

In the United States, recent laws have mandated equality in the labor market. Although women earn in the aggregate only 60 to 70 percent of men's earnings, the acceptance of the concept of comparable worth holds promise for future employment equalization. Progress has been slower in the political arena, where the number of women holding positions of power is nowhere close to their numbers in the population. Also, the U.S. Congress has not approved ratification of a major UN treaty, the Convention on the Elimination of All Forms of Discrimination against Women, even though

President Carter recommended it. However, there is optimism that Congress will yet ratify the treaty.

In Argentina, the political turmoil, the Falklands war, and the suspension of the constitution have been major setbacks to women's progress toward equality. The recent restoration of the constitution, and the fresh awareness of the harm to humans that accrued when civil rights were suspended, offer hope for reforms. Although national problems, such as runaway inflation reaching crisis proportions, remain and necessarily absorb the public's attention, the need for equal women's rights is being acknowledged. Women have proven themselves capable of mobilizing and making the public aware of injustices, as the Plaza de Mayo demonstrations showed. The recent political reforms should logically lead to a new era of greater equality for women, since the old order has led to corruption by government officials, a disastrous war that the government was unprepared to win, a suspension of human rights, and the deaths of thousands of innocent victims who were unaccounted for and unavenged. Once internal economic stability has been achieved, it is likely that the general public could remain reform-minded and take steps to prevent such disasters from recurring. It is conservative speculation to assume that Argentine women, who have recently proven their capability as activists, will not allow a complete return to the old regime with its underpinning of traditional machismo and marianismo attitudes. Women in Argentina have a high literacy, education, and employment rate, and these are qualities which usually contribute to an awareness of social deprivations and to demands for more equal social and legal status with men.

Sweden has been aggressive in its desire to equalize the social and political status of women, and has probably been the most successful of the six countries discussed. Sweden recognized early that changes in role definitions for one sex must perforce entail changes for the other sex. Studies of the male role have been undertaken in order to better understand any resistance to equalization that might exist, and to determine the best method of bringing about acceptance of shared co-parenting responsibilities. Paternal leave after the birth of a baby has been an option for Swedish men for quite some time. In spite of this, more Swedish women than men take part-time jobs because of domestic responsibilities. However, women have made great progress in Sweden, and a very high percentage are to be found in positions of power in government and the economy.

Social conditions for women in Egypt have gradually been improving in urban areas. However, rural women still face extreme social restrictions such as confinement to the home, veiling, and the threat of polygyny. There is an apparent inability by the government to enforce women's right in the rural areas, where the old repressive traditions continue. The custom of female genital mutilation is still practiced, and local rules are applied in the treatment of women in spite of federal laws to the contrary. A deterrent to female liberation could be the new religious fundamentalism, which seeks to eliminate all Western influences from the culture. However, Egypt has ratified UN treaties mandating equal status for women, and has passed laws ensuring such rights. All Egyptians eventually must abide by these legal pronouncements and modify the ingrained culture where it infringes on the legal rights of women.

It seems that India is a country where progress on women's rights has been slow. The daily mass media attest to the continuance of the degrading dowry system, and to the purported accidental burning deaths of wives, which free husbands to contract for another wife and therefore another monetary dowry. Husbands apparently kill their wives with impugnity since law enforcement officials choose to believe their protestations of innocence. However, another practice, sati (the burning of widows in the husband's pyre), has been virtually eliminated by law. There are only rare instances reported in the newspapers, which affirm that legal sanctions will be meted out to those responsible for encouraging the practice. Indian women have not mobilized on a large scale to bring about reforms, and India has not signed the UN treaties mandating the elimination of discrimination against women. Only an optimistic view would suggest that the social and legal status of Indian women will be elevated in the near future.

China is a modern example of radical and sudden change in the status of women. Before 1949, China was an example of the most repressive and degrading kind of treatment of women to be found anywhere, since upon marriage women lost their previous identity and became virtual slaves in the husband's home. Foot binding mutilated their feet so that they could barely walk, and husbands often brought their mistresses to live at home with them. These practices have been eliminated, and women's status in China has been elevated through guaranteed legal rights. Today women have paid employment outside the home along with men, and social services to alleviate the double burden of domestic chores. However, Chinese men have not been encouraged to share equally in child rearing and household chores, and this burden still falls largely to women. That is, change in women's life-styles has had to occur without much change in men's life-styles, and the result has been a greater burden on some women. In spite of this, before-and-after studies in China show a great equalization of men's and women's statuses.

There has been much research concerning gender in other countries. Studies on the low status of women have analyzed the allotted roles for both sexes. However, the social-psychological realm of existence has seldom been explored in this connection. All persons have a need to feel a part of their social system, and the disparity in status between men and women in their society has seldom been questioned. The result is that women have often wittingly participated in their own oppression. The demand for dowry, formerly a Hindu middle-class phenomenon, has crossed such former barriers as class, education, and religion. It sometimes takes a bizarre occurrence such as suicide by female children (see the section on India in Chapter 8) to raise people's consciousness to the inhumanity of the system. Obviously such incidents must shock the community, but one could wonder why Indians would be appalled at such activity since they should have realized there could be brutalizing effects resulting from the extreme difference in value that their culture places on men and women.

In some countries the traditional customs persist unmodified. Since people must perforce adjust to a variety of environmental problems that face them in various parts of the world, one cannot make ethnocentric value judgments about the diverse cultures that abound. Humankind's survival in the past required living in groups, since people were as vulnerable to extinction as the dinosaur if they failed to develop a viable culture that allowed them to respond to problems collectively. The social forms (or culture) that evolved varied according to the contingencies people faced in different geographic regions. However, since social conditions have changed in modern times, the adaptations and requirements for survival need to change as well. Many of the old customs are no longer functional, and some are actually a deterrent to national progress and the well-being of citizens.

As has been demonstrated, in some countries the unequal gender status has religious origins. Religion has not been discussed as a separate topic in this book but has been included in the broad reference to culture. Unlike the United States, where church and state are guaranteed to stand separate by the Constitution, in many societies in the world religion determines a large portion of the cultural mores, and much of everyday social behavior is based on religious dogma. The religion is used as the underpinning justifying women's separate and obviously inferior sphere. For many individuals, religious belief is a great solace and a cornerstone of their sense of purpose and belonging, their adaptation to adversity, and their transcendence of present circumstances.

Concerning women, it is generally understood that the sacred books have mandated woman's place, which is therefore not to be questioned. However, history tells us that all of the major religions have experienced changes in their prescriptions and major practices from time to time. For instance, it has been suggested by scholars in the Middle East that passages in the Quran may have been misinterpreted concerning the status of women, as they are actually highly appreciated in Islam (El Saadawi 1982). In India, the powerful Hindu goddesses have been ignored; these could be positive role models for attitudes toward women (Mukhopadhyay 1982). Perhaps in many religions a reinterpretation and reemphasis could be conducive to more freedom for women without loss of the important contributions that religious belief makes in the lives of individuals.

The social fiction of oppositeness as it has been applied to females and males has been refuted by science, and only one of twenty-three pairs of human chromosomes concerns sex differentiation. Socially, the difference has not been interpreted as representing equal opposites. In Western societies the social roles undertaken by men and women have become increasingly similar as the sharply demarcated gender roles of the past have become less functional with modernization. However, the change has not followed a clear and straight path forward toward equality; there have been setbacks along the way. The changing cultural mores have not always kept up with reality. For instance, although women's labor force activity has been required by the economy, accessible and reliable day care for children has not always been available, and husbands have generally been reluctant to accept housework and nurturing responsibilities.

Since the inequality of women has it origin and basic manifestation in the home, there is a need for rethinking family roles. More flexibility is required, especially in regard to the responsibilities for nurturance of family members and home activities. Changes in the activities of one sex must perforce affect the lives of the other sex. A few planned societies, such as China, have attempted outside services to alleviate the responsibilities of working women, and these have had varying degrees of success. What has not been addressed in China is the need for co-responsibility for domestic chores. Whereas childbearing is genetically predetermined, the period of birthing and lactation is a short span in a woman's life. The other domestic activities are not genetically predetermined and are therefore learned activities. Hence, men are as capable as women of tasks such as meal preparation, home cleaning, child rearing, and caring for the elderly or infirm. The recent phenomenon of one-parent families headed by men in the United States has shown that men also can nurture children and still work outside the home successfully.

Today in most of the world men are a protected group—protected from the need to do housework and so be distracted from their jobs outside the home. However, the work women do in the home is essential for society as well as the family. Nonetheless, in the allocation of society's resources, none are assigned as rewards for these important tasks. They do not even command much respect. Housework is not officially defined as work, and it carries no monetary recompense for the time and energy allotted to it, although domestic work done outside the home is acknowledged as an occupation and commands a salary and benefits. Societies have not confronted this inconsistency; neither have they redressed the old patriarchal issue that a husband has a right to free domestic service from his wife. In order to achieve gender equality, countries must address the need to reeducate men and women concerning equal sharing of family responsibilities. Since it has always been alleged that household chores are not demeaning and that women derive a great deal of satisfaction from them, then such work should not be demeaning for men either, and they should be encouraged to share in the satisfaction.

What is there about certain tasks that they have so thoroughly been designated as women's work even today? For all human societies it is functional to allot tasks to different groups. This division of labor is a social phenomenon and not a divinely ordained one. It often follows class, age, or sex criteria, but the tasks that are assigned to various categories can vary from society to society. For instance, in some Muslim societies men handle the food shopping, while in others it is women's work, and in some African societies women are the traders, while in other societies men are.

In most cultures, however, the nonpaying daily chores within the home have been assigned to women. One has to conclude that the lack of pay contributes to the low status of women, and the low status of women is reenforced by the lack of pay. The arrangement assures men free domestic labor and less competition in the job market. The low status of women is therefore functional for men. To effect change, communal arrangements must be worked out on both the macro level and the micro level of society. Suggestions on the macro level include full-day day-care centers for children and the elderly, and communal dining facilities supplying three daily meals for workers. On the micro level, diurnal chores and nurturing responsibilities can be shared by spouses on an alternating or scheduled basis. When the concept of equality is fully accepted, the details will fall into place.

The United Nations Convention on the Elimination of All Forms of Discrimination against Women does allude briefly to "the common responsibility of men and women in the upbringing and development of their children" (Article 5), but does not specify a method to achieve male involvement. While this treaty specifies the right of maternity leave with pay and the retention of benefits for the woman, it makes no mention of the new concept of paternity leave. The recognition that either the man or the woman is capable of nurturing a baby after it is born is recognized officially in Sweden, thus opening up new possibilities for behavior and new versions of gender roles.

One of the conventions discussed in Chapter 7, the Convention Concerning Equal Opportunities and Equal Treatment for Men and Women Workers: Workers with Family Responsibilities, addresses the issue of equal treatment of workers with families. It provides that countries should pursue appropriate policies to enable women to fulfill home and work responsibilities harmoniously. Equality of opportunity is intended to come about through the development of community services and understanding on the part of employers so that they will not discriminate because a woman has family responsibilities. The treaty contemplates that, through vocational guidance and training and adjusted work rules, the women can remain integrated in the labor force. Although this is a modern treaty that came into force in 1983, nothing in it suggests that men should shoulder half the domestic activities in the home. However, without reeducation concerning traditional gender roles, there cannot be true equality between men and women. Men will still have an unfair advantage since their energies will not have to be divided between two major roles.

Rural women in Third World countries appear to have especially difficult lives. They have as much intelligence, ability, and energy as people everywhere, but their cultures have not trained them to be individualistic, incredulous, cynical, and generally objective enough to have a sense of their own exploitation, nor to have an awareness of the power of group action in effecting cultural change. Their lack of sophistication and the dirth of available alternatives make them willing coconspirators in the legitimation of the asymmetrical marital relationship. Few jobs are available for them outside the home, and women usually do not have the requisite training for those that are available. It is indispensable for them to get married, as social status, economic prosperity, and personal happiness depend on it. It is functional for them to develop "clinging vine" personalities, which include flattery and unquestioned servility, in their efforts to love, honor, and obey husbands in exchange for security in marriage. The exchange of nurturance for survival assures women continued economic dependency and inferiority, however, and assures men of domestic and sexual services. While males cannot be said to be free and independent from economic repression, and most rural men have many fewer options than their urban counterparts, the poorest rural man has a servile woman at home catering to his physical and psychological needs.

The argument has been made that global comparisons are not valid since Western women can afford the luxury of equality demands while women elsewhere must be concerned with basic survival needs such as food and shelter. This is a pernicious argument, as women in all countries must be compared to their male counterparts who, in spite of poverty, manage to have more political and personal power. Although in many Third World countries most families are not affluent and the lives of men are also difficult, one cannot look at the harsh and often brutal lives of women solely through the lens of cultural relativism.

The principle of cultural relativity stipulates that social phenomena in societies cannot be understood or evaluated meaningfully except in the light of the environmental circumstances faced by a group and the role that the value system and social structure play in adaptation and survival. Therefore, the customs of a country cannot be objectively or validly judged by outsiders, according to the principle. However, this can be an obvious rationalization of the status quo. A concept overriding cultural relativity must be the belief in human worth, the high valuation of each person regardless of sex and regardless of country. Human rights transcend economic status, politics, and religion. Every human life is at stake in inequality, as the domination over women signals the acceptance of the enslavement principle and thus the jeopardy of all people everywhere. If meaningful change is to occur, individuals must take a stand, as the United Nations has done, and rethink some long-entrenched cultural habits.

True equality between men and women in a society cannot be imagined where prevailing customs and beliefs are based on the restriction of education opportunities for women. Statistics show that in many countries a much smaller proportion of adult women than adult men are literate. A comparison of the literacy gap on the different continents is informative. In Africa, 20 percent more women than men are illiterate, in the Arab states there is a 25 percent gap, in Asia a 20 percent gap, in Latin America a 7 percent gap, in North America a 1 percent gap, and in Europe a 3 percent gap (U.S. Committee for UNICEF 1975). There has been gradual social change, however, and when those within the fifteen- to nineteen-year-old age group are compared, the literacy rates of women improve. In many countries a school enrollment boom is starting to close the education gap between girls and boys, suggesting the possible influence of the international treaties.

The interest in education has continued at the United Nations. In 1987 the General Assembly proclaimed 1990 to be International Literacy Year. An international conference titled World Conference on Education for All is planned for March 1990, to be held in Thailand. Since estimates are that nearly one-fifth of the world's population is illiterate, it is hoped that commitments from governments and concerted efforts by leaders will greatly reduce illiteracy by the year 2000. A specific goal is the prevention of the early dropout of students, especially girls.

The cultural practice of early teenage marriage symbolizes the low status of women, and it also helps perpetuate it. Early marriage and high fertility rates discourage women's equal access to education and leads to women's preoccupation with domestic responsibilities. Recent figures show a general trend toward later marriage. Statistics on the percentage of females aged up to nineteen years who are married, widowed, or divorced show these trends. In Egypt in 1960, 31.1 percent of teenaged women fit this category, while by 1976 the figure was reduced to 21.8 percent. In India in 1961, the figure was 70.8 percent, which by 1971 was reduced to 56.9 percent. By contrast, in a country such as Sweden, child marriage, widowhood, and divorce have been low for some time; in 1970 the figure was 2.5 percent and by 1980 it was 0.8 percent (United Nations 1971, United Nations *Compendium* 1989).

It must be noted that UN agencies other than those involved in treaty preparation and monitoring have become concerned with women's progress. The United Nations Development Programme (UNDP), which has had development projects in Third World countries for decades, has now become concerned that its initiatives should reflect gender-responsive programming, "with the practical and positive outcome of project appraisals from a woman-in-development perspective" (UNDP 1989:4). It is particularly concerned with the involvement of women in, and their access to, opportunities provided by UNDP, and is calling for baseline studies to assess "the actual economic roles and practical needs of women in the respective country, and an analysis of factors which restrict their full participation in and benefit from development" (UNDP 1989:6). The new emphasis on women should help elevate the status of Third World women in the future.

The leaders of Third World countries know that dependence on other powers has as its counterpart domination by other powers. Men who would be appalled at one nation's dependency on another for food do not get incensed by the fact that a woman must be dependent on a man for food. Just as dependency has its price in the political sphere, so it does on the personal level. Human emancipation requires the reduction of dependency and domination. It is not an easy struggle on either level. However, societies no longer tolerate having pariah groups based on ascribed status and euphemistically referred to as second-class citizens. In fact, in some countries women have barely been recognized as citizens at all. Modern international and government laws lead the way toward greater equality by establishing a basis for all persons to exercise legal rights and pursue equal dignity as full members of their society. A basic education as to legal rights should rank along with literacy as a government goal.

It would be naive to think that complete equality of opportunity will soon be the norm all over the world. There are many difficulties to overcome. The international community has by no means reached unanimity on some issues, and cultural differences, sharp variations in economic levels of development, and ideological contradictions abound. These can be divisive. Sometimes the interpretation of international law is extremely relative. For instance, in some countries the efforts guaranteeing rights of women can be perceived as having been accomplished if viewed from the level of law and not the level of reality. Nonetheless, there is no doubt that the enabling mechanisms for women's equal status are being put into place, although the coercive power of governments does not completely shape human destiny. On the individual level, resocialization regarding the ideals of equality between the sexes can be slow, but the incorporation of provisions of nondiscrimination in the legal system is a beginning on which to build future social interaction. Changes in legal mandates alone will not necessarily result in equality. There have to be changes in both the laws and social attitudes to bring it about, since woman's "place" is a social construction. The legal underpinnings have been installed in many countries, and the slow process of change in encrusted cultures has started. In some areas it may take a few generations before the new ideology of gender equality becomes a reality. Nevertheless, at whatever speed it happens, change is inevitable given the present social climate.

The principle of human rights is highlighted in Chapter 9 of the UN Charter, which established a link between the promotion of respect for human rights and fundamental freedoms. The United Nations has continued to address itself to a broad array of issues, including property rights, education and training, working women with family responsibilities, equal pay for equal work and for comparable work, abused women and powerlessness, and more. These are the same issues with which women in the United States have been concerned for some time.

The advancement of women and their liberation from repressive traditional attitudes and practices is an ongoing process. Without the urgings of the international community, tradition would most likely persist unquestioned as before. Thus, the creation by the United Nations of a broad consensus leading to a collective legitimation of principles offers hope. UN delegates from 159 member countries constantly discuss the ways to elevate the status of women. The concept itself, gender equality, is seldom in dispute, and in many countries it is mostly a matter of working out the details. Although it can take a long time for new ideas mandated by law to trickle down to rural areas and effect change in a traditional culture, which may have been ensconced for hundreds of years, most countries are committed to implementing change.

It should be clearly understood that equality for women is not a movement based on benevolence toward a segment of the population. In the United States, the trend toward incorporating women in all spheres of society is based on their legal rights as citizens as set forth in the U.S. Constitution. In the world arena, the concern in international law for a higher status of women and their incorporation into political, economic, and social institutions is based on the hopes for a better world in the future. The theme running through many of the declarations, resolutions, and conventions of the United Nations is that the participation of women on an equal basis in all areas of society is necessary not only for desired national economic development but also for the achievement of world peace.

Twice in half a century there has been the scourge of world war. Its horrors and inhumanities remain fresh in the minds of people everywhere. The subjugation of whole groups of people and their powerlessness in the face of abuses, outrages, and even annihilation became a sensitive issue that incensed people and made them critically aware of the need for a better world. At the outset of the formation of the United Nations, the delegates from the member countries were committed to laying the foundation for peace thereafter. It is to their credit that they realized that in many countries women were a subjugated segment of society. Women had to be included in the decision-making processes of their countries on an equal basis with men in order to achieve development and peace in the world and for the future betterment of humanity.

Women of the world can be likened to an awakening giant: So much potential has remained dormant for so long. Today women have been prodded by new laws in many countries, and their stirrings are already being noticed. Changes in female activities have occurred mostly in urban areas as the hinterlands are slower to accept innovation. An awakening has begun, however, and it is especially auspicious at this time. Today thoughtful people speculate whether humankind is an endangered species because of the many environmental problems we have spawned, which seem to multiply yearly and could become overpowering. In the search for solutions, all adult minds have potential. Human beings are maleable at birth, and both women and men have an equal innate capacity to learn whatever is required to contribute to a viable and non-repressive society. It is unconscionable to ignore the intellectual input of half the human population. Men and women working together in all aspects of the political and economic realms of human existence can indeed result in a better world in the future. Old solutions are not always effective. Today's problems are not solved by violence or brawn but by rethinking standard practices and introducing necessary innovations. With education and freedom from bondage to home responsibilities, half the human population can, along with men, contribute ideas and work toward a global community offering improved lives for individuals and peace between nations. As Plato stated: "Those who have lamps will pass them to others." (Jones 1958:153).

Almost all member countries of the United Nations have signed the Declaration of Human Rights, and many have ratified the treaties concerning the status of women. It is hoped that in the not-so-distant future, the gap between proclamation and performance in the various countries—that is, the gap between human rights ideals and human rights realities—will be eliminated. The elaboration of international standards at the United Nations, the publicizing of human rights violations, and the continuing diligence toward building an effective system for the protection of human rights for women as well as men are innovations whose time has come.

Bibliography

Abbott, Edith. *Women in Industry.* New York: D. Appleton and Co., 1910.

AFSCME v. State of Washington. 578 F. Supp. 846 (W. D. Wash. 1983) rev'd, 77 F.2d 1401 (9th Cir. 1985).

Ahs, Stig. "Sweden: The Changing Role of the Male." Summary of a Swedish *Report by the Working Party for the Role of the Male.* Ministry of Labour, Stockholm, 1986.

Alexander, Shana. *State-by-State Guide to Women's Legal Rights.* Los Angeles: Wollstonecraft, 1975.

Almquist, Elizabeth McTaggart. "Race and Ethnicity in the Lives of Minority Women." In Jo Freeman (ed.), *Women: A Feminist Perspective.* 3d ed. Palo Alto: Mayfield Publishing Co., 1984.

Amsden, Alice H. (ed.). *The Economics of Women and Work.* New York: St. Martin's Press, 1980.

Andersen, Margaret L. *Thinking about Women: Sociological and Feminist Perspectives.* New York: Macmillan Publishing Co., 1983.

Argentina. *Report to the Committee on the Elimination of Discrimination against Women* [CEDAW]. CEDAW/C/5/Add. 39/Amend. 1/New York: United Nations, Dec. 7, 1987.

Babcock, Barbara Allen, Ann E. Freedman, Eleanor Holmes Norton, and Susan C. Ross. *Sex Discrimination and the Law: Causes and Remedies.* Boston: Little, Brown and Co., 1975.

Bagdikian, Ben K. "Conglomeration, Concentration and the Media." *Journal of Communication* 301 (1980): 59–64.

Bandura, A., and R. Walters. *Social Learning and Personality Development.* New York: Holt, Rinehart, and Winston, 1963.

Barbanel, Josh. "Candidates Vow to Fight Abortion Rule." *New York Times,* July 4, 1989, pp. 31, 34.

Bartholomew, Paul C. *Summaries of Leading Cases on the Constitution.* 11th ed., rev. Joseph F. Menez. Totowa, N.J.: Littlefield, Adams and Co., 1981.

Berman, Harold J. (ed.). *Talks on American Law.* New York: Vintage Books/Random House, 1961.

Bernard, Jessie. *The Future of Marriage*. New York: World Publishing, 1972.

Bhasin, Kamla. "The Predicament of Middle Class Indian Women—An Inside View." In Kamla Bhasin (ed.), *The Position of Women in India*. Srinigar: Arvind Deshpande, 1972.

Black, H. C. *Black's Law Dictionary*. 4th ed. rev. St. Paul: West Publishing Co., 1968, P. 1427.

Blackstone, W. *Commentaries on the Laws of England*. Oxford, England, 1765.

Blau, Francine D. "Women in the Labor Force: An Overview." In Jo Freeman, (ed.), *Women: A Feminist Perspective*. 3d ed. Palo Alto: Mayfield Publishing Co., 1984.

Boston Women's Health Book Collective. *The New Our Bodies, Ourselves*. New York: Simon and Schuster, 1984.

Bradwell v. Illinois. 83 U.S. (16 Wall.) 130, 21 L.Ed. 442 (1873).

Brantingson, Charlie. *Swedish Women as Entrepreneurs*. Stockholm: Business and Industry Information Group, May 1983.

Briggs v. City of Madison. 536 F. Supp. 435 (W. D. Wisc. 1982).

Brown, Barbara A., Ann E. Freedman, Harriet N. Katz, and Alice M. Price, with Hazel Greenberg. *Women's Rights and the Law*. New York: Praeger Publishers, 1977.

Brown v. Board of Education, 347 U.S. 483 (1954).

Brownmiller, Susan. *Against Our Will: Men, Women and Rape*. New York: Bantam Books, 1975.

Bullough, Vern L. *The Subordinate Sex: A History of Attitudes toward Women*. New York: Penguin Books, 1974.

Calhoun, Arthur W. *A Social History of the American Family: From Colonial Times to the Present*. Vol. H, *From Independence through the Civil War*. Cleveland: Arthur H. Clark Co., 1918.

Calvera, Leonor. "Argentina: The Fire Cannot Be Extinguished." In Robin Morgan (ed.), *Sisterhood Is Global*. Garden City, N.Y.: Anchor Press/Doubleday, 1984.

Carmody, Denise Lardner. *Women and World Religions*. Nashville, Tenn.: Abingdon Press, 1977.

Carter, President Jimmy. Exec. Doc. R., 96th Cong., 2d Sess., 1980.

Cary, Eve, and Kathleen W. Peratis. *Woman and the Law*. Skokie, Ill.: National Textbook Co., 1981.

Childs, Marquis W. *Sweden: The Middle Way on Trial*. New Haven, Conn.: Yale University Press, 1980.

China. *First Periodic Report to the Committee on the Elimination of Discrimination against Women* [CEDAW]. CEDAW/C/5/Add. 14. New York: United Nations, May 25, 1983.

Cogley, John, (ed.). *Natural Law and Modern Society*. Cleveland: Meridian, 1966.

Corne v. Bausch and Lomb, Inc. 390 F. Supp. 161 (D. C. Ariz. 1975) at 163–64.

Corning Glass Works v. Brennan. 417 U.S. 188 (1974).

Craig v. Boran. 429 U.S. 190, 97 S. Ct. 451, 50 L.Ed.2d 397 (1976).

Crites, Laura L. "Wife Abuse: The Judicial Record." In Laura L. Crites and Winifred L. Hepperle (eds.), *Women, the Courts, and Equality*. Newbury Park, Calif.: Sage Publications, 1987.

Crites, Laura L., and Winifred L. Hepperle (eds.). *Women, the Courts, and Equality.* Newbury Park, Calif.: Sage Publications, 1987.

Crossette, Barbara. "India Studying 'Accidental' Deaths of Hindu Wives." *New York Times,* January 15, 1989, p. 10.

Dahl, Robert. *Who Governs?* New Haven, Conn.: Yale University Press, 1961.

Davidson, Laurie, and Laura Kramer Gordon. *The Sociology of Gender.* Chicago, Ill.: Rand, McNally and Co., 1979.

Davis, Elizabeth Gould. *The First Sex.* New York: Penguin Books, 1973.

de Beauvoir, Simone. *The Second Sex.* New York: Vintage Books/Alfred A. Knopf, 1952.

Deckard, Barbara Sinclair. *The Women's Movement.* 3d ed. New York: Harper and Row, 1983.

Defunis v. Odergaard. 416 U.S. 312 (1974).

Degler, Carl N. *At Odds: Women and the Family in America from the Revolution to the Present.* New York: Oxford University Press, 1980.

DeGlopper, Donald R. "The Social System." In Robert L. Worden, Andrea Matles Savada, and Ronald E. Dolan (eds.), *China: A Country Study.* Washington, D.C.: U.S. Government Printing Office, 1988.

DePauw, Linda Grant, and Conover Hunt. *Remember the Ladies: Women in America 1750–1815.* New York: Viking Press, 1976.

de Rivera, Alice. "On Desegregating Stuyvesant High." In Robin Morgan (ed.), *Sisterhood is Powerful.* New York: Vintage Books, 1970.

Diaz v. Pan American World Airways, Inc. 401 U.S. 950 (1971).

Doe v. Bolton. 410 U.S. 179 (1973).

Dorsen, Norman. *Our Endangered Rights: The ACLU Report on Civil Liberties Today.* New York: Pantheon Books, 1984.

Dunn, Erica, and Judy Klein. "Women in the Russian Revolution." In *Women: A Journal of Liberation* 1, no. 4 (Summer 1970): 22–26.

Durkheim, Emile. *The Division of Labor in Society* [1893]. New York: Free Press, 1964.

EEOC Guidelines on Discrimination because of Sex. Section 1601.2(b)(1).

Egypt. *First Report to the Committee on the Elimination of Discrimination against Women* [CEDAW]. CEDAW/C/5/Add. 10. New York: United Nations, Feb. 3, 1983.

Egypt. *Second Report to the Committee on the Elimination of Discrimination against Women* [CEDAW]. CEDAW/C/13/Add. 2. New York: United Nations, May 14, 1987.

Eisenstadt v. Baird. 405 U.S. 438 (1972).

El Saadawi, Nawal. *The Hidden Face of Eve: Women in the Arab World.* Boston: Beacon Press, 1982.

Epstein, Cynthia Fuchs. *Women in Law.* New York: Basic Books, 1981.

Fact Sheets on Sweden: Equality between Men and Women in Sweden. Stockholm: The Swedish Institute, May 1987.

Feinman, Clarice. "Women Lawyers and Judges in the Criminal Courts." In Imogene L. Moyer (ed.), *The Changing Roles of Women in the Criminal Justice System.* Prospect Heights, Ill.: Waveland Press, 1985.

Flexner, E. *Century of Struggle.* New York: Atheneum Publishers, 1971.

Fogel, Walter. *The Equal Pay Act: Implications for Comparable Worth*. New York: Praeger Publishers, 1984.

Fox, Mary Frank. "Women and Higher Education: Sex Differentials in the Status of Students and Scholars." In Jo Freeman (ed.), *Women, A Feminist Perspective*. 3d ed. Palo Alto: Mayfield Publishing Co., 1984.

Freeman, Jo. "Women, Law, and Public Policy." In Jo Freeman (ed.), *Women: A Feminist Perspective*. 3d ed. Palo Alto: Mayfield Publishing Co., 1984.

French, John, and Bertram Raven. "The Bases of Social Power." In D. Cartwright (ed.), *Studies in Social Power*. Ann Arbor: University of Michigan Institute for Social Research, 1959.

Friedman, Leslie J. *Sex Role Stereotyping in the Mass Media: An Annotated Bibliography*. New York: Garland Publishing, 1977.

Friedmann, Wolfgang. *Law in a Changing Society*. 2d ed. New York: Columbia University Press, 1972.

Friendly, Fred W., and Martha J. H. Elliott. *The Constitution: That Delicate Balance*. New York: Random House, 1984.

Fritz, Sara. "The President Tackles His 'Gender Gap.'" *U.S. News and World Report*, Nov. 8, 1982, pp. 52–53.

Frontiero v. Richardson. 411 U.S. 677, 93 S.Ct. 1764, 36 L.Ed.2d 583, 1973.

Galanter, Marc. "The Modernization of Law." In M. Weiner (ed.), *Modernization*. New York: Basic Books, 1966.

Galbraith, John Kenneth. *Economics and the Public Purpose*. Boston: Houghton Mifflin Co., 1973.

Geis, Gilbert. "Criminal Abortion." In Simon Dinitz, Russel R. Dynes and Alfred C. Clarke (eds.), *Deviance Studies in Definition, Management and Treatment*. New York: Oxford University Press, 1975.

Gerbner, George, and Larry Gross. "Living with Television: The Violence Profile." *Journal of Communication* 26 (1976): 173–99.

Gilman, Charlotte Perkins. *Women and Economics* [1898]. New York: Harper Torchbook, 1966. Quoted in Babcock, Freedman, Norton, and Ross (eds.), *Sex Discrimination and the Law*.

Glazer, Nora, and Helen Youngelson Waehrer (eds.). *Woman in a Man-Made World*. 2d ed. New York: Rand, McNally and Co., 1977.

Goesaert v. Cleary. 335 U.S. 464, 69 S.Ct. 198, 93 L.Ed. 163 (1948).

Goffman, Erving. *Interaction Ritual*. New York: Anchor Books, 1967.

Goldberg, Susan, and Michael Lewis. "Play Behavior in the Year-Old Infant: Early Sex Differences." *Child Development* 40 (1969): 21–30.

Gough, Kathleen. "The Origin of the Family." In Jo Freeman (ed.), *Women: A Feminist Perspective*. 2d ed. Palo Alto: Mayfield Publishing Co., 1979.

Greenhouse, Linda. "Supreme Court, 5–4, Narrows Roe v. Wade, Upholds Sharp State Limits on Abortions." *New York Times*, July 4, 1989, pp. 1, 10.

Griswold v. Connecticut. 381 U.S. 479 (1965).

Grove City College v. Bell. 465 U.S. 555, 104 S.Ct. 1211, 79 L.Ed.2d 516 (1984).

Gutis, Philip S. "Family Redefines Itself, and Now the Law Follows." *New York Times*, May 28, 1989, Section 4, p. 6.

Haddad, Y. Y. "Islam, Women and Revolution in 20th Century Arab Thought." In Y. Y. Haddad and E. B. Findley (eds.), *Women, Religion, and Social Change*. Albany: State University of New York Press, 1985.

Haddad, Yvonne Yazbeck, and Adair T. Lummis. *Islamic Values in the United States.* New York: Oxford University Press, 1987.

Halberstam, Malvina, and Elizabeth F. Defeis. *Women's Legal Rights: International Covenants—An Alternative to ERA?* Dobbs Ferry, N.Y.: Transnational Publishers, 1987.

Hale, Sylvia M. "Male Culture and Purdah for Women." *Canadian Review of Sociology and Anthropology* 25, no. 2 (1988): 276–298.

Hall, Robert E. "The Abortion Revolution." In Arlene Skolnick and Jerome Skolnick (eds.), *Family in Transition.* Boston: Little, Brown and Co., 1971.

Hall, Robert E. (ed.). *Abortion in a Changing World.* Vol. 2. New York: Columbia University Press, 1970.

Hammer, Jalna. "Violence and the Social Control of Women." In Gary Littlejohn, Barry Smart, John Wakeford, and Nira Yuval-Davis (eds.), *Power and the State.* New York: St. Martin's Press, 1978.

Hardin, Garrett. "Abortion—or Compulsory Pregnancy." In Kenneth C. W. Kanmeyer (ed.), *Confronting the Issues: Sex Roles, Marriage and the Family.* Boston: Allyn and Bacon, 1975.

Harris v. McRae. 448 U.S. 297, 100 S.Ct. 2671, 65 L.Ed.2d 784 (1980).

Henkin, L. "Foreign Affairs and the Constitution" at 1017 (1972:146). Quoted in Halberstam and Defeis, *Women's Legal Rights*, p. 55.

Hoffman-Ladd, Valerie J. "Polemics on the Modesty and Segregation of Women in Contemporary Egypt." *International Journal of Middle East Studies* 9, no. 3 (Summer 1987): 25–50.

Hollander, Nancy Caro. "Women: The Forgotten Half of Argentine History." In Ann Pescatello (ed.), *Female and Male in Latin America.* Pittsburgh: University of Pittsburgh Press, 1973.

Hommes, Regina W. "The Measurement of the Status of Women." In Marry Niphuis-Nell (ed.), *Demographic Aspects of the Changing Status of Women in Europe.* Hingham, Mass.: Kluwer Boston Inc., 1978.

Hoult, Thomas Ford, Lura F. Hinze, and John W. Hudson. *Courtship and Marriage in America.* Boston: Little, Brown and Co., 1978.

JämO. "The Act Concerning Equality between Women and Men at Work." (SFS 1980:412 amended 1980:888, 1982:92). Stockholm, 1984.

Janeway, Elizabeth. *Man's World, Woman's Place: A Study in Social Mythology.* New York: Dell Publishing Co., 1971.

———. *Powers of the Weak.* New York: Alfred A. Knopf, 1980.

Johnson, P. "Women and Power: Toward a Theory of Effectiveness." *The Journal of Social Issues* 32 (1976): 99–110.

Jones, Anne. "Women Who Kill Their Batterers." In Marilyn Safir et al. (eds.), *Women's Worlds, From the New Scholarship.* New York: Praeger Publishers, 1985.

Jones, Hugh Percy. *Dictionary of Foreign Phrases and Classical Quotations.* Edinburgh, Scotland: John Grant Booksellers, Ltd., 1958.

Kagan, Jerome. "Acquisition and Significance of Sex Typing and Sex-Role Identity." In Martin Leon Hoffman and Lois Wladis Hoffman (eds.), *Review of Child Development Research.* New York: Russell Sage Foundation, 1964.

Kagan, Jerome, and Michael Lewis. "Studies of Attention to the Human Infant." *Merrill-Palmer Quarterly* 2 (1965): 21–30.

Kahn v. Shevin. 416 U1S. 351 (1974).

Karmen, Andrew. "Women Victims of Crime—Introduction." In Barbara Price and Natalie Sokoloff, (eds.), *The Criminal Justice System and Women.* New York: Clark Boardman, 1982.

Kay, Herma Hill. *Sex-Based Discrimination.* 3d ed. St. Paul, Minn.: West Publishing Co., 1988.

Kay, Herma Hill, and Christine A. Littleton. "Feminist Jurisprudence." In Herma H. Kay, *Sex-Based Discrimination.* 3d ed. St. Paul, Minn.: West Publishing Co., 1988, pp. 884–887.

Kaye, Judith S. "Women Lawyers in Big Firms: A Study in Progress toward Gender Equality." *Fordham Law Review* 57, no. 1 (Oct. 1988): 125.

———. "Historical Observations: Yesterday, Today and Tomorrow." (Talk given at a symposium on women and the courts.) *The New York State Bar Journal* 61, No. 4 (May 1989): 12–15, 52.

Kidder, Robert L. *Connecting Law and Society.* New York: Prentice-Hall, 1983.

Kipnis, David. *The Powerholders.* Chicago: University of Chicago Press, 1976.

Kirkpatrick, Jeane. "Incentives to Participation: The Presidential Elite." Paper presented at the annual meeting of the Southwestern Political Science Association, San Antonio, Texas, March 1975.

Kohlberg, L. "A Cognitive-Development Analysis of Children's Sex-Role Concepts and Attitudes." In E. Macoby (ed.), *The Development of Sex Differences.* Stanford, Calif.: Stanford University Press, 1966.

Komarovsky, Mirra. *Women in the Modern World.* Boston: Little, Brown and Co., 1953.

Kristeva, Julia. *About Chinese Women* (translated from the French by Anita Barrows). London: Marion Boyars Publishers Ltd., 1977.

Kuhl, Anna F. "Battered Women Who Murder: Victims or Offenders?" In Imogene L. Moyer (ed.), *The Changing Roles of Women in the Criminal Justice System.* Prospect Heights, Ill.: Waveland Press, 1985.

Leonard, Karen. "Women in India: Some Recent Perspectives." *Pacific Affairs* 52 (1979): 95–107.

Liddle, Joanna, and Rama Joshi. *Daughters of Independence.* London: Zed Books, 1986.

Literary Digest. Jan. 6, 1912, p. 6. Cited in Philip S. Foner, *Women and the American Labor Movement.* New York: Free Press, 1979.

Little, Cynthia Jeffress. "Education, Philanthropy, and Feminism: Components of Argentine Womanhood, 1860–1926." In Asunción Lavrin (ed.), *Latin American Women.* Westport, Conn.: Greenwood Press, 1978, pp. 235–251.

Luker, Kristin. *Abortion and the Politics of Motherhood.* Berkeley, Calif.: University of California Press, 1984.

Lynn, Naomi B. "Women and Politics: The Real Majority." In Jo Freeman (ed.), *Women, A Feminist Perspective.* 3d ed. Palo Alto, Calif.: Mayfield Publishing Co., 1984.

McDougal, Myres S., Harold D. Lasswell, and Lung-Chu Chen. "Human Rights for Women and World Public Order: The Outlawing of Sex-Based Discrimination." *The American Journal of International Law* 69 (July 1975): 497–533.

MacKinnon, Catherine. *Sexual Harassment of Working Women.* New Haven, Conn.: Yale University Press, 1979.

Mansbridge, Jane J. *Why We Lost the ERA*. Chicago, Ill.: University of Chicago Press, 1986.

Marbury v. Madison. 1 Cranch 137, 2 L.Ed. 60 (1803).

Martin, Susan Ehrlich. "Sexual Harassment: The Link between Gender Stratification, Sexuality, and Women's Economic Status." In Jo Freeman (ed.), *Women, A Feminist Perspective*. 3d ed. Palo Alto, Calif.: Mayfield Publishing Co., 1984.

Mead, Margaret. *Sex and Temperament in Three Primitive Societies*. New York: Dell, 1968.

Meadows v. Ford Motor Company. 62 FRD 98 (W. D. Ky. 1973) (FEP Cases 732).

Meritor Savings Bank FSB v. Vinson. 477 U.S. 57, 106 S.Ct. 2399, 91 L.Ed. 2d 49 (1986).

Merton, Robert K. *On Theoretical Sociology*. New York: Free Press, 1967.

Minai, Naila. *Women in Islam: Tradition and Transition in the Middle East*. New York: Seaview Books, 1981.

Minattur, Joseph. "Women and the Law: Constitutional Rights and Continuing Inequalities." In Alfred D. Souza (ed.), *Women in Contemporary India: Traditional Images and Changing Roles*. Delhi: Manohar Book Service, 1975.

Minor v. Happerset. 88 U.S. (21 Wall.) 162, 22 L.Ed.627 (1874).

Mischel, Walter. "A Social-Learning View of Sex Differences in Behavior." In E. Maccoby (ed.), *The Development of Sex Differences*. Stanford, Calif.: Stanford University Press, 1966.

Missouri v. Danforth. 428 U.S. 52, 44 U.S.L.W. 5197 (1976).

Missouri v. Holland. 252 U.S. 416, 432, at 434 (1920).

Morgan, Robin (ed.). *Sisterhood Is Global*. Garden City, N.Y.: Anchor Press/Doubleday, 1984.

Moynihan, Daniel Patrick. "Social Science and the Court." *The Public Interest* 54 (Winter 1979): 12–31.

Mukherjee, Prabhati. *Hindu Women: Normative Models*. New Delhi: Orient Longman, 1978.

Mukhopadhyay, Carol. "Sati or Shakti: Women, Culture and Politics in India." In Jean F. O'Barr (ed.), *Perspectives on Power: Women in Africa, Asia, and Latin America*. Durham, N.C.: Duke University Press, 1982.

Muller v. Oregon. 208 U.S. 412 (1908).

Muñoz, Susana. "Las Madres: The Mothers of Plaza de Mayo." Documentary aired on "P.O.V." (Point of View), New York, New York, Channel WNYC, June 27, 1989.

National Information Bank on Women in Public Office (NIB). Fact Sheet: *Women in U.S. Congress in 1987*. New Brunswick, N.J.: Rutgers University, Eagleton Institute for Politics, 1987.

National Organization for Women (NOW). *Dick and Jane as Victims: Sex Stereotyping in Children's Readers*. NOW task force study by Central New Jersey Chapter. Princeton, N.J.: National Organization for Women, 1972.

Neubardt, Selig. "At Last! A Feminist Supreme Court!" *Women's News* 7, no. 12 (Aug. 1989): 17.

O'Flaherty. Wendy D. *The Origins of Evil in Hindu Mythology*. Berkeley, Calif.: University of California Press, 1976.

Orr v. Orr. 440 U.S. 268, L.Ed. 2d 306 (1979).

Page, Joseph A. *Peron, a Bibliography*. New York: Random House, 1983.

Parrillo, Vincent N. *Strangers to These Shores*. 1st ed. New York: John Wiley and Sons, 1980, p. 25.

People v. Liberta. 64 NY2d 152, 474 N.E.2d 567, 485 NYS2d 207, 105 S.Ct. 2029, 85 L.Ed.2d 310 (1985).

People v. Rincon-Pineda. 538 P.2d 247 (Sup.Ct. Calif. 1975).

Phillips v. Martin-Marietta Corp. 400 U.S. 542 (1971).

Pierce, Christine. "Natural Law Language and Women." In Vivian Gornick and Barbara K. Moran (eds.), *Woman in a Sexist Society*. New York: Basic Books, 1971.

Planned Parenthood of Central Missouri v. Danforth. 428 U.S. 52 (1976).

Popenoe, David. *Disturbing the Nest: Family Change and Decline in Modern Societies*. New York: Aldine deGruyter, 1988.

Rathus, Spencer A. *Human Sexuality*. New York: Holt, Rinehart and Winston, 1983.

Raven, Bertram. "Social Influence and Power." In I. Steiner and M. Fishbein (eds.), *Current Studies in Social Psychology*. New York: Holt, Rinehart and Winston, 1965.

Reed v. Reed. 404 U.S. 71 (1971).

Reid, Donald Malcolm. "Cairo University and the Orientalists." *International Journal of Middle East Studies* 19 (Feb. 1987): 51–76.

Renzetti, Claire M., and Daniel J. Curran. *Women, Men and Society*. Boston: Allyn and Bacon, 1989.

Reskin, B. A., and H. I. Hartmann (eds.). *Women's Work, Men's Work: Sex Segregation on the Job*. Washington, D.C.: National Academy Press, 1986.

Richardson, Laurel. *The Dynamics of Sex and Gender*. 3d ed. Boston: Houghton Mifflin Co., 1988.

Richmond-Abbott, Marie (ed.). *The American Woman: Her Past, Her Present, Her Future*. New York: Holt, Rinehart and Winston, 1979.

Rittenmeyer, Steven. "Of Battered Wives, Self-Defense and Double Standards of Justice." *Journal of Criminal Justice* 9 (1981): 389–396.

Roe v. Wade. 410 U.S. 113 (1973).

Ross, Susan Deller, and Ann Barcher. *The Rights of Women*. New York: Bantam Books, 1983.

Safilios-Rothschild, Constantina. *Toward a Sociology of Women*. Lexington, Mass.: Xerox College Publishing, 1972.

Sail'er Inn, Inc. v. Kerby. 5 Cal3d1, 485 P.2nd 529 (1971).

Sanger, Margaret. "Women and the New Race" (1920). In Miriam Schneir (ed.), *Feminism: The Essential Historical Writings*. New York: Vintage Books, 1972, pp. 325–334.

Schaefer, Richard T. *Sociology*. 3d ed. New York: McGraw-Hill, 1989.

Schneir, Miriam (ed.). "Married Women's Property Act of 1960." In Miriam Schneir (ed.), *Feminism: The Essential Historical Writings*. New York: Vintage Books, 1972.

Schultz, T. Paul. "Women's Work and Their Status: Rural Indian Evidence of Labour Market and Environment Effects on Differences in Childhood Mortality." In Richard Anker, Mayra Buvinic, and Nadia H. Youssef (eds.), *Women's Roles and Population Trends in the Third World*. London: Croom Helm, 1982.

Schulz, Muriel R. "The Semantic Derogation of Women." In Barrie Thorne and

Nancy Henley (eds.). *Language and Sex: Difference and Domination*. Rowley, Mass.: Newbury House, 1975.

Schur, Edwin M. *Law and Society: A Sociological View*. New York: Random House, 1968.

―――. *Labeling Women Deviant: Gender, Stigma, and Social Control*. New York: Random House, 1984.

Schwartz, Felice N. "Management Women and the New Facts of Life." *Harvard Business Review* 1 (January-February 1989), pp. 65–76.

Schwartz, Herman. *Packing the Court: The Conservative Campaign to Rewrite the Constitution*. New York: Charles Scribner's Sons, 1988.

Scott, A. C. "The Value of Housework: For Love or Money?" *Ms*, July 1972, pp. 56–58.

Scott v. Sanford. 19 Howard 373; 15 L.Ed. 691 (1857).

Selznick, Philip. "Sociology of Law." Paper prepared for the *International Encyclopedia of the Social Sciences* 9, David L. Sills, (ed.). New York: Macmillan and the Free Press, 1968, pp. 50–59.

Shenon, Philip. "Ex-H.U.D. Chief Linked to Housing Lobby Bid" in *New York Times*, June 28, 1989, p. 14.

Shortridge, Kathleen. "Poverty Is a Woman's Problem." In Jo Freeman (ed.), *Women: A Feminist Perspective*. 3d ed. Palo Alto, Calif.: Mayfield Publishing Co., 1984.

Simons, Marlise. "Abortion Has New Front in Western Europe" in *New York Times*, June 28, 1989, p. 1.

Simpson, Peggy. "The War Has Just Begun" in *Ms*, Sept. 1989, p. 88.

Spencer, Cassie C. "Sexual Assault: The Second Victimization." In Laura L. Crites and Winifred L. Hepperle (eds.), *Women, the Courts, and Equality*. Newbury Park, Calif.: Sage Publications, 1987.

Sprogis v. United Air Lines, Inc. 44 F.2d 1194 (7th Cir.), *cert. denied*, 404 U.S. 999 (1971).

Stacey, Judith. "When Patriarchy Kowtows: The Significance of the Chinese Family Revolution for Feminist Theory." *Feminist Studies* 2, no. 2/3 (1975): 64–112.

State v. Smith. 85 N.J. 193, 206, 426 A2d 38 (1981).

State v. Wanrow. 559 P.2d 548 (1977).

Stein, Leon. *The Triangle Fire*. Philadelphia, Pa.: Lippencott, 1962.

Stern, Marianne. Interviewed in Charlie Brantingson, *Swedish Women as Entrepreneurs*. Facts and Interviews. Stockholm: Business and Industry Information Group, 1983.

Stevens, Evelyn P. "Marianismo: The Other Face of Machismo in Latin America." In Ann Pescatello (ed.), *Female and Male in Latin America*. Pittsburgh: University of Pittsburgh Press, 1973.

Strainchamps, Ethel. "Our Sexist Language." In Vivian Gornick and Barbara Moran (eds.), *Woman in a Sexist Society*. New York: Signet, 1971.

Sumner, William Graham. *Folkways* (1906). Reprinted New York: Mentor Books, 1960.

"The Supreme Court: Excerpts from Court Decisions on the Regulation of Abortion." *New York Times*, July 4, 1989, p. 13.

Sweden. *First Periodic Report to the Committee on the Elimination of Discrimination against Women* [CEDAW]. CEDAW/C/5/Add. 8. New York: United Nations, December 15, 1982.

———. *Second Periodic Report to the Committee on the Elimination of Discrimination against Women* [CEDAW]. CEDAW/C/13/Add. 6. New York: United Nations, March 26, 1987.

Sweden, Division of Equality Affairs. *Equality between Men and Women in Sweden. Government Policy to the Mid-Nineties.* (Government Bill 1987/88: 105). Division of Equality Affairs Act: Stockholm, 1988.

Sweden, Ministry of Justice. *New Swedish Family Legislation.* S–103 33. Stockholm, Feb. 1988.

Sweden, Ministry of Labour. *The Swedish Act on Equality between Women and Men at Work.* Ministry of Labour, S–103 33. Stockholm, March 1985.

Taeuber, C. M., and V. Valdisera. "Women in the American Economy." *Current Population Reports.* Series P–23, no. 146. Washington, D.C.: U.S. Government Printing Office, 1986.

Tien, H. Yuan. "A Talk with China's Wang Wei." *Population Today* 16, no. 1 (January 1988). Washington, D.C.: Population Reference Bureau.

Tiger, Lionel. *Men in Groups.* New York: Random House, 1969.

Tong, Rosemarie. *Women, Sex and the Law.* Totowa, N.J.: Rowman and Allanheld, 1984.

Tresemer, David E. "Assumptions Made about Gender Roles." In Nona Glazer and Helen Y. Waehrer (eds.), *Woman in a Man-Made World.* 2d ed. Chicago, Ill.: Rand McNally, 1977.

Trost, Jan. "Swedish Solutions." *Society* 23, no. 1 (1985): 44–46.

Tuchman, Gaye. "Introduction: The Symbolic Annihilation of Women by the Mass Media." In Gaye Tuchman, Arlene Kaplan Daniels, and James Benet (eds.), *Hearth and Home: Image of Women in the Mass Media.* New York: Oxford University Press, 1978.

Turk, Austin. "Law as a Weapon in Social Conflict." *Social Problems* 23, no. 3, (Feb. 1976): 276–291.

United Nations. *Charter of the United Nations.* Signed at San Francisco on June 26, 1945, and entered into force Oct. 24, 1945.

———. *Chronicle: Perspective 1985.* (DPI/873 No. 7, Dec. 1985, 4M).

———. *Commission on the Elimination of Discrimination against Women (CEDAW).* 7th Session, Feb. 16 to Mar. 4, 1988. General Assembly Official Records: 43d Session. Supplement No. 38 (A/43/33). New York: United Nations, 1988.

———. *Compendium of International Conventions Concerning the Status of Women.* (Sales No. E88.IV.3). New York: United Nations Publication, 1988.

———. *Compendium of Statistics and Indicators on the Situation of Women, 1986.* Tables 4, 20, and 25. (Sales No. E/F.88XVII.6). New York: United Nations Publication, 1989.

———. *Demographic Yearbook 1985.* 37th issue. Department of International Economic and Social Affairs, Statistical Office. New York: United Nations, 1987.

———. *Report of the World Conference to Review and Appraise the Achievements of the United Nations Decade for Women: Equality, Development and Peace.* United Nations Publication A/CONF.116/28/Rev.1. New York: United Nations, 1986.

——. *The United Nations at Forty: A Foundation to Build On*. New York: United Nations, 1985.

——. *U.N. Action in the Field of Human Rights*. Sales No. E79XIV.6. New York: United Nations, 1980.

——. *U.N. Demographic Yearbook 1971*. Sales No. E/F.72.XIII.1, 23d issue, New York: United Nations, 1971.

United Nations Development Programme. DP/1989/24. New York: United Nations, March 15, 1989.

United Nations General Assembly Official Records, 43rd Session. Supplement No. 38 (A/43/38). New York: United Nations, 1988.

United Nations Press Release. *New York Times*, March 5, 1989.

——. L/T/4081, New York: United Nations, April 13, 1989.

U'ren, Marjorie B. "The Images of Women in Textbooks." In Vivian Gornick and Barbara K. Moran (eds.), *Woman in a Sexist Society*. New York: Signet, 1971.

United States, Bureau of the Census. "Money, Income and Poverty Studies of Families in the U.S." *Current Population Reports, 1987*. Washington, D.C.: U.S. Government Printing Office, 1987.

——. *Statistical Abstract of the U.S., 1988*. Washington, D.C.: U.S. Government Printing Office, 1989.

United States, House of Representatives. *Hearings on Sexual Harassment in the Federal Government*. Committee of the Post Office and Civil Service, Subcommittee on Investigations. Washington, D.C.: U.S. Government Printing Office, 1980.

——. *Report of the Special Committee of Lawyers of the President's Commission for the Observance of Human Rights Year 1968*. Reprinted in *House Hearings* supra n. 88, Appendix 18, pp. 339–340.

United States, National Advisory Council on Women's Education Programs. *Title IX: The Half Full, Half Empty Glass*. Washington, D.C.: U.S. Government Printing Office, 1981.

United States, National Center for Health Statistics (NCHS). "Births, Marriages, Divorces, and Deaths for 1987." *Monthly Vital Statistics Report 36 (March 21)*. Washington, D.C.: U.S. Government Printing Office, 1988.

U.S. Committee for UNICEF. *Facts about Females and Education*. New York: United Nations, 1975.

U.S. Merit Systems Protection Board (MSPB). *Sexual Harassment in the Federal Workplace: Is It a Problem?* Washington, D.C.: U.S. Government Printing Office, 1981.

Vago, Steven. *Law and Society*. New York: Prentice Hall, 1981.

Vinson v. Taylor. 22 EPD 39708 pp. 14688–14689 (DDC 1980).

Waddle, Michael L. "Physical Environment and Population." In Robert L. Worden, Andrea Matles Savada, and Ronald E. Dolan (eds.), *China, A Country Study: 1988*. U.S. Government, Secretary of the Army. Washington, D.C.: U.S. Government Printing Office, 1989.

Walum, Laurel Richardson. "The Changing Door Ceremony: Some Notes on the Operation of Sex roles in Everyday Life." *Urban Life and Culture* 2 (1974): 506–515.

Webster v. Reproductive Health Services. 109 S.Ct. 3040 (1989).

Weitzman, Lenore J. *The Divorce Revolution: The Unexpected Social and Economic*

Consequences for Women and Children in America. New York: Free Press, 1985.

————. "Judicial Perceptions and Perceptions of Judges: The Divorce Law Revolution in Practice." In Laura L. Crites and Winifred L. Hepperle (eds.), *Women, the Courts, and Equality.* Newbury Park, Calif.: Sage Publications, 1987.

Wertheimer, Barbara M. "Union is Power: Sketches from Women's Labor History." In Jo Freeman (ed.), *Women, A Feminist Perspective.* 3d ed. Palo Alto, Calif.: Mayfield Publishing Co., 1984.

Wilkerson, Isabel. "Missouri after the Abortion Ruling: Both Sides Form Their Battle Lines" in *New York Times,* July 9, 1989, p. 19.

Willborn, Steven L. *A Comparable Worth Primer.* Lexington, Mass.: Lexington Books/D. C. Heath and Co., 1986.

Williams v. Zbaraz. 48 U.S. 358, 65L.Ed.2d 831, 100 S.Ct. 2694 (1980).

Williamson, Jane, Diane Winston, and Wanda Wooten (eds.). *Women's Action Almanac.* New York: William Morrow and Co., 1979.

Woloch, Nancy. *Women and the American Experience.* New York: Alfred A. Knopf, 1984.

Woody, Thomas. *A History of Women's Education in the United States.* Vol. 1. New York: Octagon Books, 1966.

Worldmark Encyclopedia of the Nations. Vol. 3, *Americas.* New York: John Wiley and Sons, 1976.

Index

ABOUT THE AUTHOR

WINNIE HAZOU received her Ph.D. in sociology from Fordam University Graduate School of Arts and Sciences and is currently Associate Professor at Mercy College. After introducing a course called "Women and the Law" at Mercy, Hazou realized that there was a need for a text that would incorporate in a single volume many of the topics on this subject that are of relevance to students. Her interest in women around the world was fueled by her extensive travels abroad and by having lived among people of other cultures for extended periods of time.